For our listeners

WAITING
FOR THE
PUNCH

ALSO BY MARC MARON

Attempting Normal
The Jerusalem Syndrome: My Life as a Reluctant Messiah

WAITING
FOR THE
PUNCH

WORDS TO LIVE BY FROM THE
WTF PODCAST

MARC MARON
and BRENDAN McDONALD

FLATIRON
BOOKS
NEW YORK

WAITING FOR THE PUNCH. Copyright © 2017 by Marc Maron and Brendan McDonald. Fore-word copyright © 2017 by John Oliver. All rights reserved. Printed in the United States of America. For information, address Flatiron Books, 175 Fifth Avenue, New York, N.Y. 10010.

www.flatironbooks.com

The Library of Congress Cataloging-in-Publication Data is available upon request.

Designed by Steven Seighman

ISBN 978-1-250-08888-8 (hardcover)
ISBN 978-1-250-08889-5 (ebook)

Our books may be purchased in bulk for promotional, educational, or business use. Please contact your local bookseller or the Macmillan Corporate and Premium Sales Department at 1-800-221-7945, extension 5442, or by email at MacmillanSpecialMarkets@macmillan.com.

First Edition: October 2017

10 9 8 7 6 5 4 3 2 1

CONTENTS

FOREWORD

We have a lot to thank garages for.

Sure, they can protect your car from the elements and act as a half-way house for objects not yet ready to be sent to the actual trash, but big things have famously started in garages too. Google and Apple each began in one. Even the Yankee Candle Company was apparently formed in a garage, and if that hadn't happened, you wouldn't currently be able to buy a Mango Peach Salsa candle for $27.99. They also make one called Cream Colored Ponies. Seriously. Cream Colored Ponies. Same price. They're actively just fucking with people now. I can't even begin to imagine what a Cream Colored Pony smells like in candle form, but I'm already getting a headache thinking about it. Oh, and one more thing you should know; in 2013 the Yankee Candle Company was apparently sold for $1.75 billion, so you're not laughing so hard at Yankee Candles now, are you?

The point is, huge things happen in garages.

That brings us to Highland Park, California, in 2009, when an unremarkable garage took a very funny, very broken man into its wooden womb and helped him create one of the most recognizable podcasts in the world. That podcast has featured conversations with everyone from comedians, actors, musicians, and writers to an actual sitting president.

In hindsight, Marc was always going to be extremely good at interviewing people. He's smart, constantly curious, and has an almost pathological desire to connect to people. For a man who has experimented with multiple forms of facial hair, it's perhaps surprising that there is absolutely no artifice to his conversation. His ludicrous levels of honesty act as a kind of emotional wrecking ball to even the most guarded human being. I'm British, so

I'm medically dead inside, but even I can't help opening up whenever I talk to him. He uses his honesty like a scalpel, cutting himself open in front of anyone he's talking to, and in doing so, invites you to do the same.

It turns out that the format of podcasting and Marc were made for each other. The complete lack of restrictions means he can have unedited, uncensored, long-form conversations that can be comedic, cathartic, and occasionally claustrophobic. And eight years after it began, here is that perfect podcast in book form. I'll admit that I didn't see the point of this at first. When you have something that is already in its ideal form, why insist on making it something else? It's like that Mitch Hedberg joke about comedians constantly being asked to write other things:

> When you're a comedian, everyone wants you to do other things besides comedy. . . . That's not fair. That's like if I worked hard to become a cook, and I'm a really good cook, they'd say, "All right, you're a cook. Can you farm?"

But you know what? I've really enjoyed this book. It's reminded me of conversations that had a big impact on me at the time, and I've gone back to listen to those conversations in full again. Louis CK and Marc in a raw conversation about friendship. Marc and Todd Hanson navigating a brutal powwow about wanting to die. Norm Macdonald being so funny while talking about drinking and gambling everything away that he almost makes it sound appealing. It's worth dipping into the discussions on these pages again to remember how truly remarkable they were. Plus, the beauty of this book over the podcast itself is that you don't need to skip the first seven pages where Marc plugs his stand-up dates and reads ads for butt plugs from Adam and Eve.

I do hope you enjoy it.

Viva Boomer.

—John Oliver

IN MEMORIAM

Four of the contributors to this book passed away in the years following their appearances on WTF with Marc Maron. They are Robin Williams, Garry Shandling, Sam Simon, and Mike DeStefano. Their contributions are invaluable, and they are incredibly missed.

WAITING

FOR THE

PUNCH

INTRODUCTION

When I was a kid I loved to talk to people.

Whether it was when I was very young, listening to the old men who hung out at my grandfather's appliance store in Haskell, New Jersey. Or in my twenties, talking to my mentor Gus Blaisdel at his bookstore. Or even to Pete, the schizophrenic who hung around the bagel place I worked at when I was in high school. Or any guy at any record or guitar store anywhere.

I wanted to hear stories. I wanted to be engaged by people who had interesting lives, thoughts, ideas, and information. I needed it. I think part of my compulsion was because I didn't feel whole. My dad wasn't around much and my mother was into herself. I didn't feel like I fit in. I was an overly sensitive, creative kid. I didn't feel comfortable in my body, and I was angry. I was painfully insecure, and being part of someone else's life for a while always felt like a relief. As long as I was talking to people I wasn't lost in my own fear, pain, and dark thoughts. It was like I was using them as a battery for my soul.

I started the WTF podcast out of complete desperation. I think if you listen to the first one hundred episodes they can be heard as me having celebrities over to my house to help me with my problems. They did.

Over the years it has evolved into a massive and amazing catalog of conversations with hundreds of people. They are mostly creative types: comics, actors, musicians, writers, graphic novelists, producers, playwrights, and directors. There's even a soap maker and a president. I had no idea when I became a comedian back in the mid-1980s that I would cocreate and host a hugely popular show out of the garage behind my house.

I think the pastime of chatting or candidly talking to people about anything or nothing is fading away. People don't even want to leave voice messages anymore, let alone talk. We keep a distance from each other because we can. It's odd and sad. Because just by talking to each other, we can put all the aspects and challenges and joys and horrors of life into perspective, even if that is not what we are talking about. It's relieving, comforting, and enjoyable.

Most of the people I talk to have public lives. That means they probably have a well-worn personal narrative that they churn out for interviews. Conversely, many of us may have a one-sided relationship with these public people based on that narrative or their work. We often create assumptions about a public persona that are based on either fantasy or preconceived judgments. I have them about most of my guests too. I am a fan and I am also judgmental. I go into the conversation with those assumptions and judgments and very quickly realize how limited they are. I am almost always wrong and almost always pleasantly surprised and excited that I am wrong. They are just people. We are just people.

When I interviewed Lorne Michaels, I went into it thinking he was some kind of all-powerful gatekeeper of show business. I came away thinking he's a good guy who works in a building and loves what he does. I thought Kristen Wiig might be difficult to interview because she's intensely private and had not spoken about her personal life in much detail. We had one of the more insightful conversations I can remember about fear and anxiety. When I interviewed Paul Thomas Anderson I was convinced he was some kind of mysterious, dark, brooding genius. Turns out he's extremely friendly and laid-back, almost a goofball. When I interviewed President Barack Obama I thought it would be like interviewing a president, but he's just a guy who happens to be a president.

When guests come into the garage with their narrative, I have to find a way around it. I wait until it falls away or I find something else engaging to talk about. If this doesn't happen immediately, it almost always happens around twenty minutes in. When they forget that they are talking into a microphone.

I have no idea what is going to happen when I talk to a guest. I'm not sure where the conversation will go. I don't have a plan other than to talk, to connect. I know I don't want to be talked at or through. I don't prepare in the same way other interviewers prepare because I don't see myself as an interviewer. I am a conversationalist and a somewhat needy one at that. I obviously know a bit about my guests, but other than what they have accomplished and where they come from, I keep myself in the dark. All I want out of any talk is for it to find its own groove. I want something to come up that enables us to engage authentically in that moment. Then I like to chase that moment, use it as a portal into who they are. Who anyone is in a moment isn't always about information or what's being said. It's about feelings, memory, spontaneously thinking aloud, finding common ground, being surprised because of new revelations, and being open. I listen. It took me a long time to learn how to do that. I make myself available and open in the moment.

It's always nerve-racking to talk to people and I almost always think it will be difficult. I am intimidated by some of my guests, sometimes because I'm a big fan and sometimes because they are just intimidating. When I talked with Judd Apatow, we talked about the feeling of dread we both deal with every day. It's the feeling of being on guard against some kind of impending doom, waiting for a punch to come from out of nowhere, even though it never comes. That's how it feels most of the time when I have these conversations. It's like I'm cornered and my only chance at survival is to talk my way out of it.

I am not afraid to share and even overshare about myself in conversation. This isn't something people being "interviewed" are necessarily prepared for. It throws them off. Now it's not all about them, and they have to engage on a personal level. This isn't a system I've devised or my method. It's just who I am emotionally. I need to be heard and seen. I need to put myself out there to know I exist. That was really the whole intention of the podcast. There were no expectations. I just knew I had to keep putting myself out there or I would fade away.

I had no idea the conversations would be so life changing for me and I certainly didn't anticipate them being that way for other people. I don't think I even considered what listeners' reactions would be. There was no way for me to anticipate the range of emotional reactions I've received. People from all over the world tell me the podcast helped them through a dark time, made them feel less alone, helped them get sober, helped them identify problems they had, helped them with the people in their lives, inspired them, moved them to tears, saved their lives. The effect of listening to an uninterrupted, long-form conversation with emotional ups and downs, depth and lightness, humor and sadness, is an essentially human experience. Hearing creative people talk about life's struggles and their creative process not only humanizes them but also makes listeners realize that they are just people trying to do something with their lives and, like the listener, are confronted with every obstacle available in the process. Sharing how they move through those obstacles helps others.

In a way, WTF is one long, ongoing conversation with many participants, many voices. This book is a thorough representation of that continuing dialogue, with shared viewpoints, differences of opinion, and profound insights about common themes in our lives. To be honest, I don't listen to my conversations after I have them. My producer does. So, reading these conversations, seeing them intertwined and complementing each other, was not simply like hearing them again. It was like being able to really feel what is being talked about and savor it. When people speak candidly and it is transcribed, the effect is visceral and immediate. When I read these pieces for the first time, it felt like I had never heard them before, and they moved me in a way I couldn't experience in the moment when I was having the conversations. I hope they hit you the same way.

Enjoy!

Boomer lives!

Love,
Maron

GROWING UP

"The Smaller Place It Came From"

I had my adventures and misadventures growing up, but it's the varying mixture of what I did or didn't get from my parents that really leaves a mark. The relationship we have with our parents explains how we engage with the world and other people.

Sometimes bad experiences can lead us to a place of self-realization or, at the very least, give us a great story. Sometimes our childhood experiences take a lifetime to process, if ever. These stories define us, they haunt us, but they also can liberate us.

I am positive I did not grow up properly. Does anyone, really? Something is definitely off. There are obviously many reasons for whatever emotional flaws I have as an adult, and I can trace most of them to my parents. I have grown into a place of gratitude rather than resentment toward them because it is essentially those flaws (and my struggle with them) that make me who I am. It is not really sympathetic or attractive to be actively mad at your parents after a certain age. You have to let it go at some point. It was fifty for me.

My parents left me hanging in the "Providing the Boundaries Necessary for Me to Take Chances and Succeed and Fail with the Support and Guidance Necessary to Define My Character" department. I had to put my sense of self together from scratch. I spent a good part of my life moving through the world like a kid lost at a mall. Looking to other grown-ups as role models, I learned which cigarettes to smoke from Keith Richards. I dressed like Tom Waits for most of my junior year of high school. I looked to Woody Allen to understand what it meant to be smart and funny.

My mother was a bit sarcastic and could be a little cutting. She was funny. She was always expressing herself in a creative way. My father was unpredictable and explosive at times. Sometimes that explosion would go in, sometimes out. He thought he was funny, but he wasn't. They both have a lot of energy. These are the things in the plus column.

It's always good to learn about the struggles other people went through while they were growing up. I like that Paul Scheer felt comfortable sharing with me the very difficult situation he found himself in after his parents' divorce. Same with John Darnielle from the Mountain Goats, who is still dealing with the pain his stepfather put him through. I was able to laugh in disbelief at Molly Shannon's story of complete parental irresponsibility when she got on a plane without an adult and flew to New York City accompanied only by another child. I'm glad people still tell these stories about their childhoods. It took years of me talking to people in my garage to finally get some perspective on things I went through as a kid and stop them from undermining me as an adult. Well, that and a little therapy and some specific reading and age.

CONAN O'BRIEN—TALK SHOW HOST, COMEDIAN, WRITER

I think I was an anxious kid. I was not the class clown. I was funny for my friends, but quiet in the classroom. I worked really hard, and I was kind of grim. I have to say I didn't really enjoy my childhood. I was not socially uncomfortable. I could make my friends laugh, but I was not easygoing. From fourth grade until, like, now.

SIR IAN MCKELLEN—ACTOR, ACTIVIST

The first three years of my life I didn't sleep in a bed. I slept on a mattress under a metal table in our downstairs room in case a bomb knocked the building over, and blackout material so the light didn't attract any German bombers that were coming over. Not much to eat, but quite healthy eating, rationing. Of course, when you're growing up, you know that's not the norm. I was well looked after. A lot of love in my house.

KEVIN HART—COMEDIAN, ACTOR

I grew up in Philadelphia, PA. My neighborhood is shit. North Philadelphia, Fifteenth area, Crime City. Right now I think we're third in the world in deaths, probably. New Year's we opened it up with five murders in my city.

Marc
Happy New Year.

Kevin
Yeah. It's not the best place in the world, but I love it. It's home for me. That's what I know.

MEL BROOKS—COMEDIAN, WRITER, DIRECTOR, PRODUCER, ACTOR, MUSICIAN

My mother, Kitty. Kitty Kaminsky. Raised four boys. You know, those days, diapers, you had to wash them. Yeah, I'll never forget. One time I wanted to see a movie. She gave me three deposit bottles, each one was three cents apiece. So that was nine cents. You needed a dime. She went next door to Mrs. Miller and borrowed a penny so I could make the dime. I don't know whether she was typical, but she was a wonderful, loving, caring, beautiful mother.

RUPAUL CHARLES—ACTOR, DRAG PERFORMER, SINGER, MODEL, WRITER, TELEVISION HOST

I was watching a kid the other day. He must have been about four years old, and he was so happy to be in a human body. He was just jumping around going upside down, and he was running over there, and he came running. It was like, "Oh my God. It's great. I'm a human. Look at me. Look, I can do this. I can do . . ." That's what I want to do. Just to move your hands, jump around, roll on the ground with an exhausted parent going, "Yes, you can. You can do that."

Unfortunately, when I was a kid, my parents were in their own melodrama, and so I really couldn't do that as much as possible.

Luckily for me, though, my sister Renee, she was the one who said, "You're great. You should try this. Why don't you do that?" I have that in my sister, so that was great.

JIM GAFFIGAN—COMEDIAN, WRITER, PRODUCER, ACTOR

Four boys and two girls and I'm the youngest of six. The oldest in my family is my sister Kathy, and she's, I don't know, she could be like a hundred and I wouldn't know. My brother, Mike, is, I don't know, fifties. It's all a blur. It's like, who cares? I kind of know that there's six kids over seven or eight years, they're just old.

Marc

You saw them all leave, I imagine.

Jim

Yeah, yeah, it was a little bit difficult. You're leaving me here with these people that are crazy. A little bit of the enthusiasm wanes in parents, right?

"You're still here?"

"Yeah, I'm still here."

So there was some of that, but there was also such an amount of distrust that develops in parents of that generation. They had been lied to by so many teenagers, by the time I got there, they were just like, "You're guilty!"

And I was like, "I didn't do anything wrong."

They were like, "Just go to your room."

JOHN OLIVER—COMEDIAN, WRITER, ACTOR, TELEVISION HOST

When my dad first started taking me to football games, to Liverpool games, I would make him let me wear my full Liverpool kit, so this was me at eight, nine years old. My full Liverpool kit, underneath whatever I was wearing, because there was a part of me as a child that felt if someone got injured on the field, they would just turn to the crowd and say, "Does anyone have a kit so that we can carry on?"

And I would say, "Yes, my name is John. I'm eight years old," and clearly somewhere in me, I think that this is going to turn out well. That this eight-year-old is going to physically compete with these twenty-nine-year-old super-fit athletes.

I wore cleats. You could hear this clip-clop of this eight-year-old kid going, "Let's do this."

MARIA BAMFORD—COMEDIAN, ACTOR

I used to play the violin and I used to be very good at it because, you know, I started when I was three. It was forced on me in a way that I was not conscious of until I was around eleven and then I said, "Oh, I think I'd like to quit."

They said, "No. Oh, no. You cannot. Because we have put in a lot of time and money, and you're freakishly good at it, so why not continue?" I was good at it, but I did not enjoy it at all.

PAUL SCHEER—COMEDIAN, WRITER, ACTOR, PODCAST HOST

My mom took my *"Weird Al" Yankovic in 3D* album and broke it over her knee because a song on there was called "Nature Trail to

Hell." It was on one of the devil worship lists that the church had given out. If your children have any of these albums, and one of them is a "Weird Al" album, you must find it and destroy it. That and my LL Cool J album. It was terrible. I was crying, like, "Nooooooo! My 'Weird Al' album!"

I got to tell "Weird Al" that story, which was awesome. There's nothing satanic about "Weird Al" Yankovic.

Marc

Actually, that might be Satan. You never know. He's very cunning. He's charming.

Paul

Satan comes in Hawaiian shirts.

My mom took all my action figures away and gave me Ten Commandments figures. I had Moses. Literally a Moses action figure, and he had two tablets in his hand, like the Ten Commandments. I would play with them, like I would play Batman or G.I. Joe. I'd make Moses swing down a pole and get into a Batmobile. I still had the Batmobile, so Moses would drive a Batmobile.

CONAN O'BRIEN

We were hardcore Catholic growing up. Church every Sunday. The whole nine yards. It's in my bones. I mean, as much as I've tried to evolve past it in certain ways, it's in my bones.

Marc

What are the liabilities of it, carrying it with you in your mind?

Conan

Body shame. I've been accused over the years of, "You're self-deprecating and that's your act." You know what? It really comes from finding myself very flawed. I think that's at the root of Catholicism. We're all just flawed. There's nothing we can do about it. I grew up just having a very dark self-view.

Marc

Why? Because you were too tall, or too what?

Conan

Too skinny, too tall, you know, my dick's too big.

I hate to get that out there as a rumor, but do you know what I mean?

My dick is huge, and it's got a lot of girth.

Marc

Yeah. Don't want to hurt people.

Conan

No. The thing is I was so worried for a long time. I actually had doctors say, "You're going to hurt someone with that." Then it was only later in life that I found out that this is a great gift. For years I lived with the shame of this, "My penis is too big. I hope no woman ever finds out." You live with these things, and then you eventually learn to work with them.

I was not a hypochondriac, but I probably feigned illnesses to get my parents' attention. I didn't believe I had the illness. When you're one of six kids, you've got to do anything to get some face time, so I was not beyond trying to just have something.

I remember I read *Death Be Not Proud,* the John Gunther, Jr. story. It's about a boy who's fourteen, and he gets a brain tumor. It's really touching. Everyone is supposed to read it when you're thirteen, fourteen years old, and you're supposed to just feel so terrible for the boy. I read it, and I thought, "Man, that guy is getting so much attention." I remember envying a kid with a brain tumor, and he dies at the end of the book. I remember thinking, "Man, brain tumor. That's the way to go."

NORM MACDONALD—COMEDIAN, WRITER, ACTOR

When I was very young, I was very, very, very shy and very afraid of everything. I mean, people say they're shy when they were kids, but it was a pathology for me.

This weird thing happened to me when I was young. I don't know if this means anything. It wasn't religious or anything, but it transformed me to some degree. I was so fucking afraid of everything, and if I went to a store, I'd have to walk around forever before I could even face a person in the store to buy a pack of gum. I don't know why the fuck I was like this.

Anyways, when I was nine, we lived in rural Ontario, and there was a blind friend of my dad's. My dad said, "Take him to the store." I was like, "What the fuck? I have to take this blind fucker and I'm already shy and shit?" I'm taking him to the store and then the fucker wants me to explain everything, describe everything to him, so I'm like, "There's some grass over here, and now there's a lamppost," and this guy's all happy. What is it about the lamppost? I mean, it's just a lamppost. It goes on and on, but something happened to me during this. It sounds bizarre, but something happened to me where I was actually, instead of always looking inward, which I think I'd always done before that one time, I was looking outward. Anyways, while I was talking to him, I suddenly had a sort of hysteria, like I was laughing. I started laughing, and I don't even know why I'm remembering this, but I started laughing about everything, and everything seemed very, very funny to me.

A couple weeks later, I saw a homeless guy and he started talking to me, and he was talking to me about John D. Rockefeller. He was like, "I was at John D. Rockefeller's funeral!" and all this shit, and I was laughing at him. And then he started laughing, and I was like, "It's all fucking crazy shit."

Now I find everything funny except really serious stuff.

MOLLY SHANNON—COMEDIAN, ACTOR

I was raised by my dad from the time I was really little. He was very Catholic so he was repressed in a lot of ways, but he was also really charismatic and fun and would do anything and was real wild. We would do crazy stuff, like we would go to the airport and we would be like, "Let's take a mystery trip." We would have no suitcases or anything and it was when they had those airlines where you could pay right on the airplane. Do you remember that? People Express. We would go to the airport, pick a city, and just fly to the city and then borrow clothes when we got there or buy clothes. Like crazy stuff and my dad would call in sick for me to school.

Then I hopped a plane when I was twelve. We told my dad, me and my friend Anna, "We're going to hop a plane to New York," and he dared us. We went to the airport and we had ballet outfits on and we put our hair in buns and we wanted to look really innocent and this was again when flying was really easy, you didn't need your ticket to get through.

Marc

Apparently you didn't need an adult either.

Molly

We told my dad and we saw there were two flights, we were either going to go to San Francisco or New York and we thought, "Oh let's go to New York, it's leaving early," and so we said to the stewardess, "We just want to say good-bye to my sister, can we go on the plane?" She was like, "Sure." Then she let us on. It was a really empty flight because it was out of Cleveland, Ohio, and we sat back there and then all of a sudden you just hear "Woosh!" The plane takes off and we had little ballet outfits and buns and I was like, "Hail Mary, full of grace, the Lord is with thee; blessed art thou amongst women." Then the stewardess who had given us permission to go say good-bye to my sister came by to ask if we wanted snacks or beverages and she was like, "Can I get you ladies something to eat?" She was like, "Oh, motherfucker!" We wondered if we were going to get in trouble, but she ended up not telling anyone and then when we landed in New York City she was like, "Bye, ladies. Have a nice trip."

Marc

It's such an exciting story but the irresponsibility of all the adults in this story is somehow undermining my appreciation of it. You were twelve-year-old girls in fucking ballet outfits and everybody's sort of like, "Have a good time." What world was that?

Molly

It was crazy. It was a crazy world.

We called my dad. "We did it!" He was like, "Oh God, Molly, oh jeez!" He didn't know what to do. He said, "Try to see if you could go find a hotel where you could stay and me and Mary"—my sister—"will come meet you, we'll drive there." Basically we were like, "All right, we'll try to find a hotel," but he was kind of excited because he liked crazy stuff. Basically we didn't have that much, we had just our ballet bags and a little bit of cash, so we went to a diner and we dined and dashed and we stole things. We were like little con artists.

We made it to the city. We just asked people, "How do you get to Rockefeller Center?" because I had just seen it on TV.

Marc

Nobody said, "Are you girls lost?" Nothing like that?

Molly

No, nothing. We did try to go to hotels and my dad would call and ask, "Could they just stay there until we get there?" and none of the hotels wanted to be responsible. He was like, "All right, you've got to come home, but I'm not paying for it, so try to hop on one on the way back." The flights were all so crowded, so we ended up having to have him pay for it and he made us pay it all back with our babysitting money.

He loved that kind of stuff. Like I said, he was wild. In his drinking days he would go to bars and if somebody didn't let him in he would be like, "Damn it!" He would go into the bar and knock all the glasses down. He was the kind of guy who could, maybe, get arrested. It was crazy.

Marc

I love the strange nostalgic excitement you have for this border-line child abuse.

Molly

It was complicated. He was also a very loving parent. I think it's complicated. He was also really supportive and made me feel like I could do anything, and so in that way it felt really free and wild, but then in other ways I had to learn the rules of how regular people live. From other people. Like, professionals. Like, people you pay.

JOHN DARNIELLE—MUSICIAN, WRITER

I want you to think about wherever you were when you were five. The place I grew up seemed big to me in my mind. The hallway. I remember running all the way to the end of the hallway, and running all the way back down and being exhausted. I'm running all the way to the heater at the end and back. In reality, that's two steps. Now that I've been back in the house, it's two paces. I remember running down that hallway. The distance between my room and my parents' room, which I remember being a walk, as if I have to go see Dad to talk to him about something, I'm going to walk down the hall. That's also two steps.

We had added a room while I lived there, and it was called the front room. I remembered it being a cavernous, big room with a very high ceiling. It's a fucking garage. It's where the students live now because now it's a rental unit. There's a fucking poster of Big-gie and Tupac on the front door.

I went there. I was like, "These people won't mind if I knock on their door," so I knocked. They had never heard of me. I was glad, that would have been really awkward. "Hey, it's Johnnie. Really, this is my old house. Can I come in and make you feel sad about shit?"

I walked in and looked around and just went, "Whoa. We had a piano in there and a stereo." I looked at the backyard, I looked at my old room, and I nodded and said, "Thank you," and then told my therapist about it when I got home. It wasn't too traumatic. It was interesting. It was sweet in a way. It was good to see. When you feel like you're okay with where your life is at, it's good to see the smaller place it came from.

AHMED AHMED—COMEDIAN, ACTOR

My parents immigrated to the States. I was a month old, I was like the Lion King. "Aaah, we're going to America." Then we ended up in Riverside, California, where I was raised. We were the only Arab family, not only on the block but in almost the whole city, really.

It was very middle class and a little bit lower-middle class, mostly white families, but then our high school was really racially diverse, with black, Mexican, Asian. And we were sort of considered the "thug" high school. Athletes would come and do really well there, but there was also some gang violence and that sort of thing. When I was in high school, I blended in perfectly. When I'd say my name, they'd hear "Egypt." They were always sort of mystified by it. I'd get the little jokes, like "Did you come in on your flying carpet?" And "Did you climb a pyramid?" And "Do you have camels?"

Marc

Those jokes have changed now.

Ahmed

Yeah. Now it's like "Do you fly planes?" "Are you good at chemistry?" "Do you use fertilizer every day?" "How many wives do you have?"

CONAN O'BRIEN

I remember when I was a kid thinking, "My family is weird. We're just weird." I don't know how to put my finger on it. Maybe everyone grows up that way, but I remember thinking, "We're kind of like an Irish Catholic Addams Family. There's something off with us." That was the feeling that my brothers and sisters all had, that we're an odd family. We never quite knew what we were.

AHMED AHMED

The kids would come over to my house and one of my friends walked in and my parents were praying, and he looked at me and said, "What are they looking for?" And I go, "They're praying." And he's like, "To who?"

I always had to explain what Islam was and talk about the belief of it all behind it. We were like the Arab Munsters. The weird family on the block. My mom was always cooking, stuff with spices that Americans weren't used to, like cumin, stuff like that. All these weird fumes and aromas. They're like, "Hey, what's your mom cooking? Cow brains?" Whatever. And my dad, he was a night owl, so he'd sit up 'til three, four in the morning, watering the grass, smoking cigarettes, watering by hand. So the neighbors were always like, "What are you doing out there at four in the morning?"

On top of that, because my parents ate only halal food, or kosher food, they didn't sell it back then in the 1970s in the stores, so my dad had to drive to Fontana, California, with our station wagon, and load up. He'd go to a farm and load up the station wagon with chickens, ducks, rabbits, and he'd bring it back. We had a live meat locker, basically, in our backyard. Every day around five or earlier, my mom and dad would go out to the backyard and they'd pick out a chicken, my dad would hold it down and say the Muslim prayer "Please bless this soul and let our family have sustenance," and my mom would do it. There's a way you sacrifice so the animal doesn't suffer. And it's like *Clash of the Titans*. She's holding up this head, she's got blood all over her, it was like "Aaaaah!" We were eating dinner by 9:00 p.m.

The funny thing was, the kids would come over during the day, from the neighborhood, and play with the rabbits or the chickens or whatever, and they'd come back to find that their favorite rabbit they were playing with was gone. They're like, "What happened to Fluffy?"

"We ate him. We're eating his sister tonight."

DAVE ATTELL—COMEDIAN, ACTOR

I used to work for my dad. My parents had a bridal dress, tuxedo rental shop, and I worked there from the time I was sixteen 'til I was, I guess, nineteen, which is slave, underage, whatever, right? No, I guess not.

I did everything. I cleaned the store. I was head of shipping and receiving. I sold shoes. It was me and my grandpa, so I was his boss.

My dad was a man. I one time saw my dad, with full-blown diabetes, lift a hundred-and-fifty-pound cash register, like one of these old cash registers, just by himself. I was the guy who was working out. Back then every kid in Long Island lifted weights and practiced karate. I couldn't lift it, and he just fucking lifted it, put it over there, lit a cigar, and said, "What next? What do we have to do next?" I'm like, "Only a man can do that because he knew it had to be done."

RUSSELL PETERS—COMEDIAN

My dad was a meat inspector. He worked in a chicken plant. He would come out stinking every day. My mom worked in the cafeteria at Kmart. With the Salisbury steak, you know? A great day for us would be when there was Salisbury steak left over and my mom would bring it home. Or hot dogs, we're like, "Yes!"

Everyone always asked me, "What about being a doctor or a lawyer?" I'm like, "There's none in my family."

JOE MANDE—COMEDIAN, WRITER, ACTOR

Both of my parents were trial lawyers, so there were a few years where I just didn't talk to my parents. Between my sister and I we would just get cross-examined on everything. We would be sitting at the dinner table, if they smelled anything fishy they were back on the clock and just grilling us until they figured out what the issue was or whatever.

My sister and I both handled that in different ways. I think from seventh to tenth grade, I basically just pleaded the Fifth on everything. I mean, I just didn't talk to them because I didn't want to incriminate myself, so there were a few years where I hardly ever talked to my parents.

My sister, on the other hand, she just plead insanity. My sister was just this wall of noise. Any time my parents tried to confront her on it, she'd just scream and slam her door. Actually, that's a much better tactic. I just internalized everything.

RON FUNCHES—COMEDIAN, ACTOR

I remember my first day of school. My mom was just being like, "Hey, some kids are going to like you, some kids are not going to like you for who you are. Don't ever change who you are for them. If kids like you, cool. If they don't, fuck them."

Marc

Goddamn. I wish I had your mom.

Ron

She made her own mistakes too, but she's pretty awesome.

JOE MANDE

In high school, they thought I had the most severe case of IBS they'd ever seen. They thought it was stomach cancer because I literally, for about four years, woke up every morning with just explosive diarrhea. Just every morning, that was just part of my routine.

I was at this thing for my Jewish youth group when I was like fifteen. We were on a bus in Wisconsin and we had just gone to Taco Bell. I mean, already, red flags. It's always, like, sort of Russian roulette with Mexican food. Mexican roulette. Immediately, I just knew I had to go and I was in a school bus, so there was no bathroom.

I had to go up to my rabbi at the front of the bus and say, "You know, bad things are happening to me. We really need to pull over at the next rest stop." He was like, "Yeah, I'll make sure of it," so I went to the back of the bus. The rest stop was five miles ahead and I'm just like pacing and then the bus driver just blew right past it. The next rest stop wasn't for, like, forty-five miles and my body was going to explode.

To this day, I can't listen to Tom Petty without thinking of it. I put on the *Wildflowers* album and it was the only time I've ever successfully meditated. I meditated for those forty-five minutes until the next rest stop and then I ran. My friend came into the bathroom and he said he's never heard a human body make those kinds of noises. Everyone on the bus was waiting for me, I mean, I was in there for like thirty-five minutes just evacuating. I probably hurt my body in the long run the way I was clenching every muscle. To this day I still don't know how I did it, because it was bad.

CONAN O'BRIEN

This is not my nose. My nose was completely rebuilt. I was beaten up.

I ran into a street gang. I was wearing a T-shirt that had the Irish flag on it. They were Italian. This was right near the aquarium in Boston. I was with my friend at the time. This is late high school. They beat the shit out of me, because I was a little bit of a wise guy. They said they wanted fifty cents, and I said, "No."

They said, "Why not?"

I said, "I don't feel like it."

Just as I finished that "it," the *tah* sound, I got hit so hard in the face. I remember it was over pretty quickly. I went to the emergency room, and the doctor, I'll never forget his name, Dr. Constable. He had a British accent. He looked kind of crazy. He had crazy hair, and he looked like the poet Ezra Pound.

I said, "Is my nose broken?"

He said, "Broken? Good God, man, it's a bag of bones!" I'll never forget that.

JOE MANDE

In ninth grade, I took Spanish. It was the only nonhonors class I ever took. I was very short and had braces and sweater vests. I don't know why I wore sweater vests. I thought it was cool.

I got into Spanish the first day of class and it was just me and the JV basketball team. That was the class, basically. I was like, "It'll be fine. I listen to Outkast or whatever." I sit down and they were just ruthless. They would make fun of me, they would call me names, they would choke me. I got choked a lot but it was never violent, they just would come up from behind when I wasn't expecting it. Sometimes it was piano wire. They had piano wire. They would wrap wire around my neck and I would freak out, obviously, and then they would let go and just crack up. They'd be like, "Ahh, you stupid."

Marc

"Look at him! He's frightened for the right reason."

Joe

Right, what an idiot. I was like, "How stupid of me to freak out." They would throw empty cans of soda at my head and stuff. It sucked.

That Spanish teacher was so broken, she was so done with life, so it was chaos. She looked like Newman from *Seinfeld*, so everyone called her Newman. They would call her Ms. Newman and she would respond to it. I mean, it was bad.

Then that December our principal made this big announcement that no more gambling was allowed in the hallways. Because people played dice in the hallways and stuff. The Asian kids would have break-dance competitions in between classes. I actually started doing this thing where I got really good at making it look like I was about to start break dancing. Actually, I was just trying to get through the hallway, but I would get in the middle of this big circle and it would be my turn and I would start moving around to music and pumping my shirt and making it look like I was about to dance. I would just do it until they realized I was never going to start break dancing. I would go for like two minutes without actually doing any dancing before they pushed me out of the circle.

Anyway, back to the story. Our principal, she instituted this no gambling policy. I saw an opportunity and I went up to these kids in the back of my class and I was like, "I can teach you a gambling game that you'll never get in trouble for playing if you just stop choking me." It was a clear negotiation. They thought about it, and the next day I taught them how to play dreidel for money.

For a good month, outside my Spanish class, you would walk by and see these black kids in Avirex jackets, huddled over a top. Just like, "Yo, that's a 'W' motherfucker, pay up."

ALLIE BROSH—WRITER, ILLUSTRATOR

I was never a cool kid. They made an attempt to, like, maybe I could be in that group, but I was too scared.

Marc

They reached out? They sent a representative?

Allie

They reached out and I was too scared. I was always an awkward kid. I was always behind, never knew what to do with myself, or how to be. My best friend, this kid named Joey. He was a cool kid and I never was. I always felt very intimidated by him. Much of my early life was defined by trying to get him to think that I was cool. He would give me advice on how to dress. I spent my early preteen years wearing jeans and baggy shirts—totally rocking the skater-guy look.

I didn't fit in to anybody but him. He didn't know what he was doing either. To me, he looked like he knew what he was doing.

I was like the tumor on his life. He found this group of cool friends, and I wasn't meshing with the cool friends. They could just tell. Cool kids have this sense where they just know that you aren't one of them, right? It also didn't help that about three months earlier, my friend Joey had dared me to shave my head.

I did that because he dared me to and I didn't want to look like I was chicken.

Marc

Oh, no! People who don't know who they are can't shave their heads!

Allie

Yeah, exactly! I didn't know who I was.

Marc

I did that.

Allie

It was really bad timing. It was about two weeks before I discovered that I'm interested in boys. I had no view of self before this—no self-consciousness, nothing. Then, I shaved my head and I discovered, "Wow! I am not pretty!" I had giant braces. When you do something like that—when you do something that's so obviously—it just shows that you don't know how to do the things that show people you can be one of them. They see you and they're like, "There's something wrong here."

MARIA BAMFORD

My dad sent me to a Dale Carnegie training course on How to Win Friends & Influence People. For eighteen weeks I went with some businessmen and women, and it saved me. I was super depressed. I was sleeping all day through school. I took the course and suddenly I was able to have friendships.

I just had a format of how to talk to people. Because I had so much anxiety. So after taking the course, I would say, "Hi, Marc. Marc, it's really great to see you. You know, Marc, your set was so great last night, Marc. I really mean that."

Then you listen to people and then you tell the person back what they just said, but with a positive spin on it. It was fantastic, I tell you. Like, immediate results.

Then it all crashed down when I went to college, and people on the East Coast were like, "Why are you talking like that to me? Just calm down." I think there was an air of hysteria with my Dale

Carnegie techniques in college because I was very afraid, so I'm sure they were telling me to calm down for a good reason.

GILLIAN JACOBS—ACTOR

My interests were always very different from what other kids my age were into, so I think that we didn't really have a lot to talk about, and the more they didn't understand me, the louder I talked about what I was into, so they just didn't know what to make of me.

My mom would only let me buy clothes that she approved of, so I wore a lot of sweater sets in high school because she liked sweater sets. I remember going to an outlet store and wanting to buy a skirt. It was not a revealing skirt, it was a floor-length skirt, but my mom was like, "I don't like it. The material looks cheap." She wouldn't let me buy it. I was dressed like a middle-aged woman.

AMAZING JOHNATHAN—COMEDIAN, MAGICIAN

I used to be able to bend spoons. I figured out how to bend a spoon using my mind. It was just misdirection. I would make them look away for a second and I would bend it.

I did it really well, and I did it for my physics teacher, who I really admired. He said to me, "Is that real? Are you really doing this or is it a trick?" I was really unpopular in school. I was not standing out at all. I lied and I said, "Yeah, I can really do it," thinking that would be the end of it.

Nah.

The next hour, I'm sitting in class, and I hear on the speaker, "John Szeles, please come to the principal." Shit, this has something to do with the spoon bending, I know it does.

I walk in there, there's my mom and my dad. They were called out of work. A bunch of spoons on the desk and a local reporter. I'm like, "Fuck. This is not good."

They wanted me to demonstrate my powers. My mom took me aside and said, "Can you really do this, or are you just lying?" I looked her straight in the eye, and I said, "I can really do this." It's like a snowball going downhill. I said, "I can really do it." I proceeded to bend all the spoons and they freaked out. I bent everything.

The reporter, he's chomping at the bit to do this great story with the psychic kid. I had to figure a way out of it because I figured the local magicians would bust me on it and make me a fraud. Like magicians do. Magicians, they busted Uri Geller for doing it. They'll bust me too. If it's in the paper, you can bet someone's going to come forward and go, "That's bullshit."

This is how I got out of it. I told my mom that I wanted to be a normal kid. I didn't want to be a freak at school. I just wanted to be a normal kid. I didn't want everyone looking at me like I was weird. She bought it. They all bought it. Nobody did the story, but it leaked. This is the good part. It leaked out and I didn't get that press, which I didn't want, but everyone thought I was mysterious. I got mad pussy my senior year. I was the Man Who Fell to Earth. If a chick thinks that you can read her mind or anything like that, you're in.

If I was with a girl, when they'd leave the room, I'd go through their purse, take their license out, get their birth date, know their zodiac sign, I have all the details. Would put it back fast in their purse. They come back and we'd be doing lines and all that. Let me touch your forehead for a minute. Boom! You're a Virgo.

JON GLAZER—COMEDIAN, WRITER, ACTOR

I was probably eight when my parents got divorced. I have vague memories of it, but I remember just crying and sitting on the steps and just being really upset and yelling, but I don't remember the moment. It's just all vague, but I do remember it being upsetting.

My stepdad told me about when he and my mom announced they were getting married. I was in high school. He said he was actually very impressed about how I handled it. They just told me they were getting married. I remember those first moments. I was probably fourteen and he said I just sat there quietly, just took it in. Got up from the table, went upstairs. Put on shorts and a T-shirt and my running shoes and just went jogging, but it wasn't like I could go running somewhere and then come back. We lived in this apartment complex that had a loop. They told me they were getting married and then I just left and they watched me run laps. He said he was very impressed about how I was handling this and how I was dealing with it.

I remember when my dad told me he was getting remarried the first time, I was in the sixth grade and I was taking violin lessons and he picked me up. My mom always picked me up, so right away I'm like, "All right, okay. Something's not right." And then, "Hey, I thought we'd go get a bite to eat. Anywhere you want to go." I was like, "All right, what the fuck is going on?" There was a sub shop that I liked right across the street. It was more about let's just go there. It wasn't like I was going to say, "Oh great, let's go to this great place." I just knew something was up.

We went there, but it wasn't a sit-down place. We get these sandwiches and just go sit in his car in the parking lot. It's facing the school across the street and I'm just sitting there very tight, eating my sub, and it's right next to me, tight to my chest, and I felt like I knew what was coming. I'm trying to think about what is going on. I'm like, "Oh, I think I know what's about to happen." We're sitting there and quietly eating. He's like, "Hey, so I've got some news for you. Just wanted to let you know that Shelly and I decided to get married." I can just feel my body just crunching, super tense and just not sure. Didn't know how to handle it, but it was upsetting and it shouldn't have been. It should have been like, "Oh, great. Great, good for you." Shelly was awesome. She was so cool, but I just didn't know how to handle it.

I did not say a word. I just sat there, just eating my sandwich. Probably not even eating it, but just holding it. We just sat there in silence and then eventually he started the car and drove me back to my mom's. It was really fucking weird and I don't think we've ever talked about it, not because we're avoiding it, I always just forget. I feel like I have to know what he was thinking at the moment, how he felt. So weird.

AMY SCHUMER—COMEDIAN, WRITER, ACTOR

My mom leaves my dad. Has an affair with my best friend's dad. Breaks up their family. I'm in school. We're trying to still be best friends. Like, we were best friends. It was crazy.

Marc

People forget that when you stick your dick into something that's nearby, the ripple effect is going to be fairly profound.

Amy

That vagina's going to be at a PTA meeting with your wife next week. It sucked.

Marc

So the whole town was affected by it.

Amy

Yeah. She was Hester Prynne. I was like, "I love my mom. She's my family, so fuck you guys." Then years later, I was like, "Mom, how could you do that?"

When I was sixteen, I got angry. I played volleyball pretty seriously. I was on this club team, and it was preliminaries for the Junior Olympics. My mom was a chaperone. We had to go to San Jose, from New York to San Jose. I got caught shoplifting while at this tournament, so I was benched the whole tournament. I'm standing there with my knee pads around my ankles, and my mom's just standing there for the whole weekend having to stare at me with hatred, but I could always stare right back at her and be like, "Yeah, but you ruined my life."

RON FUNCHES

My dad had a drug problem for a while. I'm assuming a few, but mostly cocaine.

Marc

That's why your parents split up, because of the drugs? Your mom was like, "Fuck this. I'm going to Chicago with the kids. When you get your shit together, give me a call"?

Ron

Yeah. He didn't call for several years. He started to get in touch a little bit later, and he was going to Portland to work in construction, and Chicago wasn't working out too well for me. My dad was never a positive influence for me. He wasn't there to parent me, but he still wants to then offer advice. He wants me to be a super Christian.

Marc

When did that come around? After the drugs left?

Ron

Yeah, of course. You've got to always replace one thing with another. I was just getting through high school, and then out of the high school just hanging out and working at canneries, or Chuck E. Cheese.

Marc

Canneries?

Ron

Where you can beans and broccoli and stuff at a factory. Any type of frozen peas. I would just have to pick out stalks of broccoli, and put them in a chute, and avoid putting my fingers close to blades. Then one day my job was to pick out rats and snakes out of the stuff. That was the last day I went.

They would just kind of get rooted up. They're not plucked out by individual farmers. They're just put all together, and when they're originally dumped they're just dirt and rocks and vegetables and dead rodents.

I let a lot of rats go through.

Marc

You did not!

Ron

Oh, yeah. Do I look like a person that touched a lot of rats?

WYATT CENAC—COMEDIAN, WRITER, ACTOR

My mother and father lived in New York City, and then they split up when I was about a year old. My mother remarried, and then maybe when I was about three, my mother, stepfather, and I moved to Texas.

My father was murdered when I was four. My grandmother, my maternal grandmother, lived in New York, so I would spend time with her, and then I would spend time with my father as well. My grandmother, even after he got killed, she did a good job of trying to keep talking about him.

He was a New York City cabdriver, and he took a fare up to Harlem, and then they robbed him and shot him.

Just recently, maybe two years ago, a friend of mine connected me to an NYPD detective who pulled up the file, and I got to see everything. I always knew where it happened, but this sort of laid it out. Once he was shot, he died instantly, and then his foot was on the gas, and the car went across the median, and crashed into some cars. Then there were some witness accounts and stuff like that. It was really amazing. Then, at the end of it all, there is the guy. They caught the guy and I had his whole rap sheet. It was weird to just see that, and to just get a fuller picture of that guy. He lives in Brooklyn. There's a whole kind of weirdness of oh, wow, this person, I've seen his whole life. I see his rap sheet.

He got a really short sentence for it. I think he was sixteen when he did it. I just think about, he was sixteen, and this thing, it just set him on a path. Weirdly enough, he was doing time in North Carolina at the same time I was in college in North Carolina. It's just strange, these little sort of intersections of life where it's like oh, we were both in North Carolina at the same time.

Marc

Different institution.

Wyatt

Exactly. Yeah, different state-run institution. Both not the best football teams. Really underperforming football teams in both situations.

Marc

Wait, so now, the dude who murdered your biological father lives in the same city as you as a free man.

Wyatt

Yeah.

Marc

Do you have any compulsion to meet him?

Wyatt

Not really, no. People have asked me that. I don't really have anything to say to the dude. If anything, there's a part of me that I look at him and what he did, and there's a sense of he is partially responsible for me being who I am. I'm not going to send him a Father's Day card, but this was a traumatic event that changed me in the way I saw the world. He's the person that did that. Who knows how different my life would be? I assume I'd probably still be in the same place, but maybe my father would have been the deadbeat that he was to my sister to me, and maybe I would have dealt with that. Or maybe I would have gone to New York and lived with him, and it would have changed my impression of him in that way.

In that way, it is, like, yeah, this one thing, that idea of the butterfly effect or something like that, here it is.

AIMEE MANN—MUSICIAN, ACTOR

My childhood was pretty fragmented. My mother left when I was three years old. There was a lot of drama around that, because she ran off with a guy and he was married, and they took me, and my father didn't know where I was. This was just a lot of drama. I was eventually found and brought back, but this was probably nine months later.

Marc

Your mom kidnapped you with this dude that she ran off with, who was also married, and took you to another state?

Aimee

Out of the country. We wound up in England, but I think we spent some time in Germany. I remember being in Amsterdam. I don't know what the plan was. I think he was going to get a job. He took his kids, because he had kids.

Marc

"Here's your new family."

Aimee

Yeah.

Marc

Was this a guy from the neighborhood, somebody that your father knew?

Aimee

Somebody who worked for my father. There's a lot of drama in it. My father had hired a private detective, but I think he found out where I was by accident, because he was in advertising. He was in the same business. In the course of doing business, my dad ran into a guy who said, "I saw the guy that used to work for you," and it was him.

I think she flew back with me, and then I was taken to my grandparents for a month, which is crazy. It's all fucking crazy. My dad told me most of this. I know her now, but I sort of didn't really see her until I got back in touch with her in my midtwenties. She obviously doesn't really want to talk about it.

Here's another detail: I think we were all staying at a hotel or something, and I was three years old, playing by myself in the parking lot, and this boyfriend hit me with a car and knocked me unconscious. Probably not on purpose, but he did yell at me for causing an accident.

Marc

I've never heard of child abuse where the child was hit by an automobile.

Aimee

Yeah. Well, look, it was only a VW bug.

Marc

Oh, you could have won.

Aimee

I could have.

TOM ARNOLD—COMEDIAN, ACTOR

When I was ten, my dad married the next-door neighbor. She had a couple kids and that was terrible. It was terrible because she'd come from a very corporal punishment background and I was the oldest and she was going to tame me. It was not a pleasant experience. I get along with her now, of course. I know it was hard for her because I was like, "Oh my God, you're taking my dad." He did ask me if he could marry her. I remember saying, "Well, yeah. Of course."

She had a chart on the fridge with check marks during the day for when my dad got home and this is how many whips you'd get. The saddest thing, and I thought of this recently because my son was born, was when I was in bed. Man, I was loaded up with the extra underwear, the padding, because I knew it was coming because there had been a lot of check marks next to my name. I could hear him saying, "Oh, come on, Ruth. I don't want to." She'd say, "Goddamn it, it's him or me." You're ten and you're hearing that. You're like, "Oh my God, I don't want my dad to get divorced." You march on down there and say, "Let's do it."

BRUCE SPRINGSTEEN—MUSICIAN, SONGWRITER, AUTHOR

How could you live in a house where there was so much kindness and great cruelty? It was very, very difficult to understand those things, and it set me very on edge. I had my own little local minefield that I had to walk every single day, which caused a great deal of anxiety and neuroticism in me. You know, I had this one great thing, but then I was always waiting for the other shoe to drop. It made me a very nervous kid.

PAUL SCHEER

My mom got divorced three times when I was a kid growing up. That was a little rough. We lived a lot in small apartments and moved around Long Island. Weird guys. Weird stepdads. I remember I had one stepdad who refused to let me call him by his name. His name was Cordell. I could not call him Cordell. He made me call him Daddy, which is, in retrospect, weird.

My dad got into a fistfight with Cordell right in front of me. That was crazy. As a kid to see your real dad and your stepdad fight, like fucking go for it. I was young. I was, like, nine or ten. I remember seeing it.

My dad and I come back from apple picking, coming in, seeing my stepdad, who was in a bathrobe. He was a truck driver for a supermarket. My dad came in, and Cordell says, "You don't say fucking hello to me, Bill?" My dad's like "I said hello to you. It's your fucking fault if you didn't hear it." All of a sudden my stepdad picked up a coffee mug, fucking whaled it at my dad's head. My dad ducked and it exploded on the wall. They just went at it, like, grappling around my kitchen table. My dad's the nicest, most well-adjusted guy, and then suddenly apples are flying. I'm throwing apples. My dad is throwing apples. They fight until they literally leave the house, like outside the front door. My dad's a pharmacist. A pharmacist fighting a truck driver. It was something like out of a Clint Eastwood movie. It was insane, insane stuff.

Hours later, I got on the phone and Cordell was on the phone in my house. My dad was on a pay phone, and they apologized to each other while I was in the middle. For my benefit, to hear them apologize to each other. They had to get together and apologize over me. Looking back on that, that was terrible.

Cordell was an abusive fuck of a dude. A terrible dick. He'd come home, literally an arm in a cast because he got into a fight at work.

I would talk back a lot. That was my thing. I got into a ton of fights all until eighth grade, and then I was like, "Oh, I got to stop this." But I was getting good at it because I was fighting a forty-year-old guy at home. When you fight this big fucking forty-year-old dude, this fat dude who is strong, literally throwing a pitchfork at me and I'm dodging a pitchfork, getting locked up in the barn.

I just learned to be more of a grappler. It was like a lot of slaps and runs or punches in the stomachs and runs. But when I was in sixth grade I got into this fight with this kid and he gave me a sixth-grade punch. Like boom, punch in the face. I remember I grabbed him by the neck and we were by a car. There was a car fender there. I was like "Whap, whap." Like, his face into a car fender. We were both suspended from school, because he started it. But I stopped that. I remember being like "I don't want to do this anymore. I don't like this."

JOHN DARNIELLE

I had fresh earrings when I was fourteen or fifteen, and that pissed my stepdad off to no end. I think I got Mom to sign off on it. He hated that. He was a left-wing political activist who beat his wife and child and was homophobic. I was getting girlie at fourteen and fifteen. I was growing my hair long, I was trying on eye shadow and rouge and stuff like that.

The day that he knocked me hard enough to actually knock out an earring, and the post dug into my neck, that was the day that I wound up getting thrown out of the house. I had to go live with my real dad.

It was a mess. The thing about that period of time was that I had at that point a strong network of friends. For the first time I was close enough to grown up that my friends weren't just my friends. They were meaningful people in my life who I talked to about my life and who I was constructing that amazing teenage life with. They know your struggle. Suddenly, there was this big blow-up day about which I remember only that he did that. He was slapping me around the face hard enough to make the earring dig into my neck and make me bleed. I went back to my room and sat there, listening to music, and my mom came down the hall to say it was time for dinner. I'd been sitting there for half an hour contemplating what I was going to do to express that I didn't deserve this and the extent of the rage, so I punched my window. I put my fist through the window. It felt like a million bucks.

I never felt so good in my whole life. It was like, holy shit, and the house melted down. My stepfather screamed that he was going to beat everybody's ass even worse. My mother is crying, my sister is crying. It was a whole terrible scene.

I'm bleeding all up the arm but I felt like a million bucks. It felt so good to show them what it felt like inside. There was no way of getting it through their heads.

That was my victory.

PAUL SCHEER

I remember Cordell having my mom held like a hostage with a handgun and seeing that as a kid. During a fight.

I say it now and I think, "Wow. That was crazy dark. That's insane." But as a kid it doesn't register like that.

I remember saying to my mom "We got to get out of here." My mom's like "No, no, no. It's okay." I was like "We got to go. We got to go."

Marc

Did he hit her too?

Paul

Yeah. He hit me, he hit her. But you know what? Never to the point where we were really hurt. I think that was always my line. "Oh well, we don't have broken arms. Or we don't have this. Or we don't have that."

He would apologize, but he was like an older brother instead of a dad. It was that kind of relationship. I think he was competitive for my mom's affection toward me, which is insane. It's, like, that's a mother and a son. You're a husband. It would come out a lot in Indian burns. You know that kind of stuff, which really hurt.

I called child protective services at one point. They came to the house and they interviewed the parents side by side. They were like, "Does this happen?" My mom's like, "No." They talked to me and I was like, "Yes." But they think, oh, the kid's lying. The parents are telling the truth. They left.

Marc

Did you get beaten for that?

Paul

Yeah. Oh yeah. Of course.

My mom rebelled in the craziest ways. My dad's so nice and great. The man she's married to right now, also wonderful and great, but with Cordell, she was like, "I want something different." She got something insanely different.

Then my mom kind of wised up at a certain point and she was like, "Oh, we're out of here." This guy has more guns than he has shirts.

This is a crazy thing. My mom pretended that he won a trip, a hunting trip. She created these envelopes. It was like, "Cordell, you won this trip." She got him plane tickets. Got him a hotel. Created this whole fantasy, seven days away for him. The minute he left the house, a moving truck pulled in and we got all of our shit out of the house and we took off. We left Cordell's farm, and we moved into a small apartment, and that was it.

JOHN DARNIELLE

My stepfather died. He died, and my sister called in the middle of the night to say, "Mike is dead." Then I went on tour a month or two later, and stuff started to crack open. It was really amazing. I started to feel free with my feelings. I tell people, I tell survivors when they come up to me in the merch line and say, "I survived abuse." I ask, "Has your abuser died yet?" and they will say, "No."

I say, "I want you to be ready because I hate to say this because you don't wish death on anybody: It's wonderful when your abuser dies, it's wonderful. It's like nothing in the world. It's like you are free." There's a feeling that you will never be free of what you were, but then there's this. Even though my stepfather was helpless at the end of his life, to know that the person who used to hurt you no longer can is very, very, very deep. It's unbelievable.

Marc

You forgive him?

John

No. Which I hate about myself, but I don't.

WYATT CENAC

My biggest fear, and it was a fear that I had as a kid, because there would be times my mother might show up somewhere or she would have somebody spy on me and do shit like that. It was a really paranoid house growing up.

I remember, one time I was supposed to leave my car at a certain place. I was picking up this girl that I was seeing at the time; we were going to go to Six Flags Amusement Park. I was supposed to leave my car on one side of town; Six Flags was on another side of town, both far from where my folks live. I go pick up the girl. She's like, "We should drive to Six Flags together. It'd be romantic," because we were supposed to ride with her sister. I was like, "Well, I don't know. My mom says—" Then she touched my leg, and it was like, "Okay, let's do it."

We drive, and I had to take the highway and my folks didn't want me on the highway. My mother used to make me carry around this cell phone, one of those big-ass car phones. Phone's ringing nonstop, the girl answers it, and I immediately hang it up, and I'm like, "What the fuck are you doing?" Then I eventually answer it, and my mother's like, "Why didn't you pick up the phone?" I was like, "I don't know if you called the right number. This is the first time it rang." I dropped the girl off, and I get home, and as I'm pulling into the driveway I see my stepfather has been tailing me at some point, and his car's coming behind mine. He picked me up somewhere on the road, followed me back to our house.

What I learned is that my mother sent somebody to go see if my car was where it was supposed to be. When it's not, she calls the police. Knowing I took it, she calls the police, thinking that the police'll pick me up, and I'll learn a lesson.

When I get home, she has opened up all my papers, anything that I had locked up. I used to keep a briefcase where I could lock things up. All that stuff is spread out on her bed and on the kitchen table. It's almost like the police have come in and raided the place, and they're just going through everything. Violating in a way that was like, this doesn't even have anything to do with the crime at hand. The crime was that I took a car on the highway; you're now looking at this as like, "Let's basically just go through all this shit." There was always that sense of violation. I never knew who was my real friend. There was a girl I grew up with. She, at one point, told me that my mother had asked her to befriend me just to report information.

Halfway through my first semester of college, I was failing out and they would send a midterm report to your house. I'm in the shower, and my roommate comes knocking on the door of the bathroom, and he's like, "Hey, your folks are on the phone." I was like, "I'm in the shower. I'll call them back." He goes back, and a minute later he's like, "They're not getting off the phone. They're saying, 'Get out of the shower.'" I'm just like, "Oh, shit." I'm thinking, "Did somebody die? What the fuck is going on?"

I go in and I don't even have to put the phone next to my ear. My mother and stepfather's screaming so loud about my grades, at that point, like, "You're failing out of everything! We will come down there!" My roommate and his girlfriend can hear the whole thing. I'm thinking, "Oh, shit. I have to get my act together, because I don't want to go back there."

That house was, there was a lot of distrust, there was a lot of yelling. It was like, "Oh, right, I don't want to go back, but I'm also not this student that she wants me to be. I have to figure out who I am, and I've got to figure out the classes I need to take to make this work so I never have to go back to that house."

LESLIE JONES—COMEDIAN, WRITER, ACTOR

I got a scholarship to Colorado State at Fort Collins, which is not only the very whitest town, it's the very purest. They have only the purest air there. The sun was killing me and I was still the best basketball player on the team because I was the only black player. Yes, I was the only black player. There was a light-skinned girl, but she really didn't count, and she didn't come to school the next year.

I didn't know that I was going to be the only black girl on the team. I walked in and I don't know how this is going to work out because I'm very militant too, so I'm very outspoken. When I walked into basketball practice, I walked in with a radio, so I'm the stereotype. Some of them girls had never even met a black person before. It was an adjustment for me and I was very lonely.

I was rebelling on all levels. My coach knew that I was at the point where I wanted to go home because he came to my apartment. I had my mattress in the living room because this was so new to me. If I could go back with my mind now, oh God, I would have run that place. I would have run Colorado. Do you understand me?

Marc

Why did you have your mattress in the living room?

Leslie

Because I was scared, I didn't want to sleep in the room. There was nobody in the apartment with me. I was fucking alone and I'm scared. I'm a kid. I was like eighteen. When he came to the apartment he was like, "Oh my God, you've got to meet people. You've got to meet other black people." He brought up the BSU on campus, the Black Student Union. "Yes, there is a building for the black people on the campus and I'm sending you there."

If you were to talk to him today, he would say that was the worst thing I ever did because I completely became a party animal.

BRUCE SPRINGSTEEN

My folks left me in 1969, which was a little unusual. Usually you're leaving them, but they left me in New Jersey and went to California. That sort of leaves you on your own to continue parenting yourself as best as you can. You know, your life is yours from that point on. That suited me. I was independent already. I had the band. I had my own little community that I was part of. I was making a few bucks on the weekend so I could survive. I was happily independent.

Of course, you're only making twenty dollars. But anybody could live on twenty dollars or forty dollars in 1969, having no dependents. Anybody could do that. You ate for three dollars a day, four dollars a day was all you needed. It was just enough money to get by and have a good time on.

TERRY GROSS—RADIO HOST

My sophomore year instead of going to college I hitchhiked cross-country. My parents were very upset about it. Now that I'm the age that I am I think, "My gosh, no wonder they were so upset." But my attitude then was, "You're not telling me what to do. I'm an adult, you don't control me anymore."

DAN HARMON—DIRECTOR, WRITER, PRODUCER

For those of us who are not prodigies, who are not blowing minds by fifteen, I think it's better to grow up in a smaller town. You have this sandbox for you. You can more easily decide at twenty-two that you want to do stand-up, or you want to be a writer.

In Milwaukee if you stood on the street corner and said, "I'm a welder," and you did that three days in a row, sooner or later someone's going to give you a job welding. The same went for writers.

We didn't get paid anything, but in the five years from when I declared myself a writer, I was working for the mayor, I was doing radio shows. Within Milwaukee I was given every opportunity that I thought I wanted. If I wanted to write a play I could write a play. If I wanted to do a radio commercial for Bacardi, there was always some ad campaign that would come through and they wanted a cheap writer. It was a nice place to cut your teeth.

PRESIDENT BARACK OBAMA

I started keeping a journal when I was around twenty. Kept it up until I went to law school, so for about seven years. Sometimes I go back and I read the stuff, and I'm still the same guy, which is good.

Stuff's changed in the sense that stuff that was bugging you, by the time you're fifty-three, either you worked it out or you've just forgiven yourself and you've said, "Look, this is who I am." I think at that age you're still trying to figure out, "Who are you? How do

I live? What's my code? What's important to me? What's not important to me?" You're sorting through all kinds of contradictions.

By the time you get into your fifties, hopefully a lot of those have been resolved. You've come to terms and come to peace with some stuff, and then some stuff you've just said, "Well, you know what, that's just who I am. I've got some flaws, I've got some strengths, and that's okay."

PAUL SCHEER

I think I had a good escape back then in a way. I loved TV and movies. I listened to Smothers Brothers albums. I had all my dad's old Smothers Brothers albums. It was fun to sit and hear that. I remember even reading an article, I think it was a Smothers Brothers article where I think they had some messed-up parents. I remember thinking, "Oh. Okay. That's cool because maybe they had messed-up parents. I have messed-up parents. It evens out."

SEXUALITY

"An Obliteration of Self"

I'm not perfect or healthy in terms of intimacy or sex. I have been very open about myself in those areas. I'm fortunate that I am a comedian and have that freedom. It's part of my act and my life. I have played a part in ruining a couple of marriages and I try to learn from my mistakes.

My sexuality and my private life at times have been shameful because I did things I am not necessarily proud of. That's human. We are all flawed. That shame is personal. Adultery is bad. Making bad sexual decisions in your life can be bad, but if you are not breaking the law and you are hetero there's some wiggle room. I am not culturally marginalized because of who I am sexually. There is no institutionalized prejudice against my desires the way there are to others.

Talking about this stuff is not always easy. Todd Glass is a friend and a great comic. I had him on the show in the early days. We talked about lots of things, but sexual orientation never came up. That's not surprising. It doesn't usually come up when two comics just sit around talking. Then Todd called a couple years later because he wanted to come on the show again, this time to talk about something specific that was very important to him. He wanted to come out publicly. It was the first time he said out loud that he is gay. I was honored and also nervous, because it was very personal and I never really had the conversation he wanted to have. I knew I just had to listen and be present for this life-changing discussion.

That moment for Todd happened in my garage, but it's happened at other times and places for a lot of people who have been on my show. Dan Savage, Kevin Allison, Judy Gold, Cameron Esposito, James Adomian, and others talked with me about coming out and the impact it had on their lives.

It's challenging for most people to be open and honest about sexuality. That's why I'm grateful for people like Jim Norton and Margaret Cho, who spoke with complete candor about their sexual proclivities. Neil Strauss told me how his life spiraled out of control when he starting living out his sexual fantasies as a professional seducer of women. Amy Schumer told me about the trouble she has remembering good sex, while the bad experiences stay right there.

I am humbled and amazed by all of these talks. It is an honor to listen to stories about personal victories on all fronts. Earning the ability to shamelessly have the freedom to love and have sex with who you want and honor your desires is an inspiration.

JON HAMM—ACTOR, DIRECTOR

Getting a professional shave—it seems like it should be luxurious and then you realize, that's what ladies do with their business all the time. And that's not luxurious at all. That's like a procedure. God bless them, like mazel tov, but holy cow, that seems brutal. And none of them describe it as anything but a horror show.

Marc

But there was a time that I remember in my life, I'm a little older than you, where that didn't happen. You just took what was there, it was fine.

Jon

You were good to go.

I honestly think that's the lesson to be learned. We're good. Whatever you got is good. We will adapt.

Marc

We will work with that. Sometimes if there's too much attention paid to the grooming, it's a little off-putting.

Jon

I agree. And it feels like there's an expectation. Of some kind of performance or something that maybe I'm not prepared to put in. If you look at a car that's clearly been souped-up, you think, I don't know, man, this probably takes a lot of skill.

AMY SCHUMER—COMEDIAN, WRITER, ACTOR

I don't have any physical memory of sex. I had sex yesterday. I don't really remember it physically. I'm like, "I know I had an orgasm, because I'm not mad," but I can't remember my last boyfriend's penis. Those sexual memories, unless it's an assault, I feel like they fade away for girls.

Marc

I think if you're remembering penises, most of the time it's not going to be in the positive.

Amy

Exactly. I know I've had satisfying sex with a bunch of people, but I don't remember it the way I remember the disappointment, you know? I remember the time I put my hand down a guy's pants and couldn't figure out which was the testicle and which was the penis. I'm, like, "Ball. Ball. This, does he have three balls because,

oh my God, no. This is his dick. That's terrible. His life is terrible."
Then I'm just pulling on something, hoping it's the right one.

JONATHAN AMES—WRITER, ACTOR

I tell women, if you want to hold on to a guy, just like every three
weeks or so, just tell him he's got a beautiful cock. Beautiful or not,
whatever they want to say. "I just like your cock." Perfect. Just say
it like every three weeks or so, not too often so the guy gets cocky
but just enough to keep him coming back for more.

ELNA BAKER—COMEDIAN, WRITER

I was a Mormon for nine years practicing, didn't drink, smoke, I
never tried coffee. I remember the first time I drank, I just remembered thinking, "Everyone is so agreeable!" I'm making so many
friends, and I didn't know why. "Tonight is so fun!"

Marc

Did that also happen with the sex?

Elna

Oh! That's another story. Do you know Landmark Forum?

Marc

Yeah, it's a self-help program. You didn't go right from Mormon to
that, did you?

Elna

Well, what happened was, I was so Mormon, but I was figuring
out what I wanted to do or not, and for Christmas, someone bought
me a Landmark Forum course, and it was expensive. The notion
of like, "What do we buy our Mormon friend? She likes cults."

The way I stopped being Mormon was that I went to the Landmark Forum and I thought it was really ridiculous the whole time, and I was judging it in my head. Then the guy called me up from the audience and he said, "I feel like you are a cynical person about this." He said, "Just try on for a minute the idea that there is no God, and that life is meaningless and empty and that there's no hope."

Marc

That guy is hilarious.

Elna

I tried on the idea. I thought of a really sad moment, when my dog died. I tried it on, and I didn't take it off, and I left, and I gave my very first blow job. To the guy I had been dating, but I probably cried the whole time, thinking about my dead dog.

Marc

Oh my God! That's the hottest thing I've ever heard. A crying blow job! Whoa!

Elna

That's how it all went downhill. I mean, I felt so bad for the guy.

Marc

I just want to hear how he coached you through that? Like, "It's okay, baby, you're doing a good job." What did he say?

Elna

"Just let the tears land."

NICK GRIFFIN—COMEDIAN, WRITER

I've done so many horrible things.

Here's a thing I did one time when I was seventeen to have sex because I didn't know how to get girls. I was in Florida on vacation with my family and we went to some little hamburger joint, a sawdust-type place, and my parents let me stay when they left. I remember I was drinking with this girl—it was eighteen at the time to drink. My parents left, we finally leave. This girl, she's like two years older than me and I have no . . . I've had sex a couple times but it was because I was drunk.

We're driving home, she's got the radio on—this is absolutely true—and The Cars come on. The song "Drive." I said, "Turn this off," and she says, "What? Why?" and I say, "Just turn it off, turn it off." She turns it off and pulls over and says, "Why?" and I said, "My girlfriend died at a Cars concert."

I said, "We went to a Cars concert, she fell down, we were on the upper deck and she fell down the stairs and never regained consciousness." I teared up. And I swear on my mother's life I had sex with that girl that night. That's a horrible, horrible thing to do, isn't it?

I've done it since. A lot of people die when I'm trying to have sex. When I'm trying to create some quick bond with somebody, there's a lot of death that happens.

AMY SCHUMER

When I hear, totally honestly, when I hear a guy say "I fuck a lot of girls," I don't believe that anyone thinks that's cool anymore, unless they're young enough to believe that. I've got guy friends who have a lot of sex and they're really unhappy. I don't know any guy that's like, "Look, life is dope, I fuck every night." Someone hurt them. They're sad. I don't think that those high fives are going around anymore.

Marc

When your book *The Game* comes out, I saw it and I thought, "Oh, Neil Strauss is doing another investigative thing. This time about pickup artists." Then I started hearing, "No, he's out there speaking. He runs workshops."

I'm like, "Wait, Neil Strauss?"

They're like, "Yeah, he's like this pussy magnet, this pickup artist, he's running these workshops, and he lives in a mansion in Malibu, and there's women all around."

I'm like, "Whoa, wait, this is the same Neil Strauss? How did that happen?"

NEIL STRAUSS—JOURNALIST, AUTHOR

Yeah, but see, you see it like I see it. I'll do a news show, and they'll be like, "Here's the biggest douche bag in the world, who just wrote the manual for men." You see it how I see it, which is, I was just a nerdy writer dude, who somehow went immersive in this community, wrote a book about it. Then, again I really got into it in the book, it wasn't just detached.

I just got a call from *Nightline,* and they're like, "We want to write about this pickup workshop, and talk to you." No, that book's ten years old, I don't want to talk about it. It doesn't go away.

What happened was, the publisher I already did a Mötley Crüe book with called me up, and he said, "Hey, I found out about this community of guys online, they don't have money, looks, or fame, and they're exchanging this knowledge on how to meet, attract, seduce women. They've got it figured out to a science." He's like, "I want you to take their information, and put it into a how-to book for me." I said, "Listen, I write for *The New York Times,* I'm a serious writer, it's not something I'm interested in. But can you give me the URL?"

I started reading this stuff, and there were all these posts with guys, with weird names like Mystery and Candor. All these weird names. And they describe, blow by blow, everything they did. I'm like, "Oh my God, this is it." Because when I was writing for *The New York Times,* I'd go to these shows, concerts, and try and meet these women. I'd have tickets to the next cool concert, and they'd come with me. I'd just always end up friendzone, no matter what I did. If I slept with someone, I would try my best to make them my girlfriend, so that I could stay with somebody for a few years and not be so lonely. Maybe a couple years' dry spell between that. I felt like these guys had the secret.

I found out that one of these guys, named Mystery, is doing his first workshop. A workshop is he meets you out in quote, "The Field." In a club, or a bar, and he shows you how to approach women, then has you do it.

It was six hundred dollars. I put the money in an envelope, terrified to meet this guy, and terrified that anyone would find out I work for *The New York Times.* Then I remember we were at the Standard Hotel. It was the cool place then, the bar there. Scott Baio was there, with this beautiful woman. Mystery walked in, started doing magic tricks, and next thing I know, Scott Baio turns to me and goes, "Is this a magic trick, or is he stealing my girlfriend?"

"Whoa, this is amazing, this guy can walk the walk." Just anyone who could talk to a woman is my hero, and this guy's walking in, stealing a celebrity's girlfriend. I'm like, that was it, I was done. Cocaine did nothing for me, but watching Mystery do this thing was my coke. My reality was blown.

Then I just tried to start to hang around him as much as I could. Eventually he's like, "I need a wingman for my workshop." I'm like, "I want to do that, just to learn what you're doing."

Marc

Is he an attractive guy, this guy?

Neil

It depends on how you see him. He's tall, he's like six feet tall, but it's funny that we go to looks. I don't think it has anything to do with looks.

Marc

Would you classify him as a guy who was once like you?

Neil

He's super nerdy, if he's not going out and putting on a whole show, it's like long, greasy hair in a ponytail, computer nerd guy. But then he'd go out, and really dress up, and act tall and confident, and become that other guy. That was an illusion.

It's embarrassing. My biggest opportunity in life was not when *The New York Times* called me and said, "Will you write for us?" It was when Mystery asked me to be his wingman. Obviously it spoke to some deep need inside me to finally really get acceptance.

Marc

There's nothing like getting sex. It's exciting, and it means a lot.

Neil

Yes, thank you for validating that. Then we started traveling around the world doing workshops, and eventually I started to get good at it. I found all the other guys who I read about in that community, and befriended them all, and learned their different tips and tricks.

The surreal thing that happened was about maybe two years into it, they did a survey in this weird world of pickup artists, of the top pickup artist. I was number one, and Mystery was number two. The student had surpassed the master.

I would decide each night, "Am I going to call someone over, or go out with someone I've met, or am I going to go out and meet new people?"

It was weird, it was like a skill set you would work on. It wasn't enough to have sex, it was like, "How can I turn getting a threesome into a science?" We'd work through all this stuff, and at this point, we're all living together in a house too. I had done an article for *Rolling Stone* about Courtney Love, and she moved into the house. We had a house with maybe six pickup artists and Courtney Love.

These guys would be in the living room, doing the pickup workshop, and Courtney Love would come careening through, topless. For some guys, that was their first sight of a female breast.

Some were guys who were really good-looking, cool guys, but they didn't know it inside, they didn't have that esteem. Other guys were over as exchange students from somewhere else, and just felt out of place in the culture. A lot of guys like that.

In retrospect, I realize what the Game was. The Game was having an overbearing, dominant, neurotic mom, having a total fear of women, and feeling like you need to have some power, or control, over the situation. It had nothing even to do with sex, it was just about self-esteem and fear.

If you're just having sex, it's pleasurable, and it's nice, and it feels good, and you enjoy people, that's great. If you're doing it to fill some hole, that's the addiction.

I was really cynical about the whole rehab, sex addiction thing. When I checked in, they said, "Anyone who masturbates is a sex addict, anyone who watches porn is a sex addict." There are some groups, not this one, that say anyone who has premarital sex is a sex addict. Basically everyone listening would be a sex addict by someone's definition.

If you already have that compulsion, it's really easy to dive into it.

Marc

Yeah, I track my entire perception of sex to seeing porn too young. It fucking hobbled me, man.

Neil

What did you see that did that?

Marc

When I was fourteen, we found a Betamax of *Deep Throat* and *The Opening of Misty Beethoven.* Then when I was fifteen, we actually had fake IDs and went to porn theaters, but the assumption at that age, especially for a socially awkward, sexually awkward kid was that's the way it's done. Anything below that, or that doesn't happen that way, is not good sex. I was fucked from the get-go.

Neil

Yeah, that's called your attraction template. It sets a template in your mind for what sex is supposed to be. Your first experience molds you, it creates those neuro-connections that don't exist.

NICK GRIFFIN

I feel the same way about sex as I do about stand-up at this point. I only feel like in the last five years that I've really gotten the hang. I had sex and I did it right and it was all fine and sex with my wife was good, but I think I just started to relax in the last five years.

AMY POEHLER—COMEDIAN, WRITER, PRODUCER, ACTOR

It's very interesting when you're no longer being sexualized what happens. When you're pregnant, men act really weird. Some of them act really into you and interested in you. A lot of guys, really they don't even want to make eye contact with you. It's very strange.

JONATHAN AMES

I feel sexuality for me has been, as an easy phrase, acting out. But acting out pain and trying to re-create psychodynamics usually of humiliation to get to a place of profound self-loathing. But sometimes, though, there is a great comfort in the humiliation because now I'm at the place that I want to be.

I was reading some book on people with sexual problems and I only read the introduction. I tend to only enjoy genre fiction, so once I pick up nonfiction, I peter out after the intros.

Anyway, this doctor wrote about people seeking an obliteration of self. He was into the idea of people with fetishes because he thought that they might be able to achieve ecstasy through the obliteration of self, like a man who's so into shoes that he will completely lose himself. I think in normal heterosexual coupling, you can have perhaps obliteration of self. Let's say you're going down on a woman and you completely lose yourself in it and just the carnality and just how beautiful she is and how sexy, you're down there. I don't know, you lose yourself. You're, like, on another planet. I think fetishes or perversions sometimes, maybe you get there faster or maybe just going down on women is the same thing as licking a shoe. I don't know.

I think that's what I've sought out, the obliteration of self. I had to get away from myself. These things are like Alice in Wonderland things. The things that might be outside the norm of human sexuality.

JIM NORTON—COMEDIAN, ACTOR, RADIO HOST

I've never had a problem with talking about myself and my own sexual shortcomings, or my own addictive behavior sexually, because anybody truly questioning it is going to be fraudulent. Even if a man doesn't cheat or get hookers, any man that acts like he doesn't comprehend how another man could pay for a blow job is a liar. I know he's a liar, and he knows he's a liar.

Any type of criticism like that, you have to meet, I think, with complete belligerence. When people are apologetic about themselves, that's when they run into trouble. People smell blood and they pounce. I've never been apologetic about the things I talk about. I'm not ashamed of it, or if I'm ashamed of it, I say, "I'm ashamed of it."

MARGARET CHO—COMEDIAN, WRITER, ACTOR

I was seeing this guy who was really, really wild and crazy. He was turned on by me going and fucking people and telling him about it. He was the most emotionally unavailable person. He only wanted to have a relationship with me so that I could be sort of like his avatar and go and do these crazy things that he was not physically capable of doing. He would jerk off and listen. I never touched him or anything.

JIM NORTON

For me, sex and sexual behavior are isolating. It's very, very dark and alone. I don't want to cruise prostitutes with friends. It's me alone being ritualistic. I would only let a hooker in the car if she approached from the right and leaned in the right side of my window. It was this weird seduction game I would play with myself.

Marc

They had to honor a fantasy before you even exchanged money.

Jim

Yeah. To me, it's too easy. They just get in and suck my dick with money and there's no seduction. Again, there's no push and pull. There's no tension. I like to have a little bit of tension, a little buildup to it. The more little pieces of the ritual you put in, the longer the ritual can go on. Once you cum, it's over.

If a girl tells me she loves me while I'm fucking her, my dick, it wilts like somebody threw fucking hot water on it. I can't keep a hard-on through that. It does nothing for me unless she's a prostitute. If a prostitute says "I love you," I'll cum immediately.

It's embarrassing to be so trapped in the Madonna-whore thing, but it's very hard for me to love the same person who I want to smell their armpits.

I don't talk about this to be shocking. I'm annoyed when people are shocked by it. I want them to enjoy the honesty of it and laugh at it. I never want them to be shocked because, to me, it's stuff that a lot of them do anyway. Come on. We're not really breaking ground here. I'm not a kid fucker.

ALI WONG—COMEDIAN, WRITER

I'm, obviously, like a perverted, gross, freaky person. Sticking my fingers up a man's butt hole, a straight man's ass, is so exciting to me. I went to Disneyland recently and I got this special hookup where I got to skip all the lines, got to go on these awesome roller coasters. None of that was more exciting to me than sticking my fingers up a straight man's butt hole.

When you're the first to do it, it's so exciting because at my age and at this point in my life, sex is 99 percent mental shit anyways. For me to get aroused, doggy-style or spanking don't cut it no more. I have to wage psychological warfare on a man in order for me to cum.

MARGARET CHO

I've always been pretty bisexual. Sometimes it depends on the girl. I usually like really butch women and also women who are very dominant, and also women who are transitioning to male bodies.

When I go through kind of a gay phase, when I'm really into women or there's this one girl that I'm just crazy about, but she doesn't live here. When we're together, I feel so powerful, like I don't need men. We don't need men at all. It feels really good.

When you can go into a universe where you just need women, that's just unbelievable. That sort of proves that I'm not gay, because I have so much invested in patriarchy. Being with a woman is a beautiful vacation from patriarchy.

Then this one girl that I really like, it just gets really complicated because she has a lot of male energy even though she looks very female. It's like she's a man in a woman's body in a female. It's hard to explain. She's super mean. I like that.

DAN SAVAGE—JOURNALIST, WRITER, ACTIVIST

Bisexuality definitely exists. I think people are a little flexible around the edges. Every once in a while, I see a woman that I am like, "Yeah, zing. I kind of feel something." It is almost invariably a lesbian firefighter. A lesbian who looks like a guy: muscles, and looks like Rolfe from *The Sound of Music,* but is a woman.

Every once in a while, I see a lesbian who blings onto my sexdar. When that happens, I do not think, "Oh my God, I must really be straight." I do not have this panic attack. Straight guys, when they see the one dude who pings onto their sex-dar, suddenly have this panic attack about what it must mean. "Maybe I am not really straight; it does not matter how much pussy I have eaten, it does not matter how much pussy I have pounded." Those guys write me every day, having just flat-out panic attacks that they must be gay.

I feel sorry for you straight guys, I really do. You are less free sexually than everybody else. I am a gay dude. I could leave here and go have sex with a woman, and nobody is going to think I am straight now. Everyone will think, "Oh, that must have been crazy. That fag Savage fucked a woman. I wonder what that was about." No one is going to say, "Damn, Savage is not a fag! He fucked a woman!"

Women can do whatever they want—they eat pussy in college, and then they can be straight-identified, and nobody says, "Not straight."

Straight guys, you are trapped. It's not a prison of your own construction solely, because straight women, when they find out that their husbands or boyfriends had one same-sex encounter, write me, panicked that it must mean he is gay. Gay guys, if we found out that some hot movie star had had one same-sex relationship or encounter, we would all insist that he had to be gay. He could not do that if he were not gay.

It's sad for straight guys. I did not like straight guys when I started writing a sex advice column. I started feeling so sorry for straight guys after about two years of reading their letters. If there is anything girlie or gay that intrigues you or interests you, it can undermine your heterosexual bona fides with other straight people, other straight guys. It induces a kind of paranoia in straight guys, that they are not sort of comfortably straight. Not all of them—individual results may vary—but they are sort of paranoid.

I used to pretend to be straight when I was fifteen years old, and really try to perform straight. I see so many straight guys who are adults who are still doing that: still trying to convince the world that they are straight. Nobody walks around once they are out of the closet and gay going, "I have got to convince everybody. I have to walk this very careful line with my playing gay, so that nobody thinks I am not gay." Straight guys have to walk this line all their lives.

JUDY GOLD—COMEDIAN, WRITER, ACTOR

People ask, "When did you know?" I knew when I was three that there was something different about me. That I wasn't like everyone else. Three.

I was cutting my hair. I wanted to look like a boy. I made everyone call me Ringo. My grandmother's like, "Judith, why are you cutting your hair off?" I just wanted to do boy things. I had no desire to play with dolls. I knew that there was something different about me, and I had different feelings about the girls. You don't know until you're an adolescent, and you become a sexual person, "That's what it is." And in the 1970s, you do not tell anyone.

My first big crush was Barbara Eden. I just loved her, I thought she was the most beautiful thing. Then, of course, teachers, and then of course Barbra Streisand, and I loved Joan Rivers too. I loved outspoken females. Phyllis Diller and Totie Fields, I loved those women.

KEVIN ALLISON—COMEDIAN, WRITER, ACTOR, PODCAST HOST

I'm about three and a half years old, when I'm looking at this statue, this Hummel statue of a boy with his pajama bottoms falling off. You can see his butt. I'm thinking, "Oh my God." I grabbed that statue and started running around the house, saying, "Look at this! You can see his heinie!"

And my brothers and sisters laughed, and then I thought, "Well, the neighbors, they ought to know about this too," so I start running out of the house to be like, "Look! Look! You can see his heinie!" All of the sudden, I feel my mom grab my collar from behind and bring me back into the house.

She said, "I'm just going to take this and put it where it will be safe," and it was gone. It was never to be seen again.

I could see a look in her eyes that was like, fearful. Put the kibosh on this.

JIM NORTON

My first turn-on was pee. I can remember being a kid and there was a brother and sister. I was either first or second grade. I lived in Edison, New Jersey. He was my age. She was a year older. I would get them both at different times. I would lay behind the shrubs and convince them to sit on my face because they both had pissed their pants a lot. I would just breathe in the urine smell through their pants. That was one of my first turn-ons as a kid, the smell of piss.

It's animal on some level. We're probably supposed to be turned on by it. When you look at it, animals mark territory. It's used for something. It would turn me on. One girl I dated used to piss her panties for me. I was like in my midtwenties. I would tell her, "I want to smell it," and just fucking lick her pussy after she had pissed her panties. I'm not into cross-dressing, but one time she pissed her panties for me, then she asked me to put them on, and I did. It was the dirtiest thing I had done until that point. She kind of blew me through her own piss panties. I know that probably has really ruined her since then, but to me it was just the start of really enjoying piss.

KEVIN ALLISON

When I was five, I convinced the boy next door, who was also five, to take our clothes off. I said, "Wouldn't this be funny if we took off all our clothes"—I had this all planned out—"and ran around your basement listening to Walt Disney's *Cinderella* soundtrack?"

"Cinderelly! Cinderelly!" And then at one point, I said, wouldn't it be funny if you bent over and spread your butt so I can see what's inside there, and that moment was like a holy grail moment for me.

He turned around and I had an erection. I was not familiar with that. He was pointing at it, laughing, and I was like, "Oh my God! what the hell is this?" And soon after, his mom came down and discovered us. And I was not allowed to hang out with the kid next door anymore.

Marc

So, no Hummel figures, no neighbor kid.

Kevin

Yeah.

JIM NORTON

I can count ten sexual partners before fourth grade. I'd say almost all of them boys, a couple girls. Oral sex. I vaguely remember someone trying to fuck me in the ass. I think they were my age. I don't count it as abuse because it was consensual between kids.

I didn't get an erection at that age. I didn't know what they were. My friend Shawn got hard-ons. He would blow me and I wouldn't get an erection. I would do him and he would get an erection. I had no idea why his penis did that. It felt good and it was secretive. We love the secretive nature of it. Girls scared me because they had something different than me.

I kicked a girl named Sue in the pussy when I was a kid. She stole my tire. I was rolling a big car tire and she took it because she was one of the dyke girls in the neighborhood. I kicked her right in the crotch and she bled. I think that fucked me up with the vagina for a while. I'd never forget her. She might have just pissed, but I know there was wet in the front of her pants. That whole area became horrifying for me.

KEVIN ALLISON

I was the space cadet, the black sheep, the gay kid in the family.

My brother Peter said to my mom, "He has got to sign up for football or he's going to become a fucking fag." Second grade, I'm eight years old and I'm taking football practice, and after like eight weeks of practice or whatever it is, the season's about to begin and I still don't know how football is played. I asked the coach, "Excuse me, before we have the first game, could you just lay out on a chalkboard, like, how does this game work?"

He said, "One team is trying to get the ball to this side of the field and the other to that side of the field," and I was like, "That's it?"

My father loved opera and football. And he would take my brothers to the football games and take me to the operas. So I just assumed that football was as meaningful as opera. Like, if you understood it, it was going to be like understanding Wagner.

JIM NORTON

I've always felt fucked-up. I know I am. It's not normal, dude. It's not normal. You know what I mean? Normal people don't do that. To me, normal is not a judgment. Normal just says it's the norm. It's common. I don't judge. For me to like piss, it is abnormal, but I don't judge it as terrible. I don't judge what I consider abnormal. It's just not common.

SACHA BARON COHEN—COMEDIAN, WRITER, PRODUCER, ACTOR

You have anti-Semitism, you have racism, but homophobia means fear of the homosexual. Where there's fear, that can turn into violence. People who don't like gay people are scared of them, and that can transition into violence pretty quickly.

There was a recent study where they showed people pictures of naked men, and they found out that the homophobes who are most likely to use violence, or use violent language against gay people, were those who had some increase in tumescence and blood flow to their groin while seeing naked men. It's guys who are struggling with their sexuality who are going to go out and beat up gay guys.

The thing about being straight or gay, they're kind of silly terms, because it's a scale. Everyone is somewhere on the scale. I'm 23 percent gay.

Marc

Oh, you figured that out?

Sacha

Yeah, I've worked it out. We did all the calculations. I'm 23 percent gay.

Marc

It's a good number.

Sacha

There's been times when I got down to 17. I got up to 31. When I was doing *Borat* and I had the man's testicles on my chin, I was up to 31.

Marc

You've done that in a couple of movies.

Sacha

Yeah. Exactly. It's a theme. It's a motif.

Everyone's on that scale somewhere. Sexuality. It's like being black or white. No one's quite all black or white. Generally people are on that scale. That's why it's difficult for people.

JAMES ADOMIAN—COMEDIAN, ACTOR, IMPRESSIONIST

I have to tell people I'm gay often. At a certain point I just assume that people know. It can get tedious to have to tell everybody.

I'm surprised that people are still surprised because I feel I've been shouting about it for years and then I'm always amazed at how little I'm actually heard. My reputation does not precede me.

KUMAIL NANJIANI—COMEDIAN, ACTOR

Sometimes it is interesting when I see my people from Pakistan who are clearly gay. I'm like, "Good for you. You probably had to fight so much to get to the point where you're wearing a scarf." Then it's like, "We're not gay yet." I definitely had kids in high school that I was like, "This guy is gay." Some of them I've looked up on Facebook. Some of them have moved here and come out. A lot of them are married with kids. They're definitely gay.

This is a thing I see a lot when I do shows in the middle of the country, like Ohio, or wherever. At some theater, the guy who's clearly very gay and in his midforties but is married with kids and runs the local theater. That happens a lot.

ANDY RICHTER—COMEDIAN, WRITER, ACTOR

My parents have been divorced for many, many years, largely because of my father's homosexuality. That was a deal breaker, apparently. They tried to overcome it, but it just got in the way, his gayness. His gayness really got in the way.

I was four when it first happened, but it was serial drama for many, many years, and in many ways, goes on to this day. They get along as much as they get along with anybody. Honestly, at this point it's more like a sibling relationship. My dad will still spend holidays with my mother. They're still family in that they have children together. Even beyond that, they're family, because my dad was my aunt's best friend in high school, my mother's older sister. My dad knew my mom since she was like a preteen, and then they fell in love later on. In retrospect, my aunt is the biggest fag hag in the world, and the fact that her best friend was this guy that went to a working-class high school in Springfield, Illinois, in seersucker suits and dusty bucks is hilarious.

My mom tells me stories like when he finally came out to her, she said that she thought he was cheating on her, but she didn't have the foggiest notion that it was with men, and she said, "Right after he said it, this whole wave of memories, of incidents, of things, that I should have seen came to me." I said, "Like what?" She says, "One time he was coming over to my house, and he was late. I got worried, he was hours late. Then he got over and he was really, really worried, and he was very upset." This is in Springfield, Illinois. "He was driving by the train station, and he said to me, 'You know all those men that hang out behind the train station? I pulled my car in there, because I wanted to ask them, "Why do you do these things? Why do you do this?" I just couldn't believe that anyone would want to do that stuff. One of them got in the car with me, and then grabbed my car keys, and said, "I'm going to run away with your car keys, and you'll be stranded here unless you give me all the money in your wallet." I had to give him all the money in my wallet.'" That was his story, and my mom was just so upset and so sympathetic. Of course, in retrospect, he got robbed by a guy he was hoping to have some kind of suck-off party with.

She said, "Looking back at it, how could I have been so naive?" It's like, "Well, you were born in 1940."

I always take people at their word. Anybody that I've ever known who's been closeted, or anything, if they talk about girlfriends or whatever, I'll think, "Okay." Then later it comes out, "Oh, they're gay." And everyone's like, "You idiot, didn't you know?" I was like, "No, because he said he had girlfriends, so I just took him at his word." I don't judge on that level, and I don't give a shit. If you say you've got girlfriends, you're straight. I'm not going to think about you any more than that. Whatever, I don't have time.

JUDY GOLD

I was fifteen when I had my first encounter with a girl. It was like, "Oh my God." It was just natural, you know what I mean? It was very natural, it was like a natural progression. It was a complete secret, it went on for a couple of years, until we graduated high school. Sneaking here, sneaking there. My mother once caught us, and she walked in the room. I'm like, "We were just playing Ouija board, what are you talking about? We were playing Ouija board, naked."

Then I went to college. It's so funny, because when you're gay, you feel like you have to try to be straight. I don't think kids feel like that anymore. But I thought, "I've got to at least try it with a guy."

I had a boyfriend, and he was six four, he was about 120 pounds, and he hated food. I was like, "I fucking love food." He would eat a plain cheese sandwich, he's like, "I only eat because I have to." He would drive the car without the radio on. He was a complete opposite of me.

He looked like Mick Jagger, and he had a huge penis. It was like, everyone knew him, because he had this huge penis. It was like ten inches long. Rip you apart at the seams. I lost my virginity to him.

I hated it. It was so unnatural to me. I didn't hate him. He was like my brother. It was like a member of my family, just really boring, and tall.

Before I lost my virginity, I said, "You have to take me to dinner and I don't want to do it in the dorms." We went to a motel. Like the ones where when the father kidnaps the kids, and then he closes the curtain, he's in there.

We go to this motel, and we do it. I hated even making out, the whole thing was unnatural, like, "I can't believe I have to do this." Then we do it. I hate it. It's just awful.

Marc

When you saw a ten-inch cock, I have to assume that frightened you.

Judy

I had nothing to compare it to, that's the other thing. He's six four, and he's really skinny. It's all cock. It's like cock, and then some little body attached to it.

Marc

The body was just a cock delivery system.

Judy

Right. He puts it in. Then it really kills, and then I went to the bathroom, and I was like, "That broke." Then I went back in the bed.

I forgot what TV show was on. It was some sitcom or something. I was like, "Good, that's comforting." He doesn't hug me, but then he was like, "We can do it again." I'm like, "No fucking way."

Then the next day was the Simon and Garfunkel concert in Central Park, and we went, and I couldn't sit. It killed so much. I was leaning against a tree. Really romantic.

That went on, and he lived in my dorm, and he had his own room. He's like, "Why don't you ever sleep in my room?" I'm like, "Because I'm gay. I'm gay." I didn't say that. Then finally, I was just like, "I can't anymore."

Recently, I was doing a gig, and his wife showed up. It was in Florida. She came up to me and said, "I'm Phillip's wife." I'm like, "Oh my God." All I kept thinking about is, "You! That big fucking dick is inside of you all the time!"

And she was like, "It's so nice to meet you." I'm like, "He made me gay." No, I didn't say that. I wanted to say that.

Marc

"I've been running from his cock for thirty years."

Judy

Yeah, exactly. Oh my God, it was so big.

That was my straight experience. I never slept with another guy, it was so unnatural to me.

DAN SAVAGE

I lost my virginity in a three-way with a guy and a girl. I was fifteen, and they were in their twenties. Technically, it was statutory rape. I was totally down with it.

It was a camping trip. It was my brother's ex-girlfriend and some guy she was messing around with. They approached me, and it happened. I do not know why it is so hard to talk about it. He had sex with her, and then I had sex with her. My first was sloppy seconds. I watched him do it, and thought, "Okay, I can do that." I had to close my eyes and pretend she was Leif Garrett or Andy Gibb or something.

I could not touch him. I knew I was gay, and I thought, "If I touch him, he is going to realize I am gay, and he is going to stop what he is doing and kill me. He will stop what he is doing and beat me up," because I saw him naked, and fucking.

I was fucking her and it was taking a while, because it is hard to pretend that she is Andy Gibb with her head on backward or whatever. I was not quite getting there, and at one point, he reached between my legs and just started playing with my balls, and I was there. That really did the trick, and it is such a closet case thinking, "Oh, he can touch me because he knows he is straight. If I touch him, he will know I am gay, and kill me." That is the sort of shit that goes on in a kid's head when they are in the closet. You are always worried about who can tell, and how much you are giving away, and when you are going to get busted and murdered.

I was able to perform with girls a few more times. It totally threw my family off the scent for a few years. That was the point of it, like, "Well, my mother is going to think I am straight." Not that I would tell them, but I'd make sure the info leaked. That was the point. My brother found out. He was mad, and then he had to forgive me, like a straight older brother would.

JAMES ADOMIAN

I think I was about twelve when I realized that what people talk about as gay was me. That me liking men and stuff, that equaled gay and I was, "Holy shit!" But also, "Oh fuck! Now what?"

I beat myself up a lot. I tried to change myself. Tried to date girls.

I think we reached a nice standstill. I think all parties are happy with me leaving the girl side of things. I would go on dates with girls and fooled around a little bit. I've had my romances with the fairer sex.

Marc

You've touched a pussy.

James

I have. Man, I have. It feels weird to talk about. Have you ever touched a dick?

Marc

I've touched my own dick plenty.

James

No other dicks?

Marc

No dicks.

James

I'm just trying to see how far, what kind of mirror image we are of each other. I have a little more experience on the girls than you do with boys.

For me, it was, "Maybe I'm one of those guys that maybe can figure it out and make it work and I could be one of those guys." After a while it's, "Why am I doing this?" It took forever.

TODD GLASS—COMEDIAN, WRITER, PODCAST HOST

I always hate using the term "gay," and that's part of why I've always been sympathetic to people that don't want to be called this anymore.

Gay. I always felt like going, "Fuck that. I'm not gay. What the fuck do I got to tell people I'm gay for? I'm not fucking gay. I'm fucking Todd Glass."

This didn't happen overnight. This happened twenty-five years ago when I started not being honest to who I was.

My friends from like seventh grade, I was meeting their wives. They say, "So what's your life? You got a girlfriend? You got a boyfriend? You got this, you got that?" It was an open forum for me to say, "You guys have known me a while" and tell them. Instead I say, "I'm still with the same girl." I get in the car, and I say to myself, "What the fuck am I doing?" I'm holding on to this to the bitter end. By the way, I probably still will in certain situations.

I'm probably never going to be able to hold someone's hand in public the rest of my life. Anybody who says, "I think Todd's doing that to himself." Well, fucking think harder. This happened over forty-seven fucking years for me. That doesn't mean I haven't made strides to be who I am.

JAMES ADOMIAN

Most of my stand-up act I spend talking about being gay. I make a point to do that everywhere I go for the last four years or so.

The worst-case scenario is somebody yells "Faggot." It's happened twice. A guy interrupted me a minute into me talking about this. It wasn't yelling at the top of his lungs, it was audible just so I could hear it from his table. "This guy is some kind of faggot," like that. Luckily he was fat so I had something to give back to him. "You're born gay, but you have to work really hard to get as fat as you are." It was a conservative crowd, so I think they were on his side.

I had a guy in North Carolina who wanted to fight me after the show, for "doing faggot shit" onstage. Luckily they didn't let him back into the club, wisely. It happens, not often, it happens, but most people are really nice people. For the most part, I practice being able to talk about controversial things in an audience that does not automatically accept it. A suburban or conservative audience.

Basically I develop a rapport with people and I try to find out what we agree on, and hopefully by the time I'm coming out on-stage in a given set, they already like me.

I played football, so I talk about being a closeted gay football player as a kid. They get an idea of where I'm coming from. It's not like I'm an alien to them.

I have a unique ability to accomplish something that not everybody can do because certain kinds of people will listen. I can make them listen to me, I can make them like me, and I have the attention of people who may not normally give any attention to a gay person. I feel in some ways I'm an ambassador into hostile territory. I could have been in the closet, I could have gone a different direction and it probably has not helped my career on paper, but I think it's worth it because we're at a point where there's a lot of homophobia that's not really on any sturdy ground. That's in the process of crumbling down.

CAMERON ESPOSITO—COMEDIAN, ACTOR

I dated men for a really long time. I dated the captain of the football team in high school. We were the class couple. I just thought nobody really cared about sex. I was a big athlete, and I was the mascot of the football team and I was on the student government. I was, like, super involved and really committed to school.

I was on top of shit! But I was a mess. I had no idea. I was in love with my best friend. I didn't know. I just thought that's how women felt. I think women also have that kind of more expansive view of the way they can be friends with each other. If dudes are really close, when you're a little kid, somebody's going to come up to you and they're going to call you a name. They're going to call you what they think you are, and maybe you'll start to wonder if that's what you are, but for women, that happens a lot less. I think you can just be a jock and you can just have really close friendships. You can have sleepovers, you can hug each other, and none of it means anything unless it does. I just thought that's how everybody felt.

I would go to sleep at my best friend's house. She had seven older brothers and sisters that no longer lived at home, and I would insist on sleeping in her bed. There were like nine other bedrooms! I just was really committed to sleeping in her bed, but I just thought that's how best friends were.

I think I had sexual feelings, but I don't think I knew what sexual feelings were. I think I was very confused. I would have dreams about women. A lot of gay women that I know had a similar experience to this.

I don't know if you have ever heard what it's like to be a teen girl, but you're all about, like, his blow job. No one's trying to figure out whether or not you're, like, "Hey, what are you jerking off to?" Nobody gives a shit. You're not supposed to be touching yourself. Women are not really taught to find what they like. Of course they're not. It's all about finding out what he likes so you can turn him on. "Oh, you made him cum, isn't that great? You did a great job."

TODD GLASS

I was afraid if people knew that, they'd be afraid like, to drink out of my cup, because they think gay people might have AIDS or something. I thought, "Should I understand that? Would I feel that way?" I wasn't educated either.

I was hoping I married someone with cancer. A girl, and she'd die. I thought, "That's what I'll tell people. I never got married again, because I never got over my wife who had cancer." I had a plan. Date a girl with cancer, then she would die. You might think, "Come on, Todd. How much are you serious here?" I'm totally serious. That went through my head. Even back then I got the ridiculousness of it, but I did think that would work.

CAMERON ESPOSITO

My boyfriend would go home after we'd be hanging out, making out in my parents' basement or something. It felt nice, because kissing feels nice, but I also felt gross. I had weird rules, like he couldn't touch my shoulders and stuff like that.

He would go home, and I just remember that I would need to stay up for like, a bunch of hours. If he left at ten or whatever, I would have to stay up 'til, like, four in the morning, and I would eat cereal, just do these really comforting things. Eat cereal, watch TV. Whatever had been happening, I just couldn't deal with it. It was so uncomfortable.

But I liked him! I couldn't understand why I would feel so uncomfortable hanging out.

I think probably it would have been misery if I had had any idea that I was supposed to feel differently than that. If you've never seen the sun, you're going to be like, "Darkness is decent! It's decent to good."

TODD GLASS

Early in my life, I made pacts. I had a friend early on that knew. There was one point in my life where I knew one person like me, and we made a pact we would never tell anybody. I was probably twenty-one. I stopped being friends with him, because I got uncomfortable and nervous. It was a horrible feeling. Like he was too gay. Obviously I want to be very clear that it was a horrible thing to do. I was nervous and scared for myself, so that's why I did a horrible thing, out of fear.

CAMERON ESPOSITO

I kissed this woman. I was dating two guys at the time, and I went to three parties that night. The night that I kissed her, I went to a party with one of the dudes that I was dating, a party with other dudes, just on-campus parties. I kissed those two dudes at the parties. Then I kissed her.

I kissed her, and it was life changing; I mean, completely. She had come with me to these parties, so we just went back to my room. We were hanging out there, finishing some wine, and then, I don't remember what she said, probably something about poverty, but I kissed her. It was my first sexual experience, it really was. I knew immediately that something was very different, and it was like watching a movie that you never understood, with the director's commentary. You never understood the movie, and then suddenly the director's explaining it and you're like, "Oh shit! That's why I never wore a top to my bikini bottoms when I was a little child, because I had some gender stuff going on," and "Oh, that's why I wanted to sleep in my best friend's bed when there were all those available beds." It all happened at once. Like a Rubik's Cube, just solved in one move.

The next morning, I woke up and I had ringworm. I had contracted ringworm in Jamaica, which is a fungus and it grows in a circle, so I had got it on my face, and it had not shown up until the morning after I kissed this girl for the first time. Which, as a Catholic person who thinks that she might be going to hell because she just discovered that she has same-sex attraction is, like, probably one of the craziest things that can happen to you. Especially if you've seen the movie *The Exorcist*. Satan's in you, it's trying to get out.

I was so ashamed of myself, and I did end up dating that girl; she was my first girlfriend, but I didn't stop dating those other guys. For years, while I dated the guys, I was totally having sex with her.

We were both finding out at the same time. There was no teacher or student. We were both very much learning how to do it, which is really cool. I wish I hadn't been as ashamed of myself and I wish I hadn't had to hide, but I'll tell you, some of the best sex you're going to have in your life is secret gay sex. Secret gay sex that you're hiding from your boyfriends.

I was so upset. I was disgusted with myself. I was disgusted with what was happening. I still have these dudes around in case I can get married, in case I can have babies, they're still around. I told my folks, because I got home for the summer and I was just a wreck. I wasn't sleeping or eating. I thought my life was over. I didn't know any gay adults. I thought, I won't be able to have normal friends, and I won't be able to have a job. I just didn't think that anything was going to be okay.

TODD GLASS

If you want to use the word "gay" and you use it without meaning any harm, you didn't do anything wrong. But once someone makes you privy to what it does, if you still want to use it, that's the problem. Not that you used it in the past, "Oh, that movie's gay," or, "That's gay," or, "This is gay." You did nothing wrong. Until someone tells you what it does when there's a twelve-year-old around, or a fifteen-year-old who's gay. It crushes their soul. What does "gay" mean in that context? It means "bad." It means "stupid." Like gay people. They're weird. They're stupid.

CAMERON ESPOSITO

I told my folks; my dad cried for five years. Like, every time I would talk to them.

I had been a good kid. My older sister was the wild one that would, like, sneak out the window, and my dad had to remove the door from the hinges to find out she wasn't in there. She was like, the *Ferris Bueller's Day Off* kid, and I was like the Cameron. Which is funny. I just realized that that's true. I am Cameron.

My parents wanted me to go to therapy. We went to therapy as a family. The three of us. I've since realized that they were probably really confused; that they just didn't have a better plan, but at the time I thought that they were trying to get reparative therapy going.

One of the most damaging things I think a gay person can hear when they're coming out is that thing where their parents are so worried for them. Because I was so worried for me, so to have that echoed back was pretty awful.

I am very aware of the fact that as much as I didn't have any knowledge, they had also no knowledge, and then they also weren't experiencing this, so I didn't know anything about being gay, but I was gay, so I knew that this felt strong and weird and real. For them, I think you just remove all those emotions and it just looks like a choice and it looks like I'm ruining my life.

They also have apologized for that. I mean, they look back on it and they realize that it was a tough time for them too, and that they're sorry that they weren't able to trust me.

I do forgive them. I do. I get it. I get why that's what happened. It also helped me in some ways, because we had such a close relationship and I was so worried about letting them down in this way that I would never be able to change. That was kind of a gift, because now I can be a stand-up comic. I've already caused the largest possible schism. There's no other way I could have been that I think would have disappointed them more in the short term, so we already went through that. Now they just kind of have to trust me a little more.

DAN SAVAGE

My dad was a Chicago cop. Busted heads at the '68 Democratic National Convention. Then he became a homicide detective for about ten years, which was weird for me when I came out to him, when I told him that I was a big faggot. He was a homicide cop in Area 6 Chicago, which was the gay neighborhood at the time. This was the 1960s and 1970s, when a gay neighborhood was not a nice place. They were kind of marginal places. They were not like coffee shops and bookstores, and they were not lovely.

Gay bars and shit were dominated by the mob then, so gay neighborhoods were kind of rough places where gay people kind of dove in, had a little anonymous sex, and then went back to the wife, or the rectory. That is where the nightclubs were, that is where the bathhouses were. It was just at the cusp where people started creating gay-borhoods, and gay communities, and coming together in the North Side of Chicago.

Clark and Diversey was the intersection in the middle of my dad's beat, and the cops called it "Clark and Perversity."

He was not a cop anymore when I came out, and he reacted fine. He was the last person I told.

When I was fifteen, he divorced my mother. He left. I was ready to come out when I was fifteen—which was really weird, kids did not come out at fifteen in 1980 when I was fifteen. They came out after college.

After my dad left, I did not have to come out to him—he was not around. He was really homophobic when I was a kid. I want to slam him for it, but I want to exonerate him at the same time, because this is what good parents thought they had to do then. They thought gay was something that grew in your child—like an inclination, or a cancer—and you could nudge them and they would not go gay. He would say shitty things about gay people because he cared about me.

When I was thirteen years old I begged my parents—all I wanted for my birthday were tickets to the national tour of *A Chorus Line*. These motherfuckers were shocked when I came out. That is like seeing your thirteen-year-old son give a blow job, and you are shocked when he comes out. "I want tickets to *A Chorus Line* for my birthday! That is all I want!"

This was thirty years ago. This was when being gay was the worst thing you could think of someone, so you did not think that about your own child—no matter how much evidence was staring you in the face.

It used to be that parents would think, "That lifestyle is going to be a horrendous struggle, so I am going to do everything I can to prevent my child from becoming gay." Which from my father meant, saying shitty things about gay people to try to convince me not to choose to be gay. Now parents know, I think, that you cannot prevent your child from being gay. The problem is not that your child is gay; the problem is the way some people are going to treat your child because your child is gay. The focus has shifted from making the gay children the problem, to making assholes like Rick Santorum and Tony Perkins the problem.

I have this really distinct memory of my dad praising Anita Bryant. This is ancient history, right? She was this antigay crusader, the very first really high-profile one, saying that gay people were a threat to civilization. A threat to the family, to the economy. That was my dad's argument too. We were a threat to the economy, because gay people did not settle down. They did not have families, so they did not buy cars and houses and washing machines, and so GE would run out of money, and the economy would collapse. That was his theory. Of course, we did not get married or have families because you would not let us, as opposed to we did not want to. We wanted to, but we could not. Ironically, of his four children, I am the one, I think, who has bought a new washing machine in his lifetime. We shop. Gay men without children shop.

My dad had encountered a lot of gay murderers and murder victims by the time he was really seeing it in me, seeing that I was gay.

When I came out, he apologized for anything he might have said or done that made me feel uncomfortable. He was the last one I came out to in the entire family, which was easy because he had moved away; he had moved to California.

My mom has six siblings, my dad has eight. I have three siblings. There are eight million cousins. Everybody lived pretty close to home base at Rogers Park in Chicago, or nearby. There were a lot of people to tell when I started coming out.

I did that shitty thing that some people do when you come out: I told my mother, and told her not to tell my father. Then my mom and dad came to see me act in a play, because I was doing plays then. There was a wedding scene for my character in this play. It was a comedy, and my mother is bawling her eyes out because she thinks, "Danny is never going to get married. This is the saddest thing I have ever seen." My father is like, "What is wrong?" and she cannot tell him. I really did not come out to my mother—I dragged my mother into the closet with me. I did that for about a year and then she was like, "We cannot keep doing this, and you have got to start telling more people."

I came out to my siblings. Then my mother basically told all of my aunts and uncles, and there were problems. I had one uncle say that he would never speak to me again, or be in the same room with me again. He is great now, and he loves me. That was the importance of actually having a big family. Maybe for five minutes it turned into two warring tribes, like "on my side" and "against me." The "on my side" tribe utterly defeated the "against me" side. My mother went to everybody and said, "If you have a problem with Danny, you have a much bigger problem with me. Got it?" My mom was tough that way.

When you come out to your family, all of a sudden they have to picture you with a dick in your ass. I hate to be crude, but that is it. When you are straight, people do not see you having sex. Coming out to my mom and dad meant burdening them with a mental image; I could see it on their faces. You tell them you are gay and they are picturing a dick going into your mouth. When my sister had a boyfriend, they do not picture her giving blow jobs. "She is straight, she has a boyfriend. There is probably something going on, but I do not have to think about it, because their relationship could be about dating and marriage and family and a future. It is about so much more than the blow job."

If you are a gay kid in the 1980s, your relationship is not about marriage, it is not about family, it is not about the future—it is about a blow job. It is about sex only.

MELISSA ETHERIDGE—MUSICIAN

When I see kids now who are openly gay, like eighteen, nineteen. Oh God, to not go through those horrible years in the closet.

SIR IAN MCKELLEN—ACTOR, ACTIVIST

The British government was passing a particularly nasty antigay law, which I took very personally. In debating this particular law, I got angry and I kicked the door open and announced on a BBC radio program I was gay.

It was Section 28 of the Local Government Act and it said because gay people have only pretended family relationships, it will be illegal to talk positively about homosexuality in any school. On the grounds that if you were to do that you would be promoting homosexuality. You would be encouraging kids to become gay, as if such a thing were possible any more than it's possible, in my view, to encourage gay kids to become straight. It was a horrible law. It is insane and cruel and unfair and ridiculous and antisocial in every possible way. In debating that with someone who approved of this new law, it was only too easy for me to say, "Will you stop talking about 'them.' You're talking about me." That shut him up. Of course I haven't shut up ever since.

It was hugely important to me because it was a great relief. I didn't understand that I had been censoring myself. I assumed that that's the way it was. You're gay. You may not show your affections in public. You may not hold hands with the person you're sleeping with. You can't put your arms on them, you can't kiss them, you can't do any of the normal things like that. You can't talk about it. You're different. Of course, when I started out being sexually active it was actually against the law to have sex. I have friends who were put in prison. Scars you for life, knowing that's a possibility. Then you restrict yourself and you see other people doing the same thing and you think this is the way that life is. You buy into the lie that homosexuality is unnatural.

It's living in a closet. It's living in a place that's dark and dusty, with old things that aren't used anymore. You certainly don't like yourself, nor do you like society that makes you like that. Once you stop all that, the relief. The joy. Proud to be gay? No, proud to SAY I'm gay. Glad to be gay. Wonderful word, "gay." Before that it was "queer," you know? Some clever activist said, "It's not working, this calling ourselves queer. Let's choose our own word. What about blue? No, that's not right. Yellow. Gold. Gay! 'Gay' is a nice word." There we go.

Everything in your life becomes better. All your relationships are improved. Better actor, I would say. A different actor. Acting became no longer a release for emotions that I wasn't allowed to have elsewhere in my life.

Marc

Do you think that maybe some of your desire to act was around that shame?

Ian

I do. I can now cry onstage. I could never cry before. It was fake. My acting was fake. My acting was disguise. Now my acting is about revelation, truth. Everything's better. I can't stop talking and telling people, "Come out. Join the human race."

DONNELL RAWLINGS—COMEDIAN, ACTOR

One of my brothers, he lives here in California. He's older than me. He's gay. It's awesome nowadays. You get points if you have a gay relative.

He just recently really came out. Black people, you've got to make an official announcement. When my brother told me one day, I was at The Improv on Melrose. He came up to me. He was like, "You know, I keep it real like you, right?"

I'm like, "What?"

He said, "See that guy over there?"

I was like, "Yeah."

"That's your brother-in-law."

I was in the middle of taking pictures and shit. It didn't register. I didn't think about it. Then I'm driving home. I'm like, "Oh, shit. My brother just introduced me to his baby daddy or somebody, right?"

I call my dad. My dad is old school. He uses the words "bitches, crackers." I'm like, "Dad. Charles just told me he was gay."

My father was like, "Yeah, man."

I was like, "Yeah."

He's like, "Yeah."

This is where I know the world has changed. My dad was like, "Man, you know I ain't with that shit. But the dude he dating is a good dude." He validated the relationship! He said it like tough. He threw the towel in on it. "The dude he's with, he's a good dude. He's a good nigga, man."

MELISSA ETHERIDGE

I obviously had this underground lesbian following. Everybody knew. It was all "don't ask, don't tell," though. I finally did an interview before my third album for a music magazine and I did my talk where I would use no pronouns, my partner, whatever. The writer changed all my pronouns to "my boyfriend" or "he." I lost my mind and I said, I have to come out because now everyone's going to think I'm lying and that's the last thing I want to do.

So I decided I was going to come out. I didn't know how. I thought I was going to do it on *Arsenio Hall*. In the meantime, I'm doing work, political work with a lot of gay and lesbian groups that helped get Bill Clinton elected. They have this inauguration ball and it's the most fun because it's all the gay people, of course. Rock and roll was back in the White House. We were there. And us gays were being gays and we were allowed to be part of the party.

So I came out at the inaugural ball there with everyone.

K.D. Lang had said some things and there were a couple of other people there. She had just come out a few months before that. She introduced me, "Melissa Etheridge," and I walk up. "Yay!" And everyone's screaming and hollering because it's one thing that I'm even just there supporting them and then I'm like, "Oh, I just want to say, I'm just so proud to be a lesbian."

Over.

It was like a match lit. Now you're on a journey, here you go.

IDENTITY

"Everybody Has a Community"

Identity is complex. On some level it defines who we are, but the choices we make around the possibilities of that identity are our own. We identify ourselves by so many things: religion, career, economics, sexual orientation, and in countless other ways. And one of the most complex sources of identity is race. It is a racial identity that cannot be hidden and it will precede you in terms of others making personal and cultural judgments just on your appearance.

On June 19, 2015, Barack Obama, the forty-fourth president of the United States of America, came to my house to talk with me in my garage. It would be a little weird if I had a conversation with the nation's first black president and we didn't talk about race. So we did. And when we did, the president said a word, a racial slur. I won't say it here. You'll read the president saying it in this chapter.

As a comic, it wasn't that jarring to me when he said it. He said it to make a point about the use of it. It was a broader statement about racism in our society, the progress we've made and the divisions that still exist.

The reaction from the news media was sadly predictable. Most outlets reduced the president's point to a grabby headline, and the talking heads shouted over each other arguing whether it was appropriate for the president to say that word. It felt dismissive, and it spoke to President Obama's larger point about why it's difficult to have these conversations about race and identity and our differences.

That's why I'm glad I can still have these conversations on my show. I've talked to many different people about different facets of identity and the struggles with identity that are very personal. I talked to Kumail Nanjiani about the culture clash he experienced as a Pakistani immigrant meeting his wife's southern family. I talked to Laura Jane Grace about accepting her identity as a transgender woman and why that allowed her to finally understand herself.

And because I have always struggled with my own identity, I can listen and learn. I am white. I am a Jew. I am a comic. I have struggled with what all of those labels really mean. I identify as a Jew but I am not that Jewish in practice. So, what does it really mean? As I write this it is 6:00 A.M. I am sitting at JFK airport. The sun is rising outside and an Orthodox Jew is davening in the sitting area in front of me. Hooded by his tallith, with tefillin on his forehead and a prayer book in his hand, he rocks back and forth. No one is looking at him but me. I know, as a Jew, we share an identity. I know that if I wanted to, I could pursue my identity to the extreme he is pursuing his. I also know I would have to change my entire life and depth of my belief system to do that. Seems like a lot of work. I don't mind watching him while I drink my Dunkin' Donuts coffee wondering about it. I'm okay with my Jewishness. I'll keep it light.

ZACH GALIFIANAKIS—COMEDIAN, WRITER, ACTOR

When my dad was younger, he and his brothers had restaurants. They opened up an all-black café in Durham, North Carolina, called the Lincoln Café. They all cooked and worked there. It was in a black neighborhood.

Growing up in the South, my dad's side of the family, they're dark. You know, they're Greek. My uncle Mike told me that in the 1950s, in the summer, he would get really tan, dark eyes, dark skin. One day he sat in the front of the bus in Durham, North Carolina, and the bus driver stops and says, "Hey, boy, you have to sit in the back."

My uncle says, "Why?"

The driver says, "Because you're a Negro, you have to sit in the back of the bus."

My uncle says, "I'm not black."

And the bus driver says, "Well, what are you?"

My uncle says, "I'm Greek."

And the bus driver says, "You can't ride the bus."

RUSSELL PETERS—COMEDIAN

I was just a kid, trying to blend in. In Canada, there was a lot of racism toward Indian people, and so it was brought to your attention very early that "this is what you are, and you shall not try and hang out with these people or these people. You should probably be quiet and shut the fuck up in that corner over there."

AHMED AHMED—COMEDIAN, ACTOR

We used to get death threats during Iran-Contra. People would call our house and say, "Go back to your country, stupid whatever." And we'd be like, "Dude, we're Egyptian. If you're going to be racist, get it right."

MAZ JOBRANI—COMEDIAN, ACTOR

Growing up, there was no Middle Eastern good guys. You know, Omar Sharif, that's forty to fifty years ago now. For my age group, I loved De Niro and Pacino and all the Italian guys because that was the closest to me. First of all, everybody loves those guys anyway, but furthermore, that was the closest I could get. I was like, "They kind of look like me," you know? They're these cool guys, that's who I'm going to grasp onto.

KUMAIL NANJIANI—COMEDIAN, ACTOR

I was eighteen when I moved here. Most of my formative years were in Pakistan. I came alone. I was eighteen.

It was always the plan. I went to an English-speaking school because the plan was always to get me out of Pakistan. For good.

Marc

Why, because your parents sensed that it was not going well there?

Kumail

The burning cars were a good hint.

I went to Iowa. I left Karachi, and I landed in Des Moines, Iowa. It's very flat. I loved Iowa. It was great for me because if I'm going from Karachi to New York, nobody is going to give a shit about me, another Pakistani in New York. If you go to Iowa, there's not that many people around. You can slowly get used to the cultural stuff. It's a gateway to the States.

The weird thing was there was so much liberal white guilt that people didn't want to acknowledge race at all. It was almost like people would go out of their way to not ask me about Pakistan.

JOE MANDE—COMEDIAN, WRITER, ACTOR

I was Jewish growing up. I went to Jewish summer camp and youth group stuff and never took that part of it seriously. When you drop a prayer book you're supposed to kiss it. We would drop it on purpose just to make out with it. Going to second base with our prayer books. We were just terrible.

Then I had this experience a couple Passovers ago. I was doing the Passover thing to see if it meant anything to me. I ended up getting conned by this Israeli guy for like $400 when I had no money. The whole time he was like, "It's a mitzvah, it's a mitzvah." I knew I was getting conned. It was crazy. This guy was awful.

I was waiting for a train, day two or three of Passover. I was following the rules, seeing if it meant anything.

Marc

Joe Mande's search for meaning.

Joe

Right. I definitely found it. This guy came up to me. He looked like Michael Chiklis. Like a tan Michael Chiklis. He was like, "Excuse me, are you Jewish?" I feel bad, but I usually say no. But I said, "Yeah." At first he just wanted to know if this was the train to Queens because he had to get to LaGuardia. Then he started telling me this weird story about how his wife and his child were at this house in Astoria and he was trying to get his shekels in order and it just made no sense. He was like, "Can you help me? It's a mitzvah. I just need you to go to this bank and help me convert shekels into dollars because I don't have a bank account in America." I was like, "Okay, sure, whatever."

Marc

Wow, this is a hustle designed for Jews.

Joe

Yeah, it was. It's also the worst hustle. It got to the point where he started asking me about my girlfriend and if she's Jewish. I said no and then he was like, "Better dump her." I was like, "Who are you?" He's like, "My grandparents didn't die in the Holocaust for you to date a Christian girl." The whole time, I'm like, "They didn't. You're clearly a liar." He keeps nailing home that it's a mitzvah, it's a mitzvah I'm helping him, we're Jewish, this whole thing. We get to the bank and I'm like, "Okay, give me your shekels." He was like, "No, you misunderstand. I need money to turn into shekels." I was like, "That's the opposite of what you said." He told me he needed

$400, he did the conversion rate. He said this many shekels and was like, "It's about $400." At the time, also, I had a broken iPod and I was waiting to buy a new iPod.

I don't know why I did this. I went and I got $400 out of my savings account and was about to hand it to the guy and then I was like, "Wait, I need your information." Okay. First of all, he said his name was Israel. From Israel. And that he owned the biggest falafel stand in Jerusalem. He was the worst con man in the world.

I don't know, to this day, I don't know why I did this. I gave him the money and then he wrote on the deposit slip, it was all in Hebrew script, "Israel from Israel," a phone number with like thirty digits, and he just walked away with all my money. I was just like, "I just gave that dude my iPod. That's my iPod." I don't know why I did it. It bothers me so much. I was like, "Well, at least I got a story out of it."

I told that story a few nights later onstage, and in the back of the room I hear someone just freak out. When I get offstage, it was Nick Kroll, and this same dude conned Nick Kroll out of like $250 on Purim. This guy knows how to find insecure twenty-three-year-old Jews going through some sort of spiritual crisis.

It's a mitzvah.

What I did was when I handed him the money, I said, "I just want you to know if you don't pay me back, I don't believe in God, so you're going to have to deal with that." Like this is some Cameron Crowe movie. He was like, "Okay," and then just skipped away. What does he care?

AL MADRIGAL—COMEDIAN, ACTOR

I get asked to do all these Latino comedy jams on a regular basis, and I'm just not that type of comic. You know the Russell Simmons's Def Comedy Jam? They have the same thing for Mexican comics and it's like, "You can come to our big local comedy slam and it's two thousand dollars for twenty minutes each day." I'm like, "Oh, that's great, four thousand bucks for a weekend."

I go to the gig and there's two thousand Mexicans in this big cafeteria. My wife looks at me and she's like, "Dude, you've got to get the fuck out of here." She's supportive like that. The guy before me was doing his entire act in Spanish and just killing. I walked up, I'm like, "What would a Latino Def Jam comedian do in this situation? What would Carlos Mencia do?" That's one of the rare times you want to ask yourself that question. I go up and I'm like, "What's up, everybody?!?!? Make some noise!!!!!" They all make some noise. This is like two thousand people. I go, "Where are all the black people at? Black people make some noise!!!!" Nothing. Not one black person there. I go, "All the white people make some noise." Nothing. Just half of me is the only white guy there.

Then I said, "What's up, Latinos?!?!?" Screams. Then I do it just by saying "fuckers" and "bro" constantly. That's the code. Just say "fuckers" and "bro." "What's up, fuckers?" "Little fucking fuckers, fuckers, bro, bro, fuckers, fuckers."

I go to the next gig and it's Stockton, California, which is this meth shithole in the middle of nowhere. I go there and the same guy who's doing his whole act in Spanish the night before and doing so well, he's just destroyed. I go, "Hey, Reuben. What's wrong? How was your set?" He's crying a little bit. He says, "They threatened my life."

I got to go up there and I can't be this character that I'm not. I'm going to be myself. And that's a bad idea. Never be yourself, try to be something better. Short story is I ended up hopping a fence while the black security guards laughed at me. That's how that gig ended.

It was because I did this "paquito" thing. Want to know how you spot a half-Mexican? Overuse the word "paquito." This guy stands up and screams, "He doesn't speak Spanish!!!!!!!!" Like Mexican Braveheart. I really tried to keep it together, but he was violently flipping me off and leading people in boos against me.

Then I finally said, "Look, you guys, this isn't exactly a dream gig for me either. I'm stuck in Stockton, of all godforsaken places. The best part about it is I get to leave and you people are stuck here for the rest of your miserable fucking lives. I'm taking the money I'm being paid handsomely and I'm going to go blow it at outlet malls on the outskirts of a very shitty city like yours, so fuck off."

That's why I had to hop the fence.

MARGARET CHO—COMEDIAN, WRITER, ACTOR

I always do my mom in my act. It's just Asianness, and the voice of whatever is ancient in me, that's sort of questioning all the stuff that I do and what I'm doing. I'm really close to my parents, so something that's always in my head are things that they say. It's a celebration of the awkwardness of being an immigrant. I think that's always going to be part of what I do and who I am.

ALI WONG—COMEDIAN, WRITER

My husband's dad is Japanese. My dad's Chinese. His mom's Filipino. My mom's Vietnamese. So we gave birth to Asia. All of it.

I speak conversational Vietnamese, but that's because I went and did this program in college and after college to learn Vietnamese. It's like the proficiency of maybe a second grader.

Marc

Which is probably kind of cute to some people.

Ali

Not to Vietnamese people. They're like, "What the fuck is wrong with you? Just speak English." I thought my mom would be excited. She's like, "This is so exhausting trying to hear your long-ass, slow, boring sentences about what time is it, basic shit. Let's talk about real shit in English, please."

KUMAIL NANJIANI

My wife is from North Carolina. She is very southern. Way southern family. They've been around forever.

I told my mom that I was dating this girl. My mom obviously freaked out. There was a lot of crying and stuff. Then to her credit, my mom was very accepting of her when she realized that I really love this woman. It's against my mom's religion, and culturally everything is against it, and our family, I'm sure people were talking about it behind her back and to her face. It was really nice that ultimately my happiness is what was most important to her.

Marc

How did your wife's family react to you?

Kumail

They were great. They called me Borat at first. I found out because we were going to a family reunion, and her uncle was like, "She said we can't call you Borat." I was like, "You guys were calling me Borat?" Emily had a serious talk with them and was like, "Don't say this, don't say this." I actually think that was their way of trying to relate to me. Borat, which I think is even the wrong continent, right? Former U.S.S.R. I think they were trying to relate to me, and Borat was the closest they could get. I'll take Borat over Bin Laden, I guess.

Marc

I think so. I think it's a little more a term of endearment, but it is ignorant still. I don't mean to be crass or insult your family, but to call you Borat, it's cute, but it simplifies things.

Kumail

It does simplify things. I think that for them that was the only way that they could relate to me, by simplifying things. They hadn't met me yet, they had seen pictures of me.

Marc

Now they know you. Can they pronounce your name?

Kumail

Yeah. I was like, "It's Kumail like e-mail but with a Ku, like Ku-mail." Then they called me E-mail for a little while. It was funny.

When I first had Thanksgiving with them, Emily had prepped them or whatever. I was sitting around with the family, and it was fine. Then I made some crack. We were talking about the airport. I made some hack joke, you know, whenever you're with the family you make a hack joke, some hack joke about getting stopped at security or something because of being brown. They laughed so hard, like way harder than I expected. They were like, "Finally, he's admitting it!"

W. KAMAU BELL—COMEDIAN, WRITER, TELEVISION HOST

I'm married, my wife is white, but I realize from being with her that her ethnic identity is Italian Catholic. Even though a very small portion of herself is Italian, but her grandfather is 100 percent Sicilian, she grew up in an Italian family, all the food, all the talking. I realized, oh, her ethnicity is Italian Catholic.

A question I get a lot from her family is, "What's your experience here?" First of all, the dynamic of somebody dating your daughter is always going to be a screwed-up thing, no matter how alike you are on the surface. Let's just start with that. I think her family was way more alerted to the fact that I was a comedian, an unsuccessful comedian in their eyes, and my eyes, than that I was black.

Certainly, there's other aspects of the family, where I would look around and be like, "I'm the only black person here at these big family gatherings," and I can't help but think about that. There were times where things would happen and I would be like, "Is this because I'm black or is this because I'm me?" I think that's a burden that the Other carries a lot, not being able to figure out what's happening.

At the time, I had really long dreadlocks, and I think that had a lot to do with it. If I had been a black lawyer, I think it would have been different, but I was a black comedian with long dreadlocks who was older than their daughter, and it was like, "What is this dude? This is not the dude we ordered." Black was maybe on the list somewhere, but it was not the top of the list.

Now, on the other hand, I couldn't sit down with her family and be like, "Let's talk about my blackness." I don't think they would have had any time for that.

I think the fact that Barack Obama is actually of a white parent and a black parent is why he's able to be president the way he has. He very much is always reaching out to white people because he had to reach out to his relatives.

PRESIDENT BARACK OBAMA

My mother was the biggest influence in my life and this wonderful woman, but I am raised without a dad. An African-American, but not grounded in a place with a lot of African-American culture, and so I'm trying to figure out how I'm seen and viewed and understood as a black man in America.

What does that mean? I'm absorbing all kinds of stereotypes and ideas from society. Like Richard Pryor or Shaft. I'm trying on a whole bunch of outfits. Here's how I should act. Here's what it means to be cool. Here's what it means to be manly. You know, you start smoking. You start drinking coffee. You've got a leather jacket.

Then at a certain point right around twenty, right around my sophomore year, I started figuring out that a lot of the ideas that I had taken on about being a rebel, or being a tough guy, or being cool, were really not me. They were just things that I was trying on because I was insecure or I was a kid. That's an important moment in my life, although also a scary one, because then you start realizing, "Well, I actually have to figure out what I really do believe and what is important and who am I really."

A lot of that revolved around issues of race and being able to say that I don't have to be one way to be both an African-American but also somebody who affirms the white side of my family. I don't have to push back from the love and values that my mom instilled in me. She instilled in me these core values that for a while I thought were corny. Then right around twenty you start realizing honesty, kindness, hard work, responsibility, looking after other people—they're actually pretty good values. They're homespun. They come out of my Kansas roots, but they're the things that ultimately ended up being most important to me and how I tried to build my life.

W. KAMAU BELL

There's a lot of racism in the alt-comedy scene.

DWAYNE KENNEDY—COMEDIAN, WRITER, ACTOR

A whole lot of nigger going on.

Kamau

Exactly. "I think he just wanted to say 'nigger.' I don't think there was a joke there." There have been many occasions, we've been at alt-comedy shows with comedians who are known and unknown and suddenly be like, "I think I got to leave," and it happens from comics you never expect it to happen with. It's weird, it's like I can't talk to white comics about it because then they think I'm crazy, because I think a lot of people think because they stand on a comedy stage and they're a good guy it can never be racist, no matter what I say.

CHELSEA PERETTI—COMEDIAN, WRITER, ACTOR

After I graduated from school, my brother and I did a Web site, Black People Love Us, which was these two white people bragging about their black friends and how well liked they are by them and testimonials from their black friends that are sarcastic implications of annoying white people. We wound up on *Good Morning America* facing off with Diane Sawyer mediating with two black people. She had one of them be pro and one be con. It was six in the morning. I was so tired I couldn't think. In general, I think I learned from it never to try to have a serious intellectual discussion about a joke. I would much rather just be like, "I thought it was funny. Bye."

DWAYNE KENNEDY

In the scheme of things, just in society, black folks are expendable. I can say "nigger" all day long without any consequence to my show business career. If I went on stage talking about "kike," that would last about one show. Not that I aspire to do that. I don't even want to do that.

W. KAMAU BELL

Racism is defined as a hate crime and I think that's not always true. It doesn't always end up in death. I feel like there's levels of racism.

Marc

I think fundamentally, racism is, "We are not the same because you are black." It's not necessarily "You are black, you should die."

Kamau

No, no, no. After you decide we're not the same, what is your next thing? I'm not going to hang out with you or I'm going to kill you?

Dwayne

I'm not going to hire you.

Marc

That's racism.

Dwayne

Which does impact your life fundamentally, eventually, in waves and ripples. "I don't mean you any harm, but I don't mean to help you in any way." When a large group of people feel like that and it becomes consensual, then it does begin to marginalize you and that does begin to impact your life. Less goods and services in your community, and less health care, and going on on on on on. Now the quality of your life is diminished a little bit, but it wasn't anybody directly doing anything, but it's this consensual thinking that pushes you away.

Kamau

It's also just the feeling of being otherized too. We were talking about this today. I was like, "I don't think white people realize how many white people there are out there." I don't think white people look around like, "There are a lot of white people out there." In that sense, I think white people take it for granted how safe that feels.

RUSSELL PETERS

The whole world speaks English. That's the funny thing, the world is smarter than we are. Because in America, we think that everybody else is stupid. Actually, no. They speak their shit *and* ours, and then, not only that, they speak ours better than we speak it.

W. KAMAU BELL

People think that white is the absence of culture in race. They think that, well, I'm not anything, I'm just an American, or I don't really know what I am. I feel like what it comes down to is if white people thought about their whiteness more, it would change the way in which they interact with other people. I don't think white people think about their whiteness enough in this country. When the news says "White people blah blah blah," every white person says, "That's not me, I'm not White People." Whereas when the news says, "Black people blah blah blah," even if I don't relate to that, I know that's me. I have to accept some responsibility for that, or I have to choose not to, but I can't act like I'm not involved in it. I feel like a lot of times white people act like they're not involved in the race discussion in any way.

There's people in this country who are filled with fear, and they're raising kids. Yes, if I'm in Brooklyn, there's a bunch of black kids on skateboards with tattoos, with their hair sprayed up, in goth bands who are like, "Yeah, I just sort of do whatever I do." You go outside of San Francisco, forty miles outside of San Francisco, there are white people who feel like they're in Texas.

Those of us in urban environments overshoot that a lot, because we think in my neighborhood it's not that way, but there's a lot more of America that's the other way.

PRESIDENT BARACK OBAMA

I always tell young people, in particular, do not say that nothing's changed when it comes to race in America unless you lived through being a black man in the 1950s or 1960s. It is incontrovertible that race relations have improved significantly during my lifetime and yours, and that opportunities have opened up, and that attitudes have changed. That is a fact.

What is also true is that the legacy of slavery, Jim Crow,

discrimination in almost every institution of our lives; that casts a long shadow and that's still part of our DNA that's passed on.

Racism. We are not cured of it.

And it's not just a matter of it not being polite to say "nigger" in public, that's not the measure of whether racism still exists or not. It's not just a matter of overt discrimination. Societies don't overnight completely erase everything that happened two to three hundred years prior.

W. KAMAU BELL

I think white people are shortchanging their community. Everybody has a community. My dad is from Alabama. I go to Alabama every year and hang out there. You can feel the community, and there's pride in the community, and sometimes that comes with a Confederate flag, but not all the time. There's a sense of "We are this thing and we define ourselves through our community," that just I think starts to not happen so much in urban environments. I just think that white people are shortchanging themselves. Have some white pride, as I say.

Marc

Be careful with that. There's a small jump from white pride to white power.

Kamau

Yeah, but I feel like white pride has been taken by bad white people. There's got to be good things to be proud about when you're white. There's got to be. The same way there's a black nationalism that is "get some guns and start taking out some white fools," and then there's the black nationalism that's like "get an Afro pick with a fist on it." That literally makes me feel better to be black.

It's by degree and direction. In America, I can't speak for the world, things move in a more progressive direction in general. This is the nature of evolution. We're talking about gay marriage now daily, we weren't ready to talk about gay people fifty years ago. This stuff is all inevitable. People are always going to pursue more freedoms and the freedom to be who they are. Get past the gay thing, because gender is coming next.

LAURA JANE GRACE—MUSICIAN

I would have this experience of extreme dysphoria and then, like, bingeing and purging, being like, "No. I'm going to be a man. This is what I'm going to do. I'm going to pretend I do not feel this way." I'm living two separate lives. I'm married, I now have a kid, we bought a house and I don't know who I am.

I fell in love and I didn't want to fall in love, but I fell in love. It was more that like I fell in love and ignored really being totally honest probably about who I was. Just like suppress, suppress, but that made me more and more unhappy, especially as I'm kind of pushed into fitting this cis-normative lifestyle of husband, wife, kid, cars in the garage.

Yeah, and then I'm like, "Oh my fucking God." The walls felt like they were coming in more and more. I probably didn't hear the word "transgender" until I was like maybe even twenty-six or twenty-seven.

I didn't understand myself. It's not like I was carrying around full knowledge of "This is who I am and I have to hide this from everybody." It was like, "Oh my God. I have all these feelings that are tearing me apart inside and I don't know how to reconcile them with life and what I'm doing and who I am. I don't know what I'm supposed to do with this." The idea of transitioning was a far-off concept that I'd only ever maybe heard about once or twice.

I dealt with these feelings to the point where I was like, "This isn't going away." The idea of whatever that meant of coming out with the way I felt and saying, "Look. I'm transgender or I'm a transsexual. This is the way I feel. I want to transition. I don't know what that means, but I want to transition." I mean, the level of information out there was like "YouTube testimonial videos," you know? Like, a couple fucking lo-fi Web sites that point you in directions, and I was living in LA at the time, staying up late watching these testimonial videos and it's like, "Okay, I think you can get on hormones. There's doctors that can do surgeries." I don't fucking know where to turn to.

I just came out to my wife and said, "I'm a transsexual. I want to transition." She didn't know what that meant.

You're in this stupid fucking high-stress situation where you're like, "Okay, I got to go into some shitty department store to buy clothes that I don't even want to wear really because it's not my style, but this is the only way I can fucking relax and really express this fucking way I feel. To calm this tension that I feel inside of me because otherwise I'm going to fucking snap on someone and just lose it."

You feel like you're almost having an affair and you are hiding something and it's like, "Why can't I just fucking be who I am whenever I want to be who I am?" By owning it, I've been able to feel a lot more comfortable and confident in a "fuck you" way, in a punk rock way. When you're hiding it you feel shameful and that in turn makes you feel defensive and closed off as opposed to being open about and just being out there and being like, "Look, I am who I am. You may not fully understand that and I don't really care, but I am who I am and I have a right to be here. I have a right to shop in this store. I have a right to do whatever I want and don't have to explain it to you or justify it to you. I'm just going to do it, and if you have a problem, it's your problem."

Hope you can deal with that problem.

LENA DUNHAM—ACTOR, WRITER, DIRECTOR, PRODUCER

A lot of people thought that the world had equalized itself. We've gotten where we need to go. We're good. It's behind us. It isn't, and

I feel anger and frustration every day, some of it intellectual and some of it very visceral about the way women and women's stories are handled in the industry in which I've chosen to make myself a part.

I feel like by announcing that's a concern of yours and by making it clear that's where your passions lie, you are pushing the ball forward and encouraging other women to also announce themselves when it would be so easy to feel like you were the bummer at the party.

I think so many women are self-conscious because they love men and they're friends with men and they don't understand. "Does feminism mean that I have to be angry at all men? Does feminism mean that I have to distance myself from the guys in my life or fight back?" I'm like, "No. Feminism means that you have to take the space that you feel that you're comfortable in."

JONATHAN AMES—WRITER, ACTOR

Maybe men are getting weaker and weaker, all this estrogen in the water. Maybe a weakening of the male is a good thing, since men are so destructive. I mean, they're good at building highways, but they're also good at blowing up highways. I guess, what I've been moving toward would be greater parameters for masculinity or maleness. I don't think I'll achieve them in my life.

RUPAUL CHARLES—ACTOR, DRAG PERFORMER, SINGER, MODEL, WRITER, TELEVISION HOST

Part of the reason people have an aversion to drag is because it breaks the fourth wall, because it is so punk rock, because it says, "You know what? Look. I'm a man. Boop. Look, now I'm a woman. Look, now I'm a cowboy. Now I'm a sailor. Now I'm this. Now I'm that. Now I'm this thing, this alien."

Ego loves identity. Drag mocks identity. Ego hates drag. Because the thing is, humans always want to identify. I'm this and I'm that. And drag is really the antithesis of that because it's like saying, "Oh, look, and I'm this. Now I'm that."

I don't identify. I don't care. You can call me whatever you want. It doesn't matter. The whole identifying thing. That's something humans do. It's part of the machine. We are programmed to say, "Well, I am this. I am that." I'm like, "You know what? I am whatever." It doesn't even matter, really, honestly.

I have this scene in my head that, with my father, where actually, on weekends he was supposed to come pick me up, and I would sit on that porch, and he would never show up. Well, let me tell you this. That scenario in my head is a benchmark. I had inevitably looked for situations to strengthen my identity as the little boy who was left behind because on some level, that identity is what drove my buggy.

Once I'm able to let go of that identity and say, "That's not me, and I don't get off on that," then the party can begin. It's very tricky because, like I said, that tail grows back, and sometimes it will creep in through someone else. "Now playing the role of Ru's father is This Guy!" Once you hit that Google Earth button and get some perspective and say, "Ah, there it is. That's it right there." First, I'm not that little boy on the porch, and second, I was never that little boy on the porch. What rocks my boat now? If I wasn't that, then what am I? Well, I love to laugh. I love to dance. I love to look at people and go and do things, and that's where the real party begins.

RELATIONSHIPS

"'Do I Like You?'"

There are a lot of different types of relationships. I've ruined all kinds. I've ruined marriages, friendships, relationships with siblings and parents, pets, business partners, plants, etc. Relationships with pets are the easiest to repair. It usually just takes a few hours and a fun snack and you're back on track. It's harder with humans, but sometimes snacks still work.

I think the element at the core of my problems with relationships is my neediness. It took me a long time to realize I was expecting way too much out of almost every relationship I've ever had with anybody and my pets. My parents didn't quite deliver, so I've kind of wandered through life looking for people to take care of me but resenting them for trying to do it. That's a lot to put on a person or a cat. It takes a lot of snacks.

With friendships I always seem to need one good one to lean on. I was never a "hang out with the guys" kind of guy. I just need one good friend who I could rely on for everything. That's a lot of pressure for a person, babysitting me and dealing with my nonstop chaos and problems, self-generated usually. Fortunately I have a little better relationship with myself now and I can ease up on others in my life. Some days I don't think I need anybody ever again. I'm fortunate that I have the podcast. It's easier for me to be open and real there because I know the person I'm talking to will leave in an hour or so. No pressure. I can get deep, reveal myself, trust the situation, and feel connected. It's when people are in my life that it becomes difficult.

Other people probably feel this way too, because so many people are totally forthcoming with me about their relationships. I've had married couples, like Bonnie McFarlane and Rich Vos, tell me secrets about the other. I've had longtime friends, like Cheech and Chong, tell me why they had a falling-out. People tell me why they got divorced. Others tell me why they're still married to their high school sweethearts.

I'm not great at relationships with women, but I've been in many, so at the very least I have experience, up to a point. That doesn't mean I'm much better at it, but I know how to handle it. The first time I was married I was with her about nine years, married for three and a half. I didn't really want to be married, but I thought it would be a good thing for me. I thought it would straighten me out. It didn't. I left her for a woman that did straighten me out, but I drained her. I was with her for about eight years, married for three and a half. The first wife wanted to have kids but I couldn't handle it. The second one said this: "You think I want to bring kids into this?" So, no. I've had many semi-long-term relationships since the marriages and I almost got married again, which really would have been a bad idea.

I keep trying. I don't need to be married again. I don't need kids. I don't need to live with anyone. At this point in my life I just want to do what I want to do when I want to do it. That's a tough dating profile. I'm with someone now who has her own life and identity and does something completely different from what I do and owns her own house. It's perfect. It's working out.

Ultimately the common problem with all of my relationships was me. I was pathologically selfish. Over the last decade I have been humbled into allowing myself to be empathetic and understanding. I now know that others aren't there solely to make me feel better or put up with my shit. It only took me until I was in my late forties to realize this.

The longest relationship I've had in my life is with my two cats, Monkey and LaFonda. We're all enjoying getting old together and I know when they are sick of me and what to do about it. Snacks.

ANDY RICHTER—COMEDIAN, WRITER, ACTOR

Being married, the thing is, a fart at night, you are aware of it. There have been times where I have been lying in bed and had to get up and go into the bathroom to fart, just out of kindness for my wife, because I don't want to wake her up with the foul stench of my rotting innards.

PRESIDENT BARACK OBAMA

Having grown up the way I did without a dad, moving around a lot, my mom sometimes gone because of the nature of her work, it was very important to me to be a good dad. Part of, I think, the attraction to Michelle originally, in addition to her being really good-looking and smart and tough and funny, was she had this opposite experience growing up. It was really *Leave It to Beaver*: Dad, mom, brother. Lived in the same place for her entire childhood. Family everywhere, and so she helped ground me in a way that allowed my kids to have this base for themselves that I never had.

Conversely, I think Michelle would be the first to admit that part of her attraction to me was that her living in the same place all her life in this very traditional sense sometimes made her less adventurous and less open to doing new things. She has seen me as a way to instill in our kids this willingness to take a flyer on something, try it out, do something new.

When we first started dating I'd always give myself kind of a fifteen-minute leeway in terms of showing up and getting to stuff. I used to say, "You know, why are you stressing me about being late? I'm just fifteen minutes late, ten minutes late, what's the big deal?"

Then, I don't remember how long we were in the relationship when she described how her dad had to wake up an hour earlier than everybody else because he had multiple sclerosis. Just to put on his shirt and button his own shirt was a big task. If the family wanted to go see Michelle's brother play basketball, this was before the ADA—the Americans with Disabilities Act—they'd have to get there early so that her dad on crutches could hobble his way up the stairs to their seats. That mentality of not wanting to stand out and not wanting to miss something, it was a very emotional thing. It wasn't just about being late.

ROB REINER—DIRECTOR, PRODUCER, WRITER, ACTOR

I'm the empty nest now, so my wife is stuck with me. We're married now twenty-seven years. You have all these distractions. The kids, the things to think about, and then all of a sudden, "Oh, it's you? Do I like you?" But what we're discovering is that we do like each other, we really do. We like to hang with each other.

ALI WONG—COMEDIAN, WRITER

I met my husband at a wedding. He went to Sidwell, which is where the Obamas go to school. A private school in D.C. I went to the Sidwell of San Francisco. We went to school with all Jewish people. We went to this wedding in Napa where I went to high school with the bride and he went to high school with the husband.

We were the only Asian people at the wedding and everybody else was Jewish. I saw him and I was like, "We were probably raised in the same economic bracket. He's hot. I'm going to make this happen." And I did. He turned out to be a lot more interesting and weird and fun than I had expected. It keeps going that way.

JUDY GREER—ACTOR, WRITER

I'm into being married, I've got to say. I don't think I would like it if I didn't like my husband so much. I can see how marrying the wrong person would make you want to kill yourself or make your life miserable. I totally married the exact perfect person. I would recommend marrying Dean Johnsen. I can't say I would recommend anyone else.

We have two different houses. We do spend the night together somewhere but we don't—

Marc

At a third location?

Judy

Ha-ha, yeah. We have a conjugal visit trailer between the two houses. I'm kidding. I'm kidding about the trailer. I have a house that I had when I met him and then he has a house that he had when he met me. We didn't change that setup.

Marc

This seems unorthodox but interesting. That seems like almost a perfect situation.

Judy

Yeah. It works out pretty well. Once we got married, I was like, I'm going to try to spend every night with him because we're married, but every once in a blue moon, we won't spend the night together.

I really feel like this is going to solve the seven-year-itch problem because when the seven-year-itch happens, if that's really a thing, we will be moving in together for the first time because his son will then go away to college.

Marc

Do you think it's going to come to a point where you're like, "I don't need this house anymore"?

Judy

No. I really like my little house. I'm an only child. I like having my space. It's working. I have a lot of crap in my car all the time, but it's working. I remember my first few years having boyfriends and I'd have a bag in my car all the time, full of stuff. Then it's like, "Yay, I own a house and I'm getting married. I'm not going to. . . ." Now I'm back to the bag in my car.

SCOTT IAN—MUSICIAN

I met Pearl in 2000. She is absolutely a transcendent type of person and I saw that in 2000 when she was in a blue latex rubber cop dress, singing backup for Mötley Crüe, who Anthrax was opening for. It was like love at first sight, but I have no game, nothing, I don't know how to pick up chicks.

We became drinking buddies because it was a sober tour at the time for Mötley. Pearl and the other backup singer Marty, this other girl, they were hanging out with Anthrax on the Anthrax bus. As a band, we hit it pretty hard every night. They started hanging out with us, so we were drinking buddies for a month. Then Mötley's management calls and says we need to take a cut in our pay on the tour because tickets weren't selling so well, blah blah blah. We can't, we're just scraping by as it is on this. So they say, "We can't keep paying you, you'll just have to go home."

Bummer. I had nothing against the dudes in the band. I get it, it's business. I was bummed because I wasn't going to see Pearl for six more weeks until she got home to Los Angeles.

I was losing my mind, so I would go to this bar, Daddy's, every night on Vine, where my neighbor worked. I would get a ride with him and I would start drinking at five and then drink until the bartenders were done drinking at like four.

Then I would walk home, I lived right by Canter's Deli at the time. I would walk back home four miles because I think if I didn't walk, I would literally die, I would be so drunk.

But I had this light named Pearl. I had this focus and I knew she was coming home at the beginning of September. She gets home from tour and I call her, "Hey, there's these bands playing at the Troubadour tonight. Do you want to go?" She was like, "Sure." I had written her a letter. Wrote her a letter and FedEx'd it to her on tour, and I told her how I felt about her. This was a really heartfelt four-page letter. She never answered that. We would talk all the time, but she never brought it up. Like, "I'm in love with you." We would still talk, but she never brought up the letter and I didn't have the balls to ask her about the letter. I just figured we're friends, that's it. I'm crushed but we'll be friends. At least I can be friends with this rad lady.

We went out that night to the Troubadour. I brought my friend Kenny because I was nervous. We just fell right back into the same thing. We ordered some drinks and hung out and watched some bands, hung out that night and then wound up saying, "What are you doing tomorrow night?"

"Nothing."

"Do you want to hang out?"

That was September 9, 2000; we've been together ever since.

Eventually, I asked, "What about the letter?"

She told me, "It was so amazing, every time I would try to respond or write a letter back, I would just tear it up. I was so blown away by your letter." Of course then me, the idiot, was waiting around to make a move on her. She felt the same way about me.

Obviously everything worked out because it's sixteen years later. I finally met the woman I was supposed to meet.

JIM GAFFIGAN—COMEDIAN, WRITER, ACTOR

Jeannie and I write together.

Marc

Are there moments where Jeannie says, "Jim, Jim, you're eating yogurt like a monkey. You should talk about that," or do you not have those moments?

Jim

I would never eat yogurt, but . . .

JEANNIE GAFFIGAN—WRITER, PRODUCER, ACTOR
Well yeah, there are moments where I'll introduce a topic, but a lot of it is just going over topics and just beating the hell out of them. Just having two people's minds dissect that one thing.

Marc
Here's how that would have gone when I was married: She would say something. I'd say, "What, you don't think it's good?" She would say, "No, I'm not saying that." I'd say, "But why would you rewrite it like that?" She'd say, "I just think it would be funnier." I'm like, "Why don't I just not fucking do the joke then?"

Jim
Right.

Marc
Never got very far with that.

Jeannie
Well, there's conversations like that too.

Marc
Oh, good.

Jim
It's like any creative process.

Jeannie
I'll beg him to do something. He'll say, "That, no."

Jim
That's not going to work.

Jeannie

But it didn't work one time! I'm like, "One audience?!? You're going to waste that on one audience!"

BONNIE MCFARLANE—COMEDIAN, WRITER, DIRECTOR

Porn stars always say how they have the best job. I feel like they always say that because people were, like, "You're not going to go into porn, are you?" People tell you don't do it, then they realize, "Ugh, now I've got to just keep this up for the rest of my life." They say, "No, I made the right decision."

That's how it is with me marrying Rich Vos. It's too late to say I made a mistake.

Marc

No other comics ever thought that you marrying Rich was anything but a nice gesture on your part.

Bonnie

Since we've been married, I've never been allowed to have my own soda when we're out for dinner. He wants to bring soda into restaurants all the time.

Marc

That doesn't make it good for Jews when he does things like that.

Bonnie

No, I know. Then he says I'm anti-Semitic because I'm constantly like, "Stop doing that!"

Marc

Does he bring popcorn to the movies?

Bonnie

Yes.

Marc

Oh, no.

Bonnie

If they ever start a policy where they open up people's purses, oh, God, it will be so embarrassing.

The first time I ever went to a movie with him, he smoked in the movie theater because he still smoked back then. He'd just take two drags and then somebody would come in and look around and not see it.

Marc

Oh my God. What a pain in the ass.

Bonnie

And I said, "I'm in love."

When I really fell in love with him was the one time when we were first going out. We were having sushi and he said to me that he was a genius. He was, like, really talking about himself as a genius.

Marc

Wait, is this Rich Vos?

Bonnie

Yes.

Marc

Okay, go ahead. I just want to make sure I know who you're talking about.

Bonnie

I never heard anyone talk about themselves like that before.

RICH VOS—COMEDIAN

Bonnie McFarlane, that's my wife.

Marc

Jesus, what the hell? Why the fuck did she marry you?

Rich

Because, first of all, I'm a genius. That's one. I mean that goes without saying.

I don't know. It's so weird. When we started dating, the first time I met her I was at the Comedy Cellar. She came downstairs. I knew she dated Mark Cohen. I was working with Cohen and he's miserable. He's fucking miserable. I go, "What's the . . ."

"Me and my girlfriend just broke up."

I knew nothing about him. "We just broke up." He's heartbroken. I go, "Look, I've been through divorce. It's not a big deal. You'll get through it, you'll get through it." But he's going through that right then.

Years later I'm at the Comedy Cellar ready to go onstage and Bonnie walks down the stairs. She says, "Oh, you're that guy on *Last Comic Standing*." That was the first thing. I'm looking at her, I'm thinking, "Oh you're the comic that's gone out with other comics." But she looks hot. She watched my set. I didn't bomb, but it wasn't a good set. She even left in the middle of it. Because I was too nervous. I wanted to impress her. I was on a date too with a hairdresser from *The View*, who was very attractive. Bonnie came down the stairs and the first thing I said to her was, "Oh yeah, I know you. I'd hit on you but I'm on a date." That's the first thing I ever said to her. So already she thinks I'm a creep.

I called the club the next day. I asked the manager, "Estee, can you give me that girl's phone number?"

Estee called Bonnie and Bonnie said, "Do not give him my fucking phone number."

So I went down there another night. She was there. We went out for pizza. We had pizza. Cut to me going down on her in the car a little bit.

Marc

That was the first date? That's unorthodox. That's what you went with? I'm going to go down on her in the car.

Rich

I had to show that I'm a giver. I didn't ask her to go down on me. A lot of comics would. Not me.

Marc

You're a real prince.

Rich

Hey, it was a Mercedes. It wasn't a crappy car. It was a nice car.

Then we just started dating a little. When I'd come to LA, we'd fool around. She was great. She was perfect. I was in LA taping something. I'm staying at a great hotel. She came over in the day, we went to the pool, and we ended up going to my room. We had sex and she got up and left. Are you crazy? She left!

Marc

You must have thought that was the best thing ever. You're like, I'm in love.

Rich

I thought, "This is it. This is it."

CAROL LEIFER—COMEDIAN, WRITER, PRODUCER, ACTOR

I like funny people. I don't think people realize, when you're coming up as a comic, and especially at that time, every night I went out to a comedy club. You're at the clubs with other comics and you're doing three sets a night.

Marc

I dated a couple. It makes sense, but the only difficult thing about it is that there is a point where someone's going to overshadow the other one. To be supportive effectively becomes difficult when your egos are involved, or if opportunities are had by one or the other, it becomes a mess. Did you find that?

Carol

It's complicated, it's definitely a complicated situation, and I always look at something like the Academy Awards, when Julia Roberts won the Oscar and she was with Benjamin Bratt. I always watch them up onstage and it's like, "Bye-bye relationship."

It's just too hard. In having a successful relationship now, having someone who's not in the business really has worked better for me.

Marc

Am I going to get married again?

JANEANE GAROFALO—COMEDIAN, WRITER, ACTOR

I would assume you would. You seem to be a romantic in that way. I don't know why you're not just content to live with people, but you seem to like to get married. There's nothing wrong with getting married. It's marrying the right person. I myself have never wanted to be married either. I have no problems living with people, I just don't want to be married.

FRED ARMISEN—COMEDIAN, ACTOR, MUSICIAN

There's always a way, if you really like someone, to keep them in your life. It doesn't have to be dating.

Marc

So why would you get married again?

Fred

Because it's so intoxicating. It's so exciting. This is going to sound very shallow, but I get lost in fantasy a lot.

Marc

Really? The guy who does characters?

Fred

I would hope that I had a place where I didn't get lost in it, but the fantasy of this person. This is something that's happened to me a million times. I have a problem with intimacy where all of a sudden there's a real person there.

I'm trying to fix this. I'm trying to get better at this, but something happens in me where it's almost like an amnesia. It's almost like waking up and going, Where am I? Who is this person? Why is this person looking me directly in the eye and having a conversation?

Marc

Who usually ends it, you or her?

Fred

It's me becoming impossible. I shut it down. There's infidelity, there's cheating. It's the most chaos I've had in my life.

I say these things because I'm not finished being a person. A person who I can be intimate with is a person who I don't have sex with. Like Carrie Brownstein. I find true intimacy there. I know that I have it. I know that I'm not shut down.

CARRIE BROWNSTEIN—MUSICIAN, COMEDIAN, WRITER, ACTOR

Fred and I hit it off. We did not date. Which I'm certain is why we're still really good friends. He would agree.

Marc

Was there a discussion?

Carrie

Yeah, there have been discussions.

Marc

Is it an ongoing discussion?

Carrie

We revisit that. But now for sure, we need to just be friends.

DAN HARMON—DIRECTOR, WRITER, PRODUCER

Whenever I'm going back to therapy I'm going because I'm in danger of fucking up with somebody who deserves better. I shut down. It's all negative space. It's all "what's not there." I don't do anything bad. I never cheat, I don't even flirt. I don't compete. I also don't make a lot of eye contact. I go into a domestic kind of cocoon. Stop having sex, I stop taking showers, I focus on my work.

CHELSEA PERETTI—COMEDIAN, WRITER, ACTOR

I max out in relationships it seems like at a year or two. I get cheated on, or . . . I don't know. This is where I feel like I will be alone perhaps forever, but I do feel like things get uninteresting or something. I get that thing of like, "Oh, maybe there's someone else who has something better." And then you get to see that everyone has flaws eventually once you're a year in or something. Also, I don't feel like I'm always myself until a year in, and that's also problematic. I've been cheated on actually many times, so. . . .

Marc

How do you handle that?

Chelsea

Depression. I shut down emotionally. Sometimes I'll try to work it out, and then I break up with a person, and then I go through a period of total relief and feeling powerful. I feel freed of things.

I think I'm evolving, but it's very hard for me to just say, "This doesn't really feel like it's working. Let's not go further." Instead I'll say, "This doesn't feel like it's working, but we have so much fun eating dinner," and just, "Let's give it two more years. I like cuddling." You know?

Marc

Yeah, I don't know how the hell to get out of things. I usually wait until it explodes into some dramatic mess.

Chelsea

Yeah, me too, but my goal as a human being is to be able to be more honest about "This doesn't really feel like it's working."

AMY SCHUMER—COMEDIAN, WRITER, ACTOR

I feel, with men, like if you and I were together, say we're married, and you have sex with someone else, that doesn't necessarily mean anything about your feelings for me. I believe that's true for men.

Marc

But if you were in that relationship, would you be able to make that distinction?

Amy

Two, three years ago, no fucking way. Like, run for your life, but now, I don't know. I don't want to ever find out about it, especially if it didn't mean something to you. Because I believe that something's going on with you. People go through phases. It would be very hurtful, but I don't believe that having sex with someone else necessarily affects your feelings for the person that you're with.

Marc

Have you ever dated an enraged dick Jew?

LENA DUNHAM—ACTOR, WRITER, DIRECTOR, PRODUCER

Like fifteen of them. It was my specialty before my current relationship.

I was raised by a decidedly nonabusive man and by an intensely self-actualized feminist, and then when I found my way into the world as an adult woman embarking on my sexual life, and saw that I had this incredible drive to find myself in dark situations where I wasn't being treated with the respect that I thought I or even any human deserves.

I would have walked right out if somebody screamed in my face or was abusive to me in any physical way. It was much more just like people who have a dark relationship with themselves, an uncomfortable relationship with their sexuality and expressed that through hate and disdain for the women that they're with, disguised as humor and a need to be obliterated half of the time.

I got all the dark stuff of dating a comic minus the pleasure of dating somebody funny. They're needy people who want to pretend that they don't need you. Needy people who want to pretend you're not an important role in their life. People who aren't happy for you when you're successful. People who don't believe in you. People who act like they're doing you a favor by being attracted to you, all of those things factor into my early dating life.

I'm not describing one boyfriend or one incident. I'm describing a chain of people and situations that I put myself through. They were painful and they took a good four years off of the evolution and health of my self-esteem, and they seemed like these cool explorations of a life that I had never known, and in reality, they were super damaging.

I do definitely have something like "look at me now" energy directed at ex-boyfriends and I don't really want to own that. But how can you help it? You must have some of that toward people who you feel didn't understand?

Marc
My second wife said, "You're not going to be famous until you're dead."

Lena
Really? You're alive.

Marc
I'm alive.

Lena
And a lot of people really like you.

Marc
Yeah, yeah. Trying to accept that now.

Lena

I feel really safe with a lot of the men in my life. I feel safe with my dad and I feel safe with my boyfriend Jack and I feel safe with Judd Apatow and I feel safe in my cast, but sometimes I feel like I go into a situation with a guy I don't know ready to feel mistreated or manhandled and I'm pleasantly surprised when it doesn't happen.

Marc

The way I've explored that lately is that I was in a relationship for three and a half years. I don't even think she really liked me. There was an age difference and we both had other problems, but it became clear that I was interchangeable and that she didn't really like me necessarily. The way I framed it in my head is that everything was going pretty well for me at that point, but I didn't hate myself. So I needed to outsource that job.

NICK GRIFFIN—COMEDIAN, WRITER

Somebody was talking to me the other day about going to marriage counseling, and they said marriage counseling generally doesn't help the marriage but it does point out what's wrong with it by a third party. I remember we went to counseling and she said, "He doesn't do this," and I thought to myself, "I don't do that. And I'm not going to." I knew she was absolutely right and she hit it right on the head and I thought we're not moving forward. There's nowhere to go because I'm not going to do that.

It was my fault for the most part, I think, pretty much.

Once you walk out of marriage counseling, there's no resolution and you don't feel better, so even if you're still married there's just waiting until next week. There's no having sex in between the sessions.

NATASHA LEGGERO—COMEDIAN, WRITER, PRODUCER, ACTOR

I met this guy who was Australian, and he was like forty-two
and I was twenty-two. I gave up my New York apartment, my
rent-controlled apartment. I moved to Australia to be with him.
I thought he was so sophisticated. I got there and he was a con
artist.

I was like, "God, these guys are so lame in New York! I want
someone who knows what a wine list looks like and how to read a
wine list." I just wanted someone sophisticated.

So I meet this guy, and he kind of looked like Mick Jagger, he
had this cool striped blazer and he was really soft-spoken. He was
like, "I just came back from this new festival called Burning Man."
It was the first year of Burning Man. He was like, "I'm making a
documentary on the information super highway," which was the
Internet, obviously. He was like, "I do book reviews for the *Australian Financial*." He did book reviews, he was an intellectual prop-
erty lawyer. He was just fascinating to me! I was like, "Oh my
God! I can't believe that I met this person."

Then we had a few dates. He would take me to the Algonquin
Hotel. We would meet at the Algonquin and eat at the Ivy!

He went back to Australia. I was like, "Oh my God, I'm going
to be with this man!" My older friends were like, "Natasha, I've
known people like this. I don't think you should go." I am like,
"No, No. I am going to go." Then finally, I gave up all of my stuff
and I went there. I was, like, twenty-two. I got there and in my
mind I was like, "We are going to literary parties!" Because he does
book reviews, he's a lawyer, and he must be rich.

I get there. First, he picks me up from the airport and he looks
worried. I think he couldn't believe that I came. It looked like he
hadn't slept.

I am like, "Oh, when are we going to start eating caviar?" And
we go to his little shack. It's a fine, little studio apartment. He
draped purple felt all over the walls to try to make it fancy. There
was IKEA furniture. I was kind of disoriented because of the flight

to Australia. I was like, "I am just going to lie down." I lay down, and I woke up to the *Seinfeld* theme song. He was like, "*Seinfeld*'s starting!" He watched television all day. I was in Australia with this guy who I thought was my dream man, and he would just want to watch television and John Candy movies.

Then it started. I couldn't answer the phone. He was getting money from other women. He was just a crazy person. The signs were every day. We would get into three fights every day. He would be like, "Don't use that! That is not the knife you use to butter the bread!" He would get really mad at me for stuff like that. I would bring him his coffee in the morning. He would be like, "How could you expect me to look at that much liquid this early in the morning! It's too full!" I think I had Stockholm syndrome or something.

We didn't have any money. I was like, "I thought you were a book reviewer?" Then I would see him reading the want ads. He was like, "Well, we need some money, Wiener." He would call me Wiener. He was like, "We need some money! You need to go out and get a job." I got this waitressing job and he would sit there and stare at me while I would wait tables! Then they fired me. Then I got a job at a brothel answering phones for, like, a day because he got really mad.

He would take the money. It would be, like, thirty or sixty dollars, and spend it all on champagne and picnic food. He was like, "We have to walk this way because the roses will be blowing. The eastern winds are right now. If we walk up this street, even though it's longer, we will get the smell of the roses."

I would be in his house, so I started digging through his shit. I was like, "What is happening here? I know something is wrong." I remember getting on my hands and knees. I was like, "God, please give me a sign." Then the phone rang. He was like, "Wiener, I need you to take your university money and put it in the mailbox." I'm like, "Why? That's my money! That's $1,200!" He was like, "Just do as I say!"

I get down there, and there is this girl bawling. She's like, "Give me that money!" I was like, "What? I thought it was for Alex?" She is like, "No! He needs to pay for my abortion!"

I asked him, "Did you have sex with her?" He would just say, "I was with no one." I would be like, "No, but did you do it?" He would just keep repeating, "I was with no one." I think that is a tactic that con artists use. I forget. It's called something. You just keep repeating something until the person believes it.

Marc

It's called lying.

Natasha

I believe he had some kind of antisocial personality disorder, maybe.

This is how people like that lie: I remember we were on a date at someone's house back in New York, and they were playing Neil Young. I was like, "Oh, I love Neil Young. My favorite Neil Young album is *Hawks and Doves*."

He was like, "You know *Hawks and Doves*?"

I was like, "Yes!"

In my head, in New York, I was like, "I have to move there! This man knows my favorite album!"

I remember once when I was in Australia, I was looking through his music. I was like, "Don't you have *Hawks and Doves*? I feel like listening to that." He was like, "What's that?"

He was such a unique person and very funny. We would be on the bus and he would be like, "Excuse me! Driver!" He would act like we were in a limo, on the bus. Everyone hated him in Australia. People were like, "Who is this guy?" People were worried about me. Strangers were like, "Are you okay?" He would be like, "Excuse me! Is this bus going to blah-blah, driver?" The bus driver was like, "Read the sign." Alex would flip his scarf and be like, "Are you assuming, sir, that I can read?" He would say these crazy things to people.

One time we were at the store and I saw him stealing potatoes.

He would steal things. I would be like, "Alex, you can't steal!" I was raised really well. I would be like, "We have to pay for this!" He would try to dine and dash.

He always told me his dad was a doctor and his mother was from French royalty. "My mother would have loved you, your ankles are so small. That's a sign of good breeding." He was always telling me all of these things. Then when I went through all of his stuff one day, I found his birth certificate. It said his dad was an electroplater, which is a very low factory job.

I told my mom I needed $2,000 for a plane ticket back. It was only $800 and I paid for him to go back with me. Then we moved back to New York.

He was like, "I am not traveling all the way back to America without going to the Lake District in England!" We went to Thailand with my mom's money. I ended up paying her back.

He had such a feeling that he should have everything. He was so charming. He would ask to be upgraded to first class and people would upgrade us. I don't know how he did it.

Marc

You are impressed with this guy!

Natasha

I've looked him up. I can't find him anymore.

He was just so funny. I never heard someone saying you had to take a certain route so you could smell the roses.

Marc

No, it's sweet, in a way. You were able to forgive all of this insanity. I am glad that he just took you for a ride for a little bit of money, in retrospect.

Natasha

Not much money.

Marc

His lie was enchanting to you. You're like, "This is it." Even when you got there and realized it was a lie, he sort of committed to behaving like that. You're like, "That's pretty good." Right?

Natasha

Yes. The problem was, when you are lying like that at that level, every day you are telling lies, you get mad for no reason.

I remember I was wearing these shoes once, when we were in London on our way back. He was like, "Why are you wearing those in the daytime!" He got so mad and wouldn't talk to me. He was so crazy. For me, I was always begging him not to be mad. It was really sad. We get back to New York. We had no place to stay. We had no money. I lost my waitressing job, everything. We were living deep in Queens. Then he left me for this girl in Brooklyn who had an inheritance. He probably knew he had limited time left with me.

It took me two or three years to recover in New York. He was always an influence in my head, I think.

MICK FOLEY—PROFESSIONAL WRESTLER, STAGE PERFORMER, AUTHOR

I stayed in character as my wrestling persona, Cactus Jack, for six months in Texas with my girlfriend. I had no way of letting her know that the guy she met was a character. I didn't know how to break it to her because she was attracted to that character.

Marc

You were having sex as Cactus Jack?

Mick

I was. Indeed I was. She started catching on because I am a nice guy. It wasn't that I would be mean to her. I was just a little out there as Cactus Jack. Then I got a phone call. I remember she specifically said to me like, "Jack." She called me Jack, didn't know my real name. She just said, "I know."

I said, "Know what?"

She said, "I know."

"What do you think you know?" She wouldn't say what she knew.

A few days later, a week, a lot of time has passed. I got a phone call and she said, "I need to talk to you." I said, "Can you tell me over the phone?" She said, "No, I need to talk to you in person." I was twenty-four, what else could it be?

Marc

You thought she was pregnant or something?

Mick

Yeah. Turns out she needed to borrow $300. I said, "Yeah, yeah." Not that I made a lot of money. That was about all I made in a week, but I said, "I can lend you money." Later that night, I said, "I can't do it. On my way over here, I promised God that if you weren't pregnant, I wouldn't have sex with you for a month." She looked at me. She said, "You're kidding me." I said, "No, I'm not kidding." I was in character.

She said, "Jack, God doesn't make deals." I screamed in my Cactus Jack voice, "Well, he made one with me!"

She said, "I thought this crazy thing was just an act, but you really are out of your mind."

It was that bond I had with myself playing this character, the promise I made. Cactus Jack would not have sex with her for a month.

Maybe I caved in after three weeks.

NICK GRIFFIN—COMEDIAN, WRITER

I have a hard time enjoying people's company for any extended period of time and I know that, so I don't want to extend it. I've said it a million times. "Look, I'm not very easy to get along with and I keep to myself and I'm pretty committed to what I do."

Marc

What they hear is, "I love you, move in."

Nick

It's the absolute truth. Eventually they wonder, "What happened? What happened?"

"I gave you the whole poop up front and now you're saying what happened? I told you what was going to happen, it's happened, and now you're upset that it's happened? That doesn't make sense to me."

DONNELL RAWLINGS—COMEDIAN, ACTOR

I love everybody. White chicks, at one point in my life, they were a lot of fun. They were easy. I like the white chicks that work for nonprofits. There's something about the peaceful bitches. I mean women, I'm sorry. Women that are like, "He's going to be my experiment." I don't want you to really accept me 100 percent. I want you to dabble in it. I want the dabbler. They're all about saving trees, whales, pit bulls, the Earth. . . .

Marc

. . . Fucking a black guy once.

Donnell

Yeah, once. Once. Dabble. Dabble. Dabble. Dabble. Then they find the person they're going to marry.

Marc

Yeah, right, of course. The Jewish guy.

Donnell

Yeah, the Jewish guy. Yep. I know the system.

CHELSEA PERETTI

I am starting to really think that I genuinely have a major fear of commitment. I choose people that always have a glaring flaw or a glaring thing that would make us incompatible, like that anyone could just . . .

Marc

I'm sorry. Didn't you go out with Jim Norton?

Chelsea

Yes.

Marc

That is not glaring. That is glowing like white-hot fire lights.

Chelsea

Me and Jim were friends for many years, and we always cracked up. It sounds stupid, but we laughed. We had long conversations. We'd go have dinner, and then there became a point where I was like, "Maybe this is something more."

BOB SAGET—COMEDIAN, ACTOR, WRITER

I've had some relationship problems in my life personally because what I've learned about myself is you throw one rock at me and I got a thousand coming back at you. I'll bring catapults. I'll bring artillery. I'll hire people. They don't even do anything wrong. They're just people. They're just human beings.

People of my ilk should be watching James L. Brooks's *As Good as It Gets* as many times as we possibly can because the Jack Nicholson/Helen Hunt relationship kind of says it all. It's like, why would you say something like that? It's just a guy who's so narcissistic and so insecure and hurt, he'll just do something that fucks it up for somebody that he cares about. It can really fuck up a good relationship. It's anger issues and it's also hurt and it's not being allowed to do what you want to do and it's also not owning your stuff. Not walking around feeling guilty, whether it be Catholic or Jew guilt.

I think the solution is to shorten the window on the angst. Shorten the argument, shorten the reason for it. Say what you want to say. I have a friend that always says this to me: "Just do a puzzle with a friend. Just do whatever you can do, shiny objects in front of yourself, change the subject in your mind." Go do something. Something. Play Zelda. Do anything.

Marc

When you lock in, do you have that moment where you feel the effect of what's aggravated you and then it's just like a switch turns?

Bob

A switch turns and the bottom of the elevator drops out. There's no rescuing anybody. Everybody's getting taken in.

It's incorrect behavior, but you can fix it. I guarantee you can fix it.

MARIA BAMFORD—COMEDIAN, ACTOR

I think I still have looked at relationships as a self-esteem-building thing and it's like, "No, I've got to really be on board with myself and my life and not try to invite anybody into it." Also, I've got to really like and respect the person, instead of just thinking, "Oh, I'm going to help him," which is horrible. Nobody wants to be helped.

You should want to be with somebody you admire. You say, "Oh, this person is really neat and a wonderful person." Not, "They're neat, they're fine, but I'm going to teach him a thing or two about a thing or two." That's totally controlling and totally manipulative, and also a put-down to the person.

RON FUNCHES—COMEDIAN, ACTOR

You can never change a person. You can never. Whoever they introduce themselves as is who they're going to be.

People can evolve. People never change. Evolving means that they still have their standard base. You can see where they're coming from. You're not going to do a 180.

That's a lesson I learned from my mom the hard way with the guy she was dating. She was hoping that she could change him.

RACHAEL HARRIS—COMEDIAN, ACTOR

If anybody's really too together and I never see them lose it, I don't trust them. Only until I see you totally fuck up, and behave really badly, like, say something shitty to someone awful, then I breathe a sigh of relief, and I'm like, okay, they're normal to me.

Marc

I say, "I don't know if someone loves me unless I can make them cry."

Rachael

I'm the crier.

Marc

That's what I mean. It's like, "Fuck you, you don't love me. If you cared about me you would fucking understand what I'm saying."

Rachael

Right, and then I say, "Yes, I do, I do, I do."

Marc

"Okay, you do, you do, I'm sorry, I'm sorry."

Rachael

Right, and then once you said you were sorry, then I'm like, "Ahhh! I'm in."

Marc

Yeah, it's over, locked in, and there you go, and that's how it goes, round and round.

PRESIDENT BARACK OBAMA

The fights you have are never about the thing you're fighting about. It's always about something else. It's about a story. It's about respect. It's about recognition, something deep.

MARGARET CHO—COMEDIAN, WRITER, ACTOR

My mother has an eating disorder and always did. My father was a terrible womanizer. She blamed her body issues on his cheating. They have a great relationship now, but they really were bad for each other. He was a sex addict, and she was emotionally crazy. Now I'm both of them. I think I'm always heartbroken, eternally heartbroken, which is why I think people are attracted to me because my heart is always open, very open all the time. That's just because I'm so smashed up.

Marc

I find that too. I know crazy people are drawn to me like a magnet, because I'm wired that way, and you've got to figure you are as well. I realized this recently in life, that because I grew up with a manic-depressive father with anger problems and completely selfish parents in general, I'm wired to accommodate those people. People who other people say, "That guy's fucking nuts," I can have him talking like a normal person and feeling sort of heard very quickly. They're drawn to me. I have that gift, which is horrible.

Margaret

Mine is I don't know they're crazy until way too late. I kind of allow them in. I just let people in.

DAVE FOLEY—COMEDIAN, WRITER, ACTOR

My first wife, I loved her when we first started dating. She was actually a girl I wanted to ask out and then I lost my job and I couldn't take her out so I didn't ask her out, and then in the meantime my best friend started dating her. They started living together, but while they were living together, she and I were getting closer and closer.

Then I started feeling like I was falling for her and because one of those nights where I said, "You know what, maybe we should stop hanging out so much because I'm starting to have these feelings and you're my best friend's girlfriend," she showed me her tits and I realized, "Maybe he's not my best friend." So then I wound up stealing my best friend's girlfriend.

Once I got into this relationship with her, I realized almost immediately, "Oh my God . . ." But in my head I'm like, "Well, I can't just break up with her. I can't. I just ruined my friendship. This has to mean something."

From then on, it was just me trying to find a way out of it in a decent way.

JUDD APATOW—COMEDIAN, DIRECTOR, WRITER, PRODUCER

After my parents got divorced, I thought, "I've got to get my shit together, I've got to get something going in this life, I really need to take care of myself."

When your parents get divorced, they just make terrible mistakes, and they fight, and you see that adults have very real flaws. I think my instinct was, "Oh my God, maybe they're wrong about all sorts of stuff they've been telling me. If my mom thinks my dad's the devil, and if my dad is enraged at my mom, then maybe some of this advice they've been giving me is wrong about things. I don't think he's the devil. He's very nice to me." It just completely threw me.

It's important that you believe your parents, like they know what they're talking about, and there's a comfort knowing they're sane. When you see them at a terrible moment, at their worst, and they're screaming at each other and it's really madness for a couple of years, my first reaction was, "I don't believe anything. I can't rely on these people because they can't rely on each other." They've bailed on each other and in some way I felt bailed on, like, "Oh, our whole family isn't important enough for you to figure out how to get along. One of you is going to leave and I'm going to see the other one randomly." It was terrible.

RACHAEL HARRIS

I've told everybody I know, "Never get divorced." Work through it, if it's possible. Divorce was so hard. But over the years, things happen. People grow apart. You know, he's not here to talk about it, and to tell his side of the story, but I will say that for me, the hardest thing was knowing that it was the right thing to do. Staying was awful. The thought of leaving was hideous and awful, but the thought of staying was worse.

MELISSA ETHERIDGE—MUSICIAN

It was horrible to have a breakup in public. Yes, it was horrible to feel like I let down a whole community because here I was regarded as this—there's this perfect relationship, I'm out, we have children. That about killed me when I thought, we're going to divorce and I've just shown the world what a gay family looks like and now we're going to end it. That just about, that broke my heart even more than really losing the relationship because I really needed to be out of that relationship. But just that I felt like I let down so many people, that was difficult.

JUDD APATOW

When your parents get divorced, life collapses suddenly. "Hey, Judd, could you come down in the living room? We need to talk to you for a minute. Mommy is moving out." You think, "Something like that is going to happen again. I don't know when it's going to happen, but I better be ready for it."

Staying ready for it is what detaches you from life. For me, that's been the great lesson of marriage, and my beautiful wife and beautiful daughters. They will not accept that. Daddy needs to be here, and needs to be happy and connected and present. It forces me to do the work, not be the guy who wants to detach.

CINDY CRAWFORD—MODEL, ENTREPRENEUR, ACTIVIST

I was twenty-six when I got married. I was young. I didn't think I was young. But I was young.

I was with Richard for six years, but I was only married for two years.

We're friendly now, but it's almost like he's gone back to being "Richard Gere" again, like a stranger, because we don't really see each other that much.

I think part of the problem in our relationship was that we were a lot of other things, but I don't know if we were ever friends. Like peers, because I was young and he was Richard Gere. Then as I started growing up and growing into myself, it's hard to change the dynamic of a relationship once you're already in it, you know?

I've been with my husband Rande now almost twenty-five years and I think why Rande and I really work is that we were friends first. I never pretended to like baseball or meditation or whatever the version is, because I wasn't trying to win him over.

It's that thing where you're on that first date and you're like, "I love that." Then six months later they're like, "Let's go to the baseball game," and you're like, "I hate baseball." They're like, "What?"

When you are with a friend you never do that and you really show your flaws from the beginning. I wasn't trying to impress Rande. We got hooked up. We had to go to a wedding together, but not as dates. He was just chaperoning me because I didn't want to go alone. We met and he didn't want to really go out with me because he was dating another model. My friend whose wedding it was said, "Well, you can go with one of these three guys." I knew the other two and I was like, "I'm not going with them, so I'll take this unknown Door Number Three." It was Rande, but he was late picking me up. I was like, "You're late." I was yelling at him the first time I met him, which was good because then when I yelled at him later on, he'd already seen that side of me.

TOM GREEN—COMEDIAN, WRITER, ACTOR, TALK SHOW HOST

When I got cancer was exactly the exact same time that Drew Barrymore and I started dating. I was doing the movie *Charlie's Angels*. We lived together for about two years and dated for two and a half years and it was great for a good chunk of that. Then it wasn't great and then we broke up.

Marc

She seems like a pretty nice person.

Tom

Yeah.

Marc

In general.

Tom

Nice enough to marry for five months, at least.

Marc

I've been married twice, man.

Tom

I think the thing is, you've got to imagine what would it be like for you—What's your first wife's name?

Marc

Kim.

Tom

What would it be like for you if every time you left your house, every day, for the rest of your life, between five and ten people, between the time you left your house and got back home, came up to you and said, "Hey, how's Kim?"

"You talked to Kim lately?"

"Oh, I remember, you're with Kim."

"Weren't you married to that Kim?"

Welcome to my life.

The tendency is to want to just rant about it. It's just so not really a viable option to go around ranting about why it went wrong. First of all, I'm sure she has a completely different opinion about why it went wrong. We don't really have any relationship anymore. I haven't talked to her in probably seven or eight years. We were living together, we were married. When she left the house that day, when we decided to get a divorce, I have never seen her since. That was over ten years ago but still, her name gets brought up every day.

It's an odd thing. You want to go, "Oh, this is what went wrong and this has happened and she did this, she did that, blah, blah, blah." Then you just sound like some jerk walking around complaining about America's sweetheart. I just chose to say nothing until now.

NICK GRIFFIN—COMEDIAN, WRITER

People ask, "How is she?" I go, "I have no idea, literally."

What's funny is that the divorce itself, I said, "This isn't working out. I'm going to move out for a little while," and she says, "If you move out we're getting divorced," and I said, "Oh, whatever." She went into the other room, she came back in with divorce papers. You can get them off the Internet, start the process. She put them down and I thought it was like a line in the sand. Like, "He won't do it." And I signed it and she walked out and then said, "You need to be out in a couple days."

I didn't really think about it very much. I ran into somebody a week after I moved out and she said, "I saw your wife the other day," and I say, "We got separated," and she says, "Yes, I thought it was weird because she was with some guy," and I was like, "Oh boy, that's not good."

AMY POEHLER—COMEDIAN, WRITER, PRODUCER, ACTOR

At this age, you have to find people that are already divorced. At least once. If you're in your forties, and you're a man, and you haven't been divorced at least once, there's something up.

SARAH SILVERMAN—COMEDIAN, WRITER, ACTOR

My parents became like brother and sister after the divorce. They're like army buddies. They went through hell together a lifetime ago, and they just love each other so much. It's really sweet. My step-mom is friends with my mom.

My mom got really sick. She has this really rare disease, and this happened in '93 to '94. My stepmother, who's terrified of needles and can't look at the sight of blood, is her blood type. She had a blood transfusion for my mom. They love each other.

My mom's new neighbors were over, and she was introducing them to my dad and my stepmother. She said, "This is Donald, my ex-husband, and this is Janice, his beautiful and incredibly patient wife."

Marc

Is your husband your first love?

TERRY GROSS—RADIO HOST

Now that I really know what love is, I'd say yes but . . .

Marc

What was the other thing?

Terry

This gets really personal. I was married once before.

Marc

For how long?

Terry

A short time and we were very close and it was a year maybe.

It makes me nervous to talk about.

I was very young. We were still in college. I was twenty, maybe. We got married quickly. I don't know. We'd already been living together for a while. Time seems different when you're young. A year is a really long time.

My parents weren't okay with anything I was doing then. I did this whole "I've got to do what I've got to do and you can't tell me," but my heart was breaking because it's like, "I don't want to hurt them," but at the same time I felt like I had to cut the string and that if I gave in that it would always feel to them like, "She's our good daughter. Everything is under control," and I just had to do it.

Marc

Did you marry the guy to sort of say, "I'm my own person?"

Terry

We loved each other. It was a beautiful relationship. It was good. At some point we were living with a group of people because it was the 1960s and 1970s and people shared the housework and the cooking and at some point I realized, "You know what I really need? I need to live alone."

I just need to find out who I am outside of the group, outside of a marriage. I was too young to be committed. I think a lot of women go through this and I think when I came of age and I started college in 1968, it was kind of understood like you grow up, you get married, you have children, and even if you have a job, that's the trajectory. I knew I wanted a different life and I knew to have that life, I needed to know who I was without picking up on what other people wanted of me or asked of me or projected on me or any of that. That required just having some room totally by myself, which I'd never had in my life.

JANE LYNCH—COMEDIAN, ACTOR, SINGER

I live with my ex. It's great. We get along, and it's great. We're room-mates. Well, we don't like sleep in the same bed, we have our own rooms.

We're like copilots in life. She's also my assistant when I need one.

She's really a perfect human being. She's even more perfect than when we dated. I have several exes where that would never happen.

I think that romance is the problem. I think the expectation that comes with romance. Romantic thinking like, this is going to be something, is going to complete me. I mean, "You complete me?" It's bullshit.

I do a live stage show. We do a medley of songs, love songs. We sing the stuff, you know we were brought up with these notions. You know, "Let it please be him," and "I won't last a day without you."

I started out singing that song "It All Depends on You," and in between each phrase I go, "You know, a romantic relationship is basically bullshit."

I basically had a renaissance in terms of thinking, and I'm done with the romance. It's stupid. I'm a happy girl right here, right now.

JILL SOLOWAY—WRITER, DIRECTOR, PRODUCER

I still have relationships with a couple of my exes. I wouldn't really spend a ton of time with any of them, because I don't think it's good to do. I'm in a new romantic relationship. No need to dabble.

That's the difference, I think. That's the difference in this rela-tionship from all others. I have no interest in getting hits. I'm not trying to find out if I can fuck this up, I just actually literally want it to last forever.

Every past relationship I thought at least every day, or every week, "Is this the right relationship? Should I get out?" I didn't really believe in the whole soul mate thing, so I just like to kind of make odd choices instead.

I actually wasn't fishing in deep enough waters, I was sort of taking anybody. Probably people I could have control over. They all felt awesome, and fun, and they felt like love, and they were intense. If somebody caught my interest I would never think to myself, "Oh, this isn't going anywhere." I really didn't believe that Mr. Right was out there, so I wasn't trying to save myself for Mr. Right. I thought it was all a big lie. I thought it was a big fucking cosmic joke that when you meet the person that's the right person you just know. I thought that was like the biggest fucking joke ever. I didn't want to play in any of those little fields, trying to attract an awesome man. That seems like a dumb game.

CONAN O'BRIEN—TALK SHOW HOST, COMEDIAN, WRITER

When I came out to Los Angeles, I met all these people. In 1985 I came out here, and over time I met all these people. It's the same cast of characters. I mean, everyone just keeps popping up, and it is funny that you're assigned a set of characters when you're born, and they keep showing up in your life. That's just how it works. I do think God, and whatever God means, I really believe that there is a force in the universe that has a sense of humor. These things are just too weird.

MEL BROOKS—COMEDIAN, WRITER, DIRECTOR, PRODUCER, ACTOR, MUSICIAN

I spend almost every other night with Carl Reiner. Three nights a week I'll be at Carl's house. Carl loves, more than anything, what he calls "reallies" that we do. Carl is so proud that we do them only for ourselves. We don't do them for an audience, we don't do them for another person. We try to really amaze each other with where we're going with our minds, you know? We're still pretty good at it.

Marc

You guys sit and hang out for an hour or two.

CARL REINER—COMEDIAN, WRITER, DIRECTOR, PRODUCER, ACTOR

About three or four hours. Sometimes while we're watching something he'll fall asleep and I won't wake him because he drives home and I'm saying, "Better he sleeps here than falls asleep behind the wheel."

Marc

What was that thing you told me about movies? You two like watching movies with certain phrases in them.

Carl

Oh yeah, that's true. The Bourne Series and movies like that. The phrases are, "Secure the perimeter! Lock all doors!" Or a character in the movie says, "Get some rest." If those words are in the movie, that movie's a good movie.

Marc

As you get older you don't see people as much anymore.

ROB REINER—DIRECTOR, PRODUCER, WRITER, ACTOR

That's true. I think it has to do with—You know that whole thing they say, where you're born alone, you die alone? That bit?

Well, I think what happens as you get older, you start thinking about that, and also that you don't want to spend any time with anybody that's going to annoy you or make it uncomfortable. As you get older, you realize that there are more and more people that annoy you. So your world keeps narrowing, and getting narrower.

I think it's unconscious. I don't think you're consciously saying, "I think I'm going to narrow my world now." No, you think, "You know, I don't really like that person that much, so why should I stay?" It's like when you're young, you'd never leave a movie theater until the movie's over. Now you go, "Why do I have to watch the last hour of this piece of crap?" Because I have such a limited time on the planet.

Marc

And now with phones and computers, it's like all the time is eaten up, unnecessarily eaten up.

Rob

Yes, and you trick yourself into believing that you're actually communicating with people. You know, I'm texting, I'm e-mailing, I'm doing. You're not talking to anybody. You're talking to a computer.

Here's the thing. You look at this show like *Friends,* right? You've got all these people, they're in their, I guess their twenties or something. They're hanging out with each other, and I guess that's what you do, you go in packs, but when you get into your thirties, your forties, your fifties, you don't do that anymore. You got kids, you hang out with them, and then when you get older you don't think, "Hey let's go and hang out at the coffee shop." You don't do it.

Marc

Maybe you get one guy.

Rob

Yeah, one guy.

Marc

I talked to your father. He says he hangs out with Mel almost every night.

Rob

Mel. Mel and my dad, virtually every single night.

Marc

That's really something.

Rob

Listen, it's wonderful that they have each other. They met each other when they were in their twenties, and to have that kind of bond, and to have that bond stick. They make each other laugh, they enjoy each other's company. They both lost their spouses recently, so they have that.

And they watch any movie that has "Secure the perimeter!" in it.

JACK BLACK—COMEDIAN, MUSICIAN, ACTOR, MEMBER OF TENACIOUS D

Kyle Gass is my jelly. Without Kyle I'm just delicious, delicious peanut butter, which is fine on its own. Actually some people prefer it, but when you add it to jelly, it makes something unbelievably delicious.

Now, why would I turn my back on my jelly? Once you find your jelly, there's just no reason to keep searching.

Marc

Was the jelly bothering you to do another record?

Jack

No, in fact the jelly was talking about breaking up. We always break up, it's a fiery relationship. Not really. Sometimes. We're like brothers. We're highly competitive with each other and there's a lot of love and there's also an endless battle for control. In the band and also in life. We're both on diets right now. Kyle won't tell you, but he's secretly hoping to win and be lighter than . . .

KYLE GASS—COMEDIAN, MUSICIAN, ACTOR, MEMBER OF TENACIOUS D

I'll tell you. Of course I want to encourage you by winning.

Jack

By winning and holding it over me.

Marc

There's no denying the fact that at some point, Tenacious D happened and then Jack Black: Movie Star happened. Now, was the jelly upset?

Kyle

The jelly did fall off the bread a little bit. It's always that. It's a half-full, half-empty sort of thing. On one hand, this partnership has been the greatest thing ever for me, but then on the other hand it's like, "Wait a minute, how come I'm not starring in my own movies? How come I can walk through an airport so easily? What's happening here?" Then you have to reconcile, "Well, I don't know. That's just the way it is."

For a while, I would just really start a lot of side projects.

There is that feeling like, "Wait, let me see how good I can do on my own." Then failing time after time, I realized that without Jack, I am nothing.

Jack

It's not true.

Kyle

I've accepted it. Really, I've become much happier.

CHEECH MARIN—COMEDIAN, WRITER, ACTOR, MEMBER OF THE DUO CHEECH AND CHONG

It was always volatile between us. We were always arguing.

We're not like best friends. People always say, "Oh, you guys must be best friends, you've known each other forever."

We're brothers!

So you can fight with your brother. But he's still your brother. That's really the kind of the connection we have.

I don't know, you come to a point where you just don't want to hear what the other guy has to say, you know? Both of us.

TOMMY CHONG—COMEDIAN, WRITER, ACTOR, MEMBER OF THE DUO CHEECH AND CHONG

I think what happened is that Cheech got divorced and I was part of the divorce settlement.

"Okay, you get Chong and I get the house."

Cheech

Yeah, yeah, okay. That's a good deal.

JACK BLACK

Kyle never ever has any interest in coming over to the house.

KYLE GASS

I haven't been invited once.

Jack

That's not true, I do invite you over.

Marc

Why don't you go there? By the way, I've received zero invites over to your ranch since you've lived there.

Jack

The Jelly Ranch.

Kyle

I think what it is, is that when we work together we see a lot of each other. I think the natural breaks are good, but I do enjoy seeing the kids when they do pop up.

Jack

Sometimes I invite Kyle over and he's like, "I've already seen that movie. I've got better things to do."

Kyle

Oh my God.

CARRIE BROWNSTEIN

Corin Tucker is still one of my best friends, so despite going through that kind of rough phase of Sleater-Kinney and then the breakup of the band, which does end up feeling a little bit divorce-like, we're still really good friends. We dated for a second when we were nineteen and twenty. She's married with two kids now.

People really focused on that even though in my mind, I'm like, "Doesn't everybody do that?" It's fine, I have nothing to hide, but it was just one of those things. I still remember reading a review after Sleater-Kinney played a show in New York, and the reviewer mentioned it. It was years later, I'd just been to Corin's wedding. But if you don't provide people with a narrative, people will provide one for you. We were never good at self-mythologizing in Sleater-Kinney. I think when you don't do that, someone will just fill it in for you.

PAUL THOMAS ANDERSON—WRITER, DIRECTOR, PRODUCER

We all kind of started out together. Me. John C. Reilly. Philip Seymour Hoffman. They had a little bit more of a résumé underneath them. Which was really helpful, even if they made four or five films, that was more than I'd done. When we were starting out, they had my back and they were really helpful. Like, "That's where craft service is," the simplest things. Just having a few movies under your belt makes a big difference.

But you know, Phil was like, he maybe had a long list of kind of not-so-great movies, but he would always be the best thing in it, you know?

When I saw him for the first time in *Scent of a Woman* I just knew what true love was. I knew what love at first sight was and it was the strangest feeling, sitting in a movie theater thinking, he's for me and I'm for him and that was it.

Strange. Believe me, when I was a kid, just like eight, nine years old, I always thought I'd have Cary Grant in my movie or Harrison Ford. But something happened when I saw him.

SAM SEDER—COMEDIAN, WRITER, DIRECTOR, ACTOR, RADIO HOST, POLITICAL COMMENTATOR

I grew up with Jon Benjamin.

Marc

You guys were best friends?

Sam

Yes.

Marc

Like, when you were ten?

Sam

No, no, we were archenemies first.

JON BENJAMIN—COMEDIAN, WRITER, DIRECTOR, ACTOR

Sam was my actual bully in junior high.

Marc

And then you became friends? Why? Because you negotiated it?

Jon

No, we became friends later, probably out of desperation.

I started prep school in seventh grade. I was a little guy. I loved disco, which was a very unpopular musical movement at the time. He was really "husky," I guess would be the best word.

Marc

So he comes up to you and he says, "Hey, Shorty!" and you go, "What, Fatty?"

Jon

Well, no. He would want to beat me up. That was the thing.

Marc

He was a "beater-upper"?

Jon

Yeah, he would chase me and stuff like that, as I remember. I was terrified of him. He was, I think, fairly serious about it—although I don't know if that was true at the time—about killing me. There was that feeling. He sort of ruined a good year in my life.

SAM SEDER

Jon's sort of like a pathological liar. I mean, he's a little bit reformed, but a lot of what he talks about, that stuff is imaginary. We were enemies, but then I think through high school I didn't really deal with him at all.

JON BENJAMIN

In any event, Sam left that prep school, and I went to college in Connecticut. This small college. My parents are dropping me off, and I'm nervous about being there. My roommate was a very strange guy from Spanish Harlem. Not many people at Connecticut College from Spanish Harlem. I open the door across the hall, and Sam Seder is there. Which I thought, at the time, was like seeing the Virgin Mary, in a bad way.

I just was like, "You've got to be kidding me, right?" That's the guy who used to beat me up for a year and a half, now he's practically my roommate. His dad is there, dropping off his clothes, and I'm like, "What are you doing here? This is going to be bad."

Then it ended up like that feel-good story you'd see on TV. We became best friends, through alcohol. We knew no one else, and he was like, "Let's go get some beer and get drunk, and go to college."

SAM SEDER

I know exactly the moment you and I met.

Marc

It was in Harvard Square.

Sam

Yes, and I had done an open mic. I was with a couple of friends who I had invited. You were walking with your soon-to-be first ex-wife. I said, "Oh, that's Marc Maron." You turned around, you were like fifteen yards ahead of us, I don't know how you heard me, or maybe you sort of sensed that there were people, and you turned around, and you said, "Is there a problem?"

That moment I remember really well, because at the time I was like, wow, he's really cantankerous, but what I came to realize was that was your way of saying, "Can you ask me for my autograph?" That was basically what you were saying. "Is there a problem?" Like, why would there be? No, we're in Harvard Square, we're walking around. I don't know, what possible problem is there? It was really you saying, "Hey, could you come over here and ask me for my autograph, please?" That's what that was, and that dynamic is really I think what I've come to understand about you.

Marc

Like when I'm doing that, I just need attention?

Sam

That was the subtext.

Marc

The subtext of "fuck you" is "come on, let's hang out"?

Sam

Right.

Marc

Yeah, that's true.

Sam

Well, it's not even just hang out.

Marc

It's like "take care of me"?

Sam

No, it's not even take care of me, it's like . . .

Marc

Celebrate me.

Sam

Yeah. Exactly.

Marc

Are we all right, me and you?

LOUIS CK—COMEDIAN, WRITER, DIRECTOR, PRODUCER, ACTOR

We're under development. You're one of the people I've known longer than almost anybody.

Marc

For some reason over the years, despite whatever happens in our lives, I feel very close to you as a friend. When you were having trouble and your marriage was falling apart, I had this idea of your life in my head and I hadn't really been in touch with you at all. And then when you told me what was going on, I was like, "Holy shit. How did I miss your entire life?" And then I got very saddened by the fact that I had been out of your life, and then some resentment happened.

Louis

We were best friends for a long time. A long, long time. It's hard. There are times when it's hard to be your friend's friend.

Marc

Well, it's not like I have any new friends.

Louis

Oh, that's good. So I wasn't replaced. Good. That would feel worse.

As far as trying to stay friends with somebody that you have a hard time thinking about what they're doing against what you're doing, focus on them needing a friend. It takes a good friend to stay with you in hard times. It takes a good friend to stay with you in good times. Everybody needs support, everybody does. So you're letting me down, if you see me doing something and you have a hard time coming to terms with it because of how you're feeling about your own life. What's really happening is you're letting me down as a friend. You're being a shitty friend by being jealous.

I coulda used you. I got divorced. I got a show canceled. I could have used a friend. Those times that were making you jealous, I was struggling. But you shut me out because you were having a hard time. And then I did it to you, out of resentment.

Marc

Well, can we get back on track or what?

Louis

Yeah. I think we can.

Marc

You understand me. Not a lot of people do. You were always able to give me a great deal of relief.

Louis

We understand each other's flaws really well. We share some, and we've known each other long enough. That's why we're able to tell each other things that we don't want to tell anyone else.

Marc

Well, I love you, man.

Louis

Yeah. Same here.

Marc

Let's just try to be better friends.

Louis

Okay.

PARENTING

"I Was Doing It the Wrong Way"

I think anyone who knows my work at all knows I am not too happy with the way I was parented. It's okay. You can't choose them. It's random. I'm not mad at them anymore. It is their fault that I struggle in the ways that I do in certain areas of my life, but life does go on. How emotionally crippled you let yourself be does become a choice if you are self-aware enough. I believe it is difficult to unfuck yourself completely, but at the very least you can train yourself to act better and hope that it will take.

I really had no idea what people were talking about when they talked about self-parenting: what it meant and that it is necessary. Obviously, I know the basics, like living alone, paying bills, shopping, cleaning myself, how to get online, and mailing a letter. The emotional component is different. It's not essential that you have to be emotionally healthy to survive. Sometimes the opposite is true. In the last decade or so it's become very clear to me that the choices I've made with my life were weird, extreme attempts at self-parenting and self-acceptance. Most of my creativity is a corrective.

As someone who is not a parent, I wind up learning a lot from people who are. Ali Wong came into my garage and pumped breast milk in the middle of our interview. It was an important moment for me, seeing that level of commitment and devotion from a new mother. A similar thing happened when I was talking with Louis CK about his kids and he got choked up recalling the emotional moment of his first daughter's birth. I've known Louis for decades, but I'm not sure I ever saw him cry. A big part of my brain is awestruck by people who put in the arduous work of parenting. It's probably why it terrified me most of my life.

The one thing I have done for the longest in my life is stand-up. I wanted to be seen, heard, and to be myself. I wanted the audience to be my parents. I wasn't looking for adoration or love because I didn't trust either. I just wanted to be myself and be accepted. I fought with audiences for years because I thought they were judging me, and of course they were. That's what they do. I would go out of my way for years to defy their liking me and I thought it was just my style. If they liked me, I would alienate them, just like a kid fights with his parents.

I would exhaust my friends, girlfriends, and audiences with needs that could never be met because the time to meet them was gone and my parents had dropped the ball. I had to put the cap on my personality and accept that those old childish needs weren't going to ever be met and that's okay. I'm okay. I'm me. That is self-parenting. It's painful. I don't think I fully processed the grief of not getting my needs met when I was a kid. I had to be humbled by life, accept that, get sober, stop yelling at girlfriends and wives, stop draining my friends, treat myself better, and be proud of what I do.

I have self-acceptance now. Age helps. I didn't really grow up until I was in my late forties. I brought myself up pretty well. I'm glad I never had kids. I just didn't want to put them through my own selfish struggle with being a grown-up. It wouldn't be fair. I have cats. They don't talk and they barely like me. It's perfect.

AMY POEHLER—COMEDIAN, WRITER, PRODUCER, ACTOR

I don't like anyone else's kids. You think having kids makes you like all kids, but it doesn't. You just like your kids. Especially if you're by yourself because you're like, I don't have my kids now.

This is the time where I'm supposed to pretend like I'm twenty-four and traveling the world by myself.

LESLIE JONES—COMEDIAN, WRITER, ACTOR

Children are crazy. We are crazy because we're full of hormones, we're full of new beginnings, we're full of veins that are being developed. We are crazy. I hate to say it like this, but they are like pets, because you have to train them. That energy goes somewhere. It's either going to go for the positive or is going to go for the negative, and my mom knew that about me because I was that kid.

My first comedy special is named Problem Child because my mom used to call me that. She sat me down one day and she was like, "You know you are a problem child, right?" It wasn't even like I was doing things on purpose, I was just a clown and I did not know it. I was just always in trouble.

ALI WONG—COMEDIAN, WRITER

So many people discouraged me from having a kid because they were like, "Why are you going to have a kid? We're never going to see you again." It's true. It's very rare to see a female comic who has a kid or is pregnant. Female stand-up comics don't get pregnant because once they do have a baby, they disappear. They become a martyr and then they stop doing stand-up, but that's not the case with male stand-up comics. Male stand-up comics, they have a baby and they get up onstage a week after the baby's born, talk about it, and then they'll complain about how the baby's shitty and they're boring and annoying and all these other shitty dads in the audience are like, "That's hilarious. I identify."

Then their fame just swells because now they're this relatable family funny man all the sudden, and they get an HBO special and a sitcom deal, and the mom is at home suffering with bloody nipples, broken pussy, career over, and so, for me, I had a lot of anxiety about it being over once I had a kid, and I was like, "I'm not going to let that happen. I don't want even being pregnant to slow me down." I planned it that way because I was like, "I need to know for myself that this is not the end."

LAKE BELL—ACTOR, WRITER, DIRECTOR, PRODUCER

I birthed at home. It was very important to me. I would do it again, even though if you asked me right after, I'd be like "Fuck you." It's just a massacre.

Also, I just had no idea that it was that hardcore. I knew birth would be insane, but I didn't know the aftermath was insane. Nobody tells you about that. You're like, "Oh, I'm injured. I am an injured person." I thought I would just kind of bounce back. I make lists, I'm kind of organized, and I felt like, all right, I'll be able to kind of troubleshoot this new priority shift.

It was just like I was hit by a wave. I didn't know what the fuck happened. I totally was depressed. All that chemical shit happened to me.

Partially I think why I wanted to do it at home was, I just was like, this is going to be my thing. I want this experience, I want to feel it, I want to be there. I'm impressed with this whole mechanism, my body's just kind of operating. I got very nervous about whether I'd know what to do. The truth is, your body knows what to do.

ALI WONG

It's just so weird to me when people have these overarching statements about what it's like to have kids because it's so different. Do we make any overarching statements about what it's like to have parents? Every parent is different and every kid is different.

Like breast-feeding. Basically, breast-feeding is super sensitive because some women don't have time, and they want to go back to work or maybe they don't have enough milk in their breasts to breast-feed. But on the west side of Los Angeles, there are these crazy lactivists that make you feel like your daughter's going to turn into a prostitute if you don't breast-feed.

CAROLINE RHEA—COMEDIAN AND ACTOR

I remember the first time I was pumping, my boyfriend walked in. I said, "If you never want to have an erection again, ever, you will watch me pump." It is the grossest. First of all, that noise. And you are literally in a pasture by yourself. But you know, it's important.

I was not going to breast-feed because I got gestational diabetes. I actually lost twelve pounds. I think it's hilarious. The only time in my life I've really consistently lost weight I was in my final trimester of pregnancy. My boyfriend was so afraid of me because I was so angry, but he says, "You know, breast-feeding is really good for the baby." I'm like, "I'm not doing that. It's disgusting!" Of course the minute the baby was born, I looked at the baby, and I'm like, "Oh my God, does she have eyelashes? Could I have some Häagen-Dazs?"

After I'd been resugared and I felt better, of course I breast-fed, and it's the most painful thing. That's what the epidural is for. It's unbelievably painful. Everyone says how natural it is. No. It's the most beautiful thing in the world, and it's totally bonding, and it's ridiculously painful. They put so much pressure on you at the hospital. They literally say to you, when they ask you if you're going to breast-feed, they say it like this, "Do you love your baby?" I'm crying, "I love my baby." You don't know that they have invisible shark teeth. Rows and rows of them. But it's the most rewarding thing and you have to do it for your baby.

LAKE BELL

When you are all of a sudden bedridden, you can't walk upstairs, and you're torn, and you're literally beaten up. There's this little thing that is insatiable, like I don't know what she needs, or I don't know what the fuck I'm doing. I also have this person that I share my life with that can go down to the shop and get something, but I can't. That's frustrating.

ELIZABETH BANKS—ACTOR, DIRECTOR, PRODUCER

Women should not be expected to bounce back. It's I think a true disservice with all this going on right now with these celebrity moms. First, I just want to remind people that celebrities generally are genetically superior human beings on a certain level anyway. They're mostly thin, they've got trainers, they work out, they've got money, they've got the ability. If you're holding up certain celebrities as your benchmark for what to look like after you've had a child, just go be with your kid for a minute. Don't get to the gym right away. It's all right.

MARY LYNN RAJSKUB—COMEDIAN, ACTOR

I never really thought about having a kid. There was one time where I called my mom and started crying out of nowhere. I was on the freeway, and I called her. I said, "I'm too old to be a young mother," but I didn't even necessarily want to be a mother. I was just having that passage-of-time thing. I was like, "Oh, I'm not having a baby in my twenties."

It was terrible when the baby was born. It was really, really hard. Your whole life as you know it is just completely shaken up and turned upside down, and pushed all over the place. Just, everything that you want to do, everything that you are doing, you can't do any of it. Even just simply waking up every three hours, and being enraged about that, and you can't, because there's this helpless creature. It pushes your buttons on every level of having to deal with being responsible for something. Everything else that you thought had meaning is just stupid. "Oh, this job or that job." This is a creature. Everything else is like, "Who cares? Who cares about all these things that I was worried about?" They don't matter when your job is to keep something alive, and to take care of it.

It didn't come natural. I didn't like it, and I didn't like the kid, and I didn't know what I was doing. The baby was terrible, and he wouldn't stop crying. I lost all sense of myself and sense of time. Then the instincts kicked in, and now I love it. It's awesome. I love it so much. My son is the greatest guy ever. The greatest guy ever. It's the hugest, massivest, suckiest adjustment. Thankfully my husband is solid as a damn rock.

LOUIS CK—COMEDIAN, WRITER, DIRECTOR, PRODUCER, ACTOR

When I had my daughter, or when her mother had her in front of me, everything changed. I just fell in love with this kid. I remember she was screaming in the delivery room, really upset. She seemed particularly upset. Kids are supposed to cry when they are born, but she seemed angry to me, and upset. You know when a kid's crying in a delivery room, everybody is smiling. "Aw, look at her cry." But I was really upset for her. They put her on this little table, and they're putting stuff around her. . . .

Sorry.

I'm unexpectedly emotional. It's not a story that I tell a lot, so. . . .

Marc

It's all right, man.

Louis

Let me have some water.

Water's good, it washes away your love for your children so you can talk without a shaking voice.

Yeah, they put her on this little table, and they were fucking jabbing shit into her, and they're just rough with her, and she's screaming. It was a C-section, so her mom is being sewn up. Her mom was just taken away.

I'm in the middle of this. I'm between her mother, who I'd been caring for. She'd been pregnant for nine months and I'd been caring for her. It all had been about the mother. The thing that happens when you have a baby is, for the better part of a year you live with the pregnancy, and it's all about that.

When the woman's in labor, you just think, "This is about getting this woman through this. When it's done, she and I are going to go home." As much as you think you understand, you don't really understand that there's someone else in there. You get through this thing that we've been taking classes about, we've been reading books about it. You just don't know until you see the kid's face that there's somebody who's now going to be with you for the rest of your fucking life. I didn't know how that would feel. But when she came out, it wasn't about my feelings. It was, "This kid is scared shitless, and she's really angry at being taken out of her mom."

There's this woman that's been the center of all this, she just got cut in fucking half in front of me. They just made a hole in her belly and took this kid out, and she's being sewn up and she's alone. This kid is over there, and she's alone, and I'm in the middle.

I went to the kid.

I got my head next to hers. She's screaming, purple face. I said, "It's okay. It's okay. You're going to be okay. It's all right. I'm here." She stopped screaming on a dime, turned, and looked right at me. Kids can't see an inch in front of them until they're a couple weeks old. But she turned her head and opened her eyes and looked at me and stopped crying. Everybody, all these practiced people, said, "Oh my God, she heard you." I just heard a voice say, "She knows who you are."

Then somebody, at that moment, stuck a fucking pin in her foot, or something, to get blood, and she screamed again. But I didn't understand that I had a role in this kid's life until that moment. So it became about this kid. She changed everything.

One way that she changed was I expected her to be unhappy. She lived in someone's belly, and she was living this perfect life. Then you're taken out to where your skin is raw, and being hit by the atmosphere, and you cough all the time. What an awful life. That's the way I always looked at it. It's just terrible. The moment you're born, you're coping. Must just be awful. Shit and piss and diapers. What an awful life. But after that bout of crying, within an hour she was breast-feeding and she was happy. I watched her eat her first meal, and I watched her shit her first shit. I saw the system start working right in front of me. She dealt with it beautifully, and I was inspired by her.

I don't like babies. I'm not wired for that. Before I had kids, I was really worried about having kids, because I don't like being around babies. I didn't like them. I didn't feel sympathy for babies in the past. I didn't know how I would get. I thought it would just be taxing to have someone screaming and crying. You don't sleep very much. They get you up in the middle of the night. I was like, "I can't do that." Pregnancy gives you some training for that, because your wife gets up in the middle of the night. She has to pee. She needs help. Pregnancy is a perfect training program for having a kid. It's the closest you can get, anyway.

What I learned was that I could do it all. I didn't mind getting up. I didn't mind being bleary and sleepy. I didn't mind her screaming and crying, because I had sympathy for her, because I wanted her to be okay.

I found out that I'm a patient person. I didn't know any of this about myself. I'm a patient person. That I had capacity for giving love and affection that I didn't know I had, and receiving it. That I was really interested in teaching her and talking to her and interacting with her. All this stuff that I never knew I had. My own anxiety about my life just went away, because I didn't give a shit. I instantly knew that I'm going to get old and die, and I wasn't afraid of it anymore, because it's about her now. It's about giving her a chance to be happy, and have her own confidence and her own life. That's what it became about. But it was a struggle. I didn't give up without a fight.

DAN HARMON—DIRECTOR, WRITER, PRODUCER

If you ever met somebody who grew up with swell parents, I'm really, really suspicious of them.

DAVE FOLEY—COMEDIAN, WRITER, ACTOR

The thing I learned from my mother, which was basically her motto for everything in life, was, "Don't fuss."

"Oh, don't fuss."

"Horrible things are happening!"

"Oh, don't fuss."

GARRY SHANDLING—COMEDIAN, WRITER, ACTOR (1949–2016)

I'm a good reactor. I said, "God, hey, give me kind of a wacky mom so I can just fucking react."

ROBIN WILLIAMS—COMEDIAN, ACTOR (1951–2014)

My mother was a very, very funny terminal optimist. Everything is wonderful, beautiful. My father is the hardcore pessimist. When I told him I wanted to be an actor, he said, "Great. Have a backup profession like welding." Between the two of them, I got this weird, not cynical, but hyperrealism and this hyperoptimism of my mother, of everything is rainbows and beauty.

PRESIDENT BARACK OBAMA

My dad was a tragic figure in a lot of ways. A brilliant man by all accounts who sort of took a leap from a tiny village in the backwaters of Kenya to suddenly the United States, getting a degree, attending Harvard, and he never managed that leap as well as he could have.

Part of the process of me writing my first book was to figure out what happened to him and how did he become who he was. He ended up becoming an alcoholic and abusive toward his several wives, and to some degree a neglectful father.

In some ways, because I didn't grow up with him, he was an abstraction to me. That stuff didn't seep into me. My mother and my grandparents, who did raise me, fortified me. Although one thing they always did that I thought was wise was they never portrayed a negative picture of him. They actually accentuated what was good about him rather than bad, which is an interesting thing. It was a good myth, and I didn't internalize a bunch of negative attitudes about who he was, and thereby didn't think that that was who I had to be.

I had the adolescent rebellion screw-up period that has been well chronicled, but it turned out that a lot of his craziness, I didn't end up internalizing it. One of the things that I always say, I've said this to Michelle, one of our biggest jobs as parents, because we're all a little bit crazy, is let's see if we can not pass on some of our craziness to our kids.

DAVID CROSS—COMEDIAN, WRITER, DIRECTOR, ACTOR

I've never sought out my father. Absolutely not. He lives in New York. I'm sure I pass by, I don't know where he is, but I'm sure I've ridden my bike past his place. My last interaction with him I was nineteen. It was on the phone.

I'm resigned to what it's going to be, and have been for a while. I've never had that, not once have I ever had that moment that I should let bygones be bygones. There's nothing in it for me except anger and bitterness and recrimination and I don't know why I would invite that in. He doesn't deserve the satisfaction, and I know I'm being obstinate. There's certainly a bit of stubbornness, but stubbornness is just something you apply to the situation.

I don't forgive him.

I don't, nor will I. I hope that I will have children someday soon, we've talked about it, and I hope I am an exemplary, good, better father for it because I know, I just cannot wrap my head around a father or mother who just doesn't care about their kids. Their level of selfishness supersedes responsibility for a child. I don't understand it, I don't get it. It's soft and silly to say I have a lack of respect for it. I loathe it, I hate it, I don't like those people, and there's no excuse.

Unfortunately, in this world, that's how a lot of people are.

I just turned ten when he left. He had just moved us back to Georgia from Syracuse. We had no money, zero, nothing. He basically left to go to Phoenix, owing a lot of money. My mom had no job, three kids. We had come from Syracuse, we got kicked out of there, and he chased this job in Georgia, which didn't pan out. I subsequently came to find out all the lies. He was not a con man. He didn't have thought-out cons. He would misrepresent himself, lie about stuff. He was so proud. He was a bit of a pathological liar, and he was the victim in everything. It was never his fault. The world was against him, and if he was fired from a job, it wasn't his fault.

Again, when you're ten, and I loved my dad, I thought he was fucking awesome, you don't really have anywhere close to the full story, but as you grow up, you come to know more stuff. He just sort of sat us down and said, "Your mom and I are going to get separated," he left, we didn't see him again until my bar mitzvah, in which he took my bar mitzvah money. Asked for it and took it. I was happy to give it to him because my dad was back in Georgia, oh my God, that's great. "Don't tell your mother."

You got it, Dad. "I need this, then I can stay here, and we can hang out."

I just don't know that level of psychotic selfishness. As I was saying before, just this idea that there's this guy who got married, had three kids. Who knows if he ever really loved my mother? I just imagine him truly thinking, you know what, I don't like this Being Married thing, I don't like this lady, maybe a kid will make me feel different, so he has a kid, and then they end up having a couple more kids. He's like, nah, it's not for me. I'll see you guys later. It's a simplistic way to view it, but that's literally the mind-set of this guy saying, "Yeah, look, I gave it a shot, guys, you can't blame me. I thought it'd be my thing, it's not, so I'm going out to the West Coast, you all take it easy. Definitely write. Call me."

In the beginning I did. He was my dad, I loved him.

DONNELL RAWLINGS—COMEDIAN, ACTOR

My dad spent time away from home in places where it wasn't too appropriate for me to visit.

Marc

What got him in there?

Donnell

He was a heroin dealer. When he first got out of prison, I kind of just started my career. This is a true story. Only thing I wanted him to do was to be proud of me. I was a stand-up comic. He came to one of my shows. I'm like, "Dad, first off, it's good to see you." I was like, "So, how'd you like the show?"

He was like, "It was . . . It was all right."

I'm like, "It was all right?"

Then he said, "Why you telling them lies about me?"

I'm like, "What lie?"

I told a joke about him selling drugs. He said, "I never sold shit two-for-fifty, nigga." He was mad that I made a joke about him being on the block. He was pissed. That's how he rounded up my set.

SUE COSTELLO—COMEDIAN, WRITER, ACTOR

I stopped talking to my family. I told my mother, "You have to treat me with respect. I can't talk to you." By stepping away and doing what I did, I realized, oh my God, I don't need them.

Marc

I had a therapist say to me once that you can train your parents, because after a certain point they will abide by your conditions because they want to have a relationship with you.

BRUCE SPRINGSTEEN—MUSICIAN, SONGWRITER, AUTHOR

There are irretrievable relationships where events have occurred that relationships don't come back from. I know plenty of people who had to sign off from their families for a variety of reasons. For good, healthy reasons and move on with their lives. That can happen. But if the relationships are retrievable, and I felt like mine was, then there's a nice payback in seeing things come closer and become a little healthier.

You look back on your anger as part of youthful misunderstandings. Of course you had your reasons and there was bad behavior. My pop could be very cruel when he was young. It's not that you let that slide. You live with it, it's a part of your life. If you're lucky, it's fuel for the fire. I mean, people don't end up in my circumstance who generally had these very placid, loving, very happy, fulfilled lives. It's not how you become a rock-and-roll star. You've got to have some chaos, tumult, disastrous relationships, humiliation at a young age, feel disempowered, enormous amount of weakness, and suddenly things start to burn, burn, burn. When that burning starts, if you take that flame and you aim it toward the right thing—powerful weapon.

RACHAEL HARRIS—COMEDIAN, ACTOR

My parents divorced when I was two and my dad moved away. I saw him once a year until I was in college and that's when I started having a better relationship with him. I was like, oh, I better know this man.

He always kept contact with us, and what was great was that when I did go to college, and I moved to New York, he got to kind of come in and be there in a way. He didn't live in New York, he lived in Alabama at the time.

I think because I wasn't living at home, and because I was in college, especially when I moved to New York, I think it was easier for my dad to deal with me as an adult than it was as a child. Unfortunately, my brother and sister didn't have that, they never got to really have that relationship with him that I did.

He passed in 2006. I was so, so glad that I'd had that relationship with him.

I got to know him as an imperfect person, and be okay with it. We often put our parents on a pedestal, and want them to be infallible, and I got to deal with the real him.

LOUIS CK

My kids were an imposition because I love them. If I didn't care about them, there wouldn't have been an issue. I would have been one of those dads, "I can't really spend much time with them, but they're there somewhere."

When you read about people, famous great guys from the past, and their kids were just completely and utterly ignored by them and everybody just thinks that was a by-product of how great that person was, and we all give them a pass for it.

I had seen a lot of *60 Minutes* episodes, where they talk about a guy, like Bill Parcells, or whoever. Look at how he's so manic, and he's so amazing. Then they talk to his wife, and she always has this kind of smile, and says, "We just know that we don't see Bill from September 1 to February 15. You know, you make a deal with yourself that that's okay. I love him." Then at the end of the episode, Morley Safer says, "They're divorced now." I always remember that, and seeing the kids going, "Dad loves football, and not much else."

I always thought, "That's really not okay. Don't have kids if you're going to do that."

PAUL THOMAS ANDERSON—WRITER, DIRECTOR, PRODUCER

My mom and my dad had four kids, me and my three sisters. Then my dad had a first marriage where he had five, so he had nine kids total.

Marc

How many do you have?

Paul

Four.

Marc

Is that just something you did because you grew up like that?

Paul

Probably. It's nice to have a lot of kids running around the house. It's like having a warm fire. Every once in a while it's like throwing a bag of cats into a warm fire and it could be a nightmare, but it's the best.

JIM GAFFIGAN—COMEDIAN, WRITER, PRODUCER, ACTOR

I have five kids and came from a family of six kids. I think we've been told that it's culturally weird to have six kids. By the way, when you think about it, if someone says, I have six cats, you think they're crazy. But what if someone really enjoys six cats and their apartment isn't covered with cat turds?

Marc

That's a long shot.

Jim

And I can afford to have my kids. I make a decent living, so as long as I can afford a decent cheeseburger, I'm all right, it's not like I need a boat.

It's like, So what? I'm going to be bald a year earlier?

What I get from these kids is immeasurable and I know it sounds like a rationalization, but it's amazing.

BOB ODENKIRK—ACTOR, WRITER, DIRECTOR, COMEDIAN

My kids are growing up, and it's great. It's nice that they're getting older, because the other option is they pass away at a young age. No, it's great that they grow up because life gets easier I think.

PRESIDENT BARACK OBAMA

The biggest fun I've had is watching my girls grow up, and they are magnificent. Look, hopefully every parent feels the way I do about my daughters, but I think they are spectacular. When Michelle and I came into office the biggest worry we had was, is this going to be some weird thing for them, and are they going to grow up with an attitude, or are they going to think that everybody eats off of china?

It turns out they're kind, they're thoughtful, they treat everybody with respect, they don't have any kind of airs. They're confident, but without being cocky. They've got great friends. They're not stuck in the bubble the same way I am. They go to the mall. They have sleepovers. They go to prom. Malia has started to drive. They're doing great, so my biggest fun has been watching them grow up.

Now, unfortunately, they're hitting the age where they still love me but they think I'm completely boring, and so they'll come in, pat me on the head, talk to me for ten minutes, and then they're gone all weekend. They break my heart. Now I've got to start thinking, "Well, what's going to replace that fun?"

ANDY RICHTER—COMEDIAN, WRITER, ACTOR

As I get older, one of the things working against my career is that I don't give a shit about anything but going home and hanging out with the kids, and swimming with them, and cooking dinner.

On this tour I did with Conan, he said at one point, "It's just really hard to do these shows, and then go home, and the very next day, someone says, 'Could you unload the dishwasher?' You're like, 'Last night, five thousand people were screaming my name!'"

I told him, "Yeah, but the dishwasher, that's the real thing. That's the thing."

There's something in me, I've never had five thousand people scream my name. Well, I have, I was on the same tour with Conan and people cheered when I came out. But that shit, I don't trust it. Unloading the dishwasher, I feel like, "I trust this. This is important." I've got to unload this dishwasher to show these people, who, like it or not, are going to be the ones wiping my ass. I've got to show them, "Look, I unloaded the dishwasher. You're going to have to roll me over in a nursing home bed someday."

BEN STILLER—ACTOR, WRITER, DIRECTOR

Working can also be a way to not stop and feel. That's something I've learned over the years. When I actually stop, there's a kind of chaos and there's not order necessarily. There's a real simplicity in working. I don't think it's a bad thing necessarily. Having kids, and learning life just doesn't happen on its own if you just go off and work all the time, forced me into figuring out "What's the balance?" I'm trying to figure that out still.

PAUL THOMAS ANDERSON

I turned to my mom the other day. She was over, and I was trying to get these four kids out of the house. I just got down on my knees and I said, "I'm so sorry for every single thing I ever did to you," and she said, "Well, you're welcome." Because it's a full-time job.

BEN STILLER

The ultimate realization when you have kids is when you think, "Okay, now I'm going to have my kids and I'm gonna right all the wrongs." Then you just realize how hard it is to be a parent, and I've made so many mistakes. Different mistakes than my parents made. Some the same, but I'm trying not to.

You just realize it's a really, really challenging thing to be a parent. I work and I know it's important to earn a living and all that, and also for creativity, but there's no way you can do that and justify it to young kids. They don't know. They don't understand why you're going away.

ADAM SCOTT—ACTOR

I went to my daughter's ballet class today, and I was watching her. All I could think about was her getting hurt. She was doing the most beautiful thing you could ever imagine. The cutest, most beautiful, incredible thing, and all I could think about was a whole fantasy scenario of tearing some guy apart who hits her in the face.

Marc

Wait, let's play that out. This is Adam Scott watching his daughter do a ballet class, and you're like, "Wow, look at that. She's really doing a great job." What happens in your head?

Adam

Well, last week, another little girl had pushed her facedown into a gymnastics mat. She got a scratch on her face. I guess it's kind of fresh that I feel protective of her. I just had this fantasy of, like, a grown man shoving her aside or slapping her across the face or something. I went through this whole thing where I just beat the shit out of him, and I started sweating and getting aggravated. While I was watching her.

Marc

You're sitting there beating the shit out of a guy you made up who just pushed your daughter out of the way.

Adam

A fictional person.

JIM GAFFIGAN

I was dropping my kids off at soccer camp, my older ones, and I brought my three-year-old. I turn around and some eight-year-old is bullying my three-year-old and I had to hold myself back from punching this kid. I do this, my wife thinks I'm crazy, like if any-one's ever rude to my kid, I go right up to them and I go, "What are you doing?" And she's like, "Jim, you look crazy." I'm like, "I don't care." Maybe my kid will say, "My dad is crazy, but he's got my back."

I grab this kid and I tried not to squeeze—I grabbed him.

My three-year-old was wearing a baseball cap and three-year-olds, they're like orangutans, right, they don't know what they're doing. This kid flipped it off my son's head and he was kind of, like, pointing it at my son. So I grabbed him by the arm and I said, "You're coming with me." I went to find a camp counselor. It's a soccer camp. The guy, it's just like this summer Manhattan soccer camp, it's nothing fancy. This guy's like, this beats being a janitor.

I said, "This kid was bullying my three-year-old son," and he looked at me like, "I don't care. I really don't care." And I was like, well, at least I did the right thing.

STEPHEN TOBOLOWSKY—ACTOR

While I was in Memphis doing *Great Balls of Fire!* is when I found out that Ann, who is now my wife, was pregnant. I had to tell somebody. I had to find somebody to tell. The first person to come in was the maid. She's knocking on the door and it was like dawn, and I said, "You know, it's a big day for me! I just found out my girlfriend is pregnant!"

She said, "I'll pray for ya, honey." That didn't cut it.

I called my mother and father, that was going to be the "Mom, Dad, guess what? I'm going to make you a grandparent again!"

Mom said, "Oh no, Stephen, no! Maybe you could get an abortion." So it wasn't exactly the vote of confidence.

I said, "No. No, we are having this child." I'd been through an abortion before with my first girlfriend. I think it was responsible for the end of our relationship. I'm not going to do this anymore. No way, man. I went down and there in the cafeteria was the stuntman of the movie, Dick. I went in and Dick was eating his eggs and grits.

I said, "Dick, I got big news, big news today! I just talked to my girlfriend. She's pregnant. I'm going to be a father."

Dick just stopped and he looked at me and he said, "Well, Stephen, you're in it now. Let me tell you, pal, when you have a child, your life will never be the same again. Ever again."

My heart kind of stopped. I was like, "Oh, okay, okay." For years, my story was the story of telling the maid, and calling Mom and Dad, and saying, "Ann, we're going to get married. We're going to have a child," and Dick's solemn blessing to me or curse or whatever it was.

Okay, the addendum. Fourteen years later, Ann and I now had two children. We're eating sushi in Studio City, California. Suddenly, I feel a pat on my shoulder. It's Dick!

I stand up and he says, "Hey, buddy!" He starts punching me in the stomach and I hate it when guys do that.

He says, "We ought to play golf sometime."

I said, "Yeah," and I look up at him and he has these huge tears coming down his face. I said, "Dick, are you all right?"

He said, "I just lost my firstborn. She died of an asthma attack. She couldn't get to the doctor in time. I had to tell someone. I'm walking down the sidewalk and I'm looking in this restaurant and I see you and your wife sitting in here eating. I knew you would understand. Let me tell you, Stephen, when you lose a child, your life will never be the same again. Ever again."

You know, a story isn't an event. An event is something that happens, but a story has a beginning, middle, and an end. You don't know what's going to happen until something else happens.

That was the addendum.

BOB SAGET—COMEDIAN, ACTOR, WRITER

I held a baby last night. This all sounds bad when I say it, but I held my friend's baby.

It sounds worse.

Adorable little girl.

It just gets worse. I really shouldn't be allowed to speak any more. There should be an injunction.

Anyway, she was just adorable. It made me think, I'm fifty-four. For me to have kids again, it's unusual. You don't want to be eighty years old and have a kid in high school. I don't want to die on my kid. Then again I wouldn't mind having a football player kid, like an eighteen-year-old boy that's a big strapping strong kid just drag me around because I can't walk anymore. Carry me like the Revolutionary War days.

HANK AZARIA—COMEDIAN, ACTOR

It freaked me out so bad, becoming a father. And my wife put no pressure on me. She was like, "I don't know if I want to do this either." I was like, "Well, if we're going to do this, we're going to have to do this now." I got obsessed with it. I started asking all my friends at my weekly poker game, "What did you guys do? Is that what you wanted? Is that why you got married, because you wanted kids? Did it change your life? Is it worth it?" They were like, "Shut up. Just have a kid or not. We don't give a shit, do whatever you want to do." I felt a lot of guilt, which was why I was so torn about having a kid.

Once that kid's born, what I didn't realize was that you're just—and especially with a preemie that comes ten weeks early—you get so grateful that they're okay. Your first thought is, "Oh my God, is he going to be all right?" Your second thought is a selfish one: "Am I going to be all right?" Am I going to be okay, if he's a special-needs kid or whatever happens? And that's part of the whole journey of this. Then you realize, just for him to be okay, you'll take it. You'll do whatever you need to do in exchange for them being all right.

For me, a selfish, narcissistic, egotistical actor, it was the only thing. I can say that he's first. Genuinely, in my heart, I can't say that about anything else.

JACK GALLAGHER—COMEDIAN, PLAYWRIGHT

When my son Liam was seven—he's a teenager now—but when he was seven he was diagnosed with autism. I didn't want to have him tested. I didn't want him labeled, because once he's labeled, he's labeled for life. I didn't know at that time we could control the label, that it didn't have to be what I thought it was going to be. Looking back, there was some denial.

He was always a smart kid. He started reading at four, he walked behind my wife and read an ad out of a newspaper from top to bottom at four. There were some social problems, issues with him. It got to the point where we needed help, and in second grade we had him tested. They said he's autistic.

When you and I are talking to each other, I'm saying something, you nod your head. Where did you learn how to do that? That's through osmosis, your parents didn't say nod your head when somebody talks to you. He didn't pick that stuff up, he has to learn that stuff. For years, we tried to get him to ask questions. We wanted him to ask a question, because he would just talk to you about his day, what he'd been doing. We'd try to have conversations, and the question we wanted him to ask was, "How was your day?" I just worked on that forever and ever, with his therapist.

It's a really weird situation, because he has to fit in to a certain degree, to function in society. I don't want him to change, that's the lesson I learned, I don't want him to change. I want him to stay as this person he is, which is completely different and unique. Honestly, a really different kind of cool, but he has to function in society.

He's one of a kind. You talk to him and you go, "Wow, this kid is interesting, he's funny, but he's different." He has to fit in to society, this is the thing as a parent, when I'm gone, I want him to be able to function. There are certain things that you have to be able to do to function. One is to engage other people. He loves other people, and he wants to talk to other people, and he wants to engage them in conversation, he just has a hard time with it.

It's very difficult to describe, he just has a difficult time with it, he just doesn't know how to do it. You have to teach him tiny steps, and things that you and I picked up, he's had to learn.

I remember walking across the playground with him at school, and he's in the fourth grade, and he said, "So how was your day?" I called my wife and said, "He just asked me how my day was." It was this giant fucking breakthrough. She said, "Liam?" I said, "Liam Gallagher asked me how my day was." I remember saying to him, "Good! Good day!"

The thing about Liam is, there are no physical cues that tell you he's different. He's not in a wheelchair, he doesn't have any muscular dysfunction. If we see people with a physical cue, you know to deal with things a little differently, but Liam is not that way. You start talking to him and it takes you about a minute to realize, "There's something a little different happening here. A little askew." That throws people off. People just blow him right off, don't want anything to do with him.

I was embarrassed of him at times, because he's my kid, and we'd be standing places, and he'd be bouncing up and down. I'd be like, "Dude, stop bouncing." Then I had this moment with him, this really revealing moment, where I was working really hard with him. I rewrote textbooks for him, I just wanted everything to work. I had this really telling moment with him where he basically told me. . . .

I was . . .

I was doing it the wrong way.

He told me he was doing the best he could, and he was really trying hard, and why was I so angry all the time?

I thought, "Shit, I'm not doing this right."

I just stepped back and I let him be himself, and I watched what he did, and I followed him. Now we have a way. He's my bud, I understand him better. It was me, it wasn't him.

I was always concerned about what people thought of me, and how I came across, and my image of what people thought of me. I think what Liam's taught me, that I try—and this isn't easy to do. Everybody says they don't care what people think about them. I have gotten to the point where I care less about what people think about me. I take criticism for what it's worth, and less to heart if I don't think it's relevant, if that makes sense. He's taught me that it's okay to be different, that it's okay to be who you are, and not try to be who everybody wants you to be, or who you think you need to be.

RON FUNCHES—COMEDIAN, ACTOR

My son's the best. He's been the best thing in my life, for sure.

Originally we thought he was deaf because he just wouldn't respond to things when you called him or when you made noises. We bring him to the doctor, and we find out that he can hear. They were like, "We need to do some more tests on him." They did some test on him. This was when he was about two years old, and they were like, "Yeah, he has classic autism."

Basically for him, and for a lot, it means nonverbal. An aversion to certain textures and noises and lights. Just developmental delays, and things of that nature.

Once we knew it became a lot easier. The hardest part was just being like, "What's wrong? What's going on? He won't sleep." He would sleep from like 2:00 A.M. to 5:00 A.M. seven days a week, and that was it. Then he'd be up singing *The Jungle Book*. It's pleasant for a few hours.

He would repeat several things for comfort. He'd watch *The Jungle Book* on the VCR, and just repeat scenes over and over and over.

You introduce things, and you add things, but it's also very rigid. You don't want him to freak out, so it becomes a battle of what you're willing to deal with.

It'll always be a thing, but he's very independent. He's not completely verbal, but does a lot of mimicking. He's very good at typing, though. He's always been on the Internet and typing things out since he was like two.

There are some things where he's really awesome. There are certain things that he's normal at, and certain things that he has trouble with. He loves cars, racing, computers. Doesn't care for baths.

Marc

What's the hardest thing in terms of dealing with it?

Ron

Other people judging.

"Why are you so tired all the time? Why is your house a mess? Why do you always give in to everything he wants?" Because if he wants something he wants it, he needs it, and he will attack you or throw fits until he gets it, so you learn to pick your battles. There's several times where people thought we were kidnapping him because he would just wig out because we couldn't afford to buy him something. "Whose kid is that going off?" We had the cops called on us a few times because he was making noise. Even now if we go somewhere together in a hotel I have to let them know ahead of time, "Don't put us near somebody else." Because when you come up to tell us about a noise complaint I'm not going to be nice to you.

The coolest part of it was learning like, "Oh, I don't have to talk. Talking's overrated. I can hang out with you all day, and not talk, and we can get things done. I know what you want for dinner. I know what you're asking me off of glances or different things."

I always wanted to be a comedian. I always knew what I wanted, and I was afraid, and I didn't think that it was normal or possible. Having him, I was like, he's not going to be a typical, normal kid, and I have to defend that, so I should be able to defend what I'm about.

Also, it was like, "I'm going to need to make money. I don't want to put him in a home, and I know I'm not going to be alive forever, and he may need care forever. I have to do something. I either have to go back to college and figure out something that I like, or I need to really do this thing that I feel that I have a calling for." Which even looking back now, even knowing that it's kind of working out, still sounds stupid.

JON GLAZER—COMEDIAN, WRITER, ACTOR

We adopted a little girl. It's a lot of money. We hired an adoption lawyer instead of an agency, which actually proved to be very helpful with how our adoption went, but yeah it's expensive. Having a baby is expensive. The hospital stuff.

I was slightly concerned about the age difference with my son, but not overly so. It's awesome. It's just watching him with her, it's unreal. He wanted a sibling for very long and was always asking about a sibling and talking about it. It was a really bizarro thing to sit down with him and talk to him about it because it all happened very quickly.

I was like, "So mommies and daddies make a baby and they put it in and then rub it and stimulate it so stuff comes out." I still had to explain that to say that we didn't do that. Someone else did and we are buying that baby. "That's why you're going to have less toys because we don't have the money for those anymore. Because we had to buy this baby." He just had a look on his face like, "All right, I understand."

We tried to get pregnant a second time. It didn't happen. Even before we had our son, we had talked about how we were both open to adoption as an option. When we were trying again and it wasn't happening, we decided to turn to adoption and we did it. Spent a large portion of last year in the process and then it all came together very quickly.

My wife met the mom, I did not, but it was very brief. The process I really have to say was not enjoyable for me at least. Part of it was you go through the clearance of background checks, security checks, FBI, fingerprints, all that stuff, and then you have to wait to get approved. Then there's home visits and all this stuff, social workers and all that. Once you're cleared, then you put your information out there.

The people putting their kids up for adoption, I can't even imagine how hard that is. For some people, maybe it's not, but you read the stories or you see these profiles of people who want to adopt and some of them are just weird. Some seem like weirdo people with religious stuff, like, we knew it was God's plan, that kind of thing. At the same time, you don't want to judge because people have just tough stories about trying to have kids. It's just like online dating. You're just putting yourself out there and hoping it happens. It can take so long, but it just made me uncomfortable to just be that open and have photos. This lady that was helping us with our profile. She's a Web person. She just kept changing the text and just trying to tell us, "Look, you've got to sell yourselves. You've got to sell this."

We'd write things like Jon is a blankety-blank and this and that and it would come back and it was all written from my wife's perspective because it's the mom connecting with the mom. There was one thing that this woman helping us wrote: "Fatherhood is the number one priority in Jon's life." I'm like, "Fucking no way. This is not who we are. This is not me." Yes, it's important, but to write that. It just was gross and she kept writing it really dramatic and flowery and just disgusting to me. It was gross and false. We kept telling her to stop doing that, please, and finally got it to where we were okay with it.

It came out of nowhere. It happened really quick. It was crazy timing. I was always worried it was going to happen in the middle of filming and we were going to miss it, and that would be it. Because it could take years, you hear these horror stories. But it happened the day after we wrapped. My mom just happened to be in town. We could take. . . .

My son Nate, we could take him out of school. And just have him . . .

Just have him be a part of the experience. . . .

I want to be able to tell the story. I'm not ashamed to cry. I just want to get through the story.

It was just great that he could be there for that moment. Because even telling him the day before, just trying to explain to your child, "Hey, we're going to pick up a baby tomorrow." It's so bizarre.

We got to the hospital. She was days old. Not even a week old. There was a lot of scrambling. But because it was our second kid, it wasn't so overwhelming. And—this is emotional too—your friends just come through for you. It's incredible.

ELIZABETH BANKS—ACTOR, DIRECTOR, PRODUCER

Both my kids were born via gestational surrogates. They're both mine and my husband's. They're biologically and genetically 100 percent me.

It's not the way I would have done it. It was literally the only chance for me to have kids that were mine.

Marc

They take your egg and they take his sperm and they fertilize it outside. Then they put it in another person.

Elizabeth

Correct. Then they grow it in another person. They bake it.

Marc

Did you use the same oven for both?

Elizabeth

I did use the same oven, yeah. Yeah it was amazing. The most amazing woman. They are—I say "they" because she has a husband who's amazing and they're an incredible couple that did this for us. They have their own kids. They have three kids.

Marc

How do you decide on a surrogate? What needs to be in place in order for them to be able to do that other than the desire?

Elizabeth

The main question you have when you go into it: "Is she going to let me make every decision as if it's mine and as if it's my body?" That's what you're really concerned about. No one is concerned that they're not going to give you the baby at the end. Your biggest concern is that they're going to force a baby on you that you don't want. That's your biggest concern, in surrogacy. Meaning, the baby has spina bifida and is going to be born severely malformed, is 100 percent going to die. If you don't believe in that, if you don't believe in giving life to something that's going to die minutes later, don't get involved with surrogacy. You need someone that you trust is going to honor your wishes about what's going on.

Marc

You're saying that if you wanted to terminate the pregnancy for whatever reason, they would have to agree to do that.

Elizabeth

Correct, because you cannot force somebody to do that.

We got two beautiful babies, thank goodness.

Marc

Does your relationship with this couple and family still exist after?

Elizabeth

Yeah. I'm writing them their Christmas cards right now.

It's amazing. The fact that we were able to have our own children, despite the fact that my womb basically doesn't work, is amazing to me. It's amazing. It was a super bummer getting there. It's not a fun path to take.

You essentially mourn the loss of your fertility. Your superiority over men is that you can carry babies. Like ha-ha, suckers, you get higher incomes but you don't get to have babies.

Suddenly I had to let go of one of those. I had to let go of my womanhood in a way. Just give over to a process that I didn't willingly go into. I went into it willingly but I didn't go into it happily. I went into it from a darker place. In the end it's all light and amazing and that's what they tell you when you start. They say in the end, there will be a baby and you'll be so happy and you'll forget everything and you do. You forget everything.

Adoption is a way to be a parent, but it is not a prescription for infertility. It's not a way for me to have my own child. It was secondary to gestational surrogacy for us, always. We've been together for twenty years, and there really is something unique and special about making a little half me, half him.

People who adopt are huge souls. I have so much respect for people that go that route. It wasn't what we chose.

Every once in a while you get someone who's like, "Why didn't you just adopt? There's so many babies out there that need love." I think they just want me to validate what they think.

SARAH SILVERMAN—COMEDIAN, WRITER, ACTOR

Maybe I'll adopt someday, but I want it to be when it's all I want. I'm crazy about kids. I love them, but I just love my life. I love being totally free and whimsical and I don't think you could do that necessarily with kids. I figure I'll wait until I'm really young grandma age.

I think a lot of people have a weird feeling of guilt over not wanting kids, and it's a silly weird social pressure that's bizarre. I love kids so much. I love playing with them. I love spending time with them, but I'll tell you, after a good half hour I'm ready to do my own thing. I'm waiting for that to not be the case anymore before I have a kid. That's not a hasty thing. I think a lot of people are really hasty about it. They have kids because they're trying to keep a man or they're trying to fix a marriage. For all the wrong reasons or they turned thirty. There's plenty of kids out there. Nobody needs you to have kids.

It's crazy because people want to have their own kids, and yet, those same people go, "Don't buy dogs from a breeder, don't buy dogs from a pet store, get them from the shelter." Well, I agree with that, but get kids from a shelter.

AMY SCHUMER—COMEDIAN, WRITER, ACTOR

I can't say right now if I'll have kids. Maybe in five, six years I'll want a kid and a family. Maybe I'll want to surround myself with unconditional love or maybe that's just because I'm starting to get afraid of dying and want somebody to carry on my genes.

I've been like, "That's not going to happen to me. I've never been interested in kids," but now, if there's a child, I'm at a party or something and somebody has a kid there, I'll sweep it up and put it on my hip. I'm like, "Whoa. How did you get up here? What are you doing up here?"

Then I'm always thrilled to put it down. I'm like, "Go back to your life." I'm never like, "Can I keep it?"

I had to watch my friend's dog. "I love your dog. I'll watch your dog for a week." A day in, I had to call in the reserves.

I'm just, like, lazy and moody and I don't want it to be about me. I don't want to have a kid to have it be about me.

TERRY GROSS—RADIO HOST

I have no children. That's intentional.

Growing up in Brooklyn when I was growing up, all the women I knew were basically full-time mothers or they were in the few professions that allowed women at the time—secretary, clerk, working in your husband's office, nurse, teacher. And I just knew I wanted a different life. I wanted out, I wanted out of the neighborhood, I wanted out of that life, I didn't want that life. I wanted interesting work, I wanted to fall in love with work and I wanted to fall in love with a person and I'm lucky I have both.

JEN KIRKMAN—COMEDIAN, WRITER

I do not want to care for something. I will hate them. I'm not interested. I have a whole life ahead of me. I don't want a kid. I don't want to love anything. It's selfless not to have kids because you're not adding to the pollution, you can do charity, you can help people. I don't believe that shit that it's selfless to have kids. It's considered selfless because you have to give up everything. You can't take a shower, you're really busy. I get that part of it. But the fact that that is what is defined as selfless nowadays makes me fucking crazy.

I didn't like kids when I was one. Gary Coleman said that once and I was like, "Yes, Gary. I totally fucking agree. They were awful to me and I think they're terrible."

I like babies. But they have too much insight. Like, they look at you and they just get something, they're from some spiritual realm where there's a lot of intelligence and then they get here and they look at you and it fucking freaks me out. I feel like I'm a mess and they see it.

JANEANE GAROFALO—COMEDIAN, WRITER, ACTOR

I have never wavered on not wanting to have kids. There was a point where I thought I probably should adopt to be socially responsible, because in the 1990s, I was financially well off and I thought it was probably the responsible thing to do, there are so many children in need of care. I have done the thing where you sponsor a kid from Guatemala. I do Feed the Children, and stuff like that. I have seven nieces and nephews. I know I don't want to have children.

I do love babies. I don't love the idea of having a teenager. I just am not interested in it. I think it's all about structure and things and the ways I don't want to live. Will I regret this decision on my deathbed? That remains to be seen.

Everybody rolls those dice. Then there's a lot of people who do everything right, and the kid still winds up with issues. Then there's parents who do everything wrong, and the kids are the most stable.

When you have kids, I do believe you become more motivated. You do get a lot more done in a day, because there is someone that's so supremely important to you, and you're so in love with this being, that it becomes effortless in certain ways to do so much.

Witnessing footage of women giving birth in the bathtub, doing natural things with the midwife or the doula. I can see that that is one of the most exciting, alive things they're ever going to feel. There is nothing that probably will ever compare to that experience those women are having, with their husbands, and the other children. It's probably a wonderful time having that baby, but cut to every other thing that comes with that. That is not probably the most wonderful time, and very few people are willing to talk about this. The realities of family living, child rearing, marriage, especially in contemporary society.

What I'm saying is, I realize one of the best things probably that ever happens to a person is child rearing. I understand this. I understand how beautiful babies are, and I intellectually get that I have missed out on something by not giving birth in the bathtub to my baby, and I'll never ever experience that kind of love, but at the same time, I don't want to pick out schools and get vaccinations, and get the driver's license and stay up all night worrying. This is a twenty-four-hour commitment of fear and anxiety, and I am not mature enough to handle that.

I'm not proud of this. I'm ashamed of this, but I am not up to the task. Again, there are millions of other people who are not up to the task either, and I wish they would realize that. Many, many people have weddings and babies because they don't know what else to do. Life feels kind of empty and they don't know how else to fill it. There are millions of ways to fill an empty life. Marriage and children are not always the best way to do that, but it's the easiest way a lot of people think.

MOLLY SHANNON—COMEDIAN, ACTOR

I love being a mom. I always wanted to be a mom, and I really feel so fulfilled. I'm so happy. I really feel like I worked really hard in my twenties and thirties, and struggling to make it, and *Saturday Night Live,* and I really killed myself with work. It was just work, work, work, work, work. Now I really feel like I've created a family, and I feel like I'm living my dream. This is all I've ever wanted. My mom died when I was little, when I was four, so for me, getting to be a mom and do all the things that she was never there for, it's very rewarding to me. It makes me feel so happy.

ALI WONG

There's a lot of joy in parenting. That part is really true. She's great, and she makes me laugh. When you become a comic that doesn't laugh out loud as much anymore, my daughter and my husband and my friends who aren't in comedy are the only things that make me laugh hysterically.

She's funny. She's sweet and all that. People are like, "Aren't you going to miss doing all the stuff you're able to do?" I'm like, "Yeah, but I get to do other stuff now."

PAULA POUNDSTONE—COMEDIAN, WRITER, ACTOR

We were riding in the car one day. I always tried to tell the kids a couple days ahead of time when I was going out of town so it wouldn't blow them out of the water. I say, "Okay, Mom's going on the big plane day after tomorrow." That's how we said it. My son was huffing and was very upset about it. I said, "Honey, you know, I have racked my brain to think of something I could do." You know? I said, "But I don't know how to do anything else."

My daughter, Allie, she was maybe seven at the time. She says, "Oh, Mom. I love it that you're a stand-up comic." Then she took this funny little pause and she said, "And don't you love it?" Which was such a great moment. I mean, she's a regular kid. She's a kid who wants more for herself. For that moment she cared about whether or not I was happy in my work, which just blew me away. It's not like I'd ever sat and talked with her about whether I was happy in my work. I try not to burden my children with all of my difficulties. She's a funny kid that way. She's a great kid.

Trust me, soon thereafter she returned to being as selfish as any other kid can be. That's just how they're supposed to be. There's nothing wrong with that.

We were walking down the street one day. We dropped her older sister off at school. It happened to be around Christmastime. I say to her, "Why don't we go over to the mall and you could talk to Santa Claus?" She was like, "Well, why would I want to do that?" I go, "Well, honey, because you sit in his lap and you tell him what you want for Christmas." She walked for a little ways and she said, "Why?" I said, "Well, have you thought about what you want for Christmas?" She said, "No." She thought about it for a little while. We walked and walked. She thought about it for a little while. She said, "I would like a Christmas bear." That was it. I almost started to weep right there on the street. I thought, "What a wonderful child I've raised that she feels she has everything she needs. There's nothing that she wants other than a Christmas bear." It was such a beautiful moment.

We walked a little farther. She said, "I thought of something else." I was like, "Ugh. There's more?" She's practically like, "Do we have time to stop and get a catalog?"

WANDA SYKES—COMEDIAN, WRITER, ACTOR

I can't believe this is my life. Me, married to this beautiful white Frenchwoman, and I have two blond-haired, blue-eyed kids. Me? Really? The country girl from Virginia? Bizarre. All the time, I wake up and I just go, "What the hell? How did this happen? How did I get here?" I am grateful, but it's just all so bizarre.

I wake up in the middle of the night—this is one of the scariest things ever. The kids are five, the twins. It's one of the scariest things ever to wake up in the middle of the night and see two little white kids standing at the edge of your bed. It's some creepy shit. It's just creepy.

"What the hell? What are these crazy little white kids doing at the edge of my bed? What kind of horror movie is this?"

"Oh, they're mine. They're my kids."

ADDICTION

"Introduce Yourself to Your Sickness"

———————

There's a weird assumption that drug and booze problems disproportionately affect creative people. I don't believe this is true. It doesn't matter what you do or who you are, the bug isn't picky. It can live in anyone. People from all over have addiction problems. Once you know you have the bug, you know it can feed on almost anything: drugs, food, booze, gambling, spending, people, sex, etc. Sometimes it's a combo.

My struggle with drugs and alcohol didn't start in earnest until 1999. I was in rehab in 1988 because I hit the wall with cocaine, but I didn't realize I had a problem. I just thought I needed a break. After that I would clean up every few years for a bit and then start up again. But 1999 was the year that it stuck. Things had gotten to the point where I realized that if I didn't stop, I would die, somehow, either from the drugs and drinking or being in a situation where shit got out of hand because of drugs and drinking.

Everyone's journey to the bottom is different. Rob Delaney told me how his alcoholism led to his arrest after a horrible car crash. Norm Macdonald found his bottom after gambling away his life savings. Artie Lange and Natasha Lyonne thought they hit their bottoms when they got hooked on hard drugs, but both found out that they had even farther to fall. Sadly, you have to get there to realize you have to change. For me it came after years of knowing I had a problem and not really dealing with it. I found myself bitter, in complete career stagnation, in a marriage I didn't want to be in anymore, and lying in bed blasted on coke with my heart pounding out of my chest, hoping it would stop beating. Fortunately, I was intercepted by an angel of recovery in the form of a beautiful woman who reached out and got me going to meetings. It was also fortunate that I wanted to be with her. So I completely turned my life upside down, destroyed it as I knew it to get sober, and more important at the time, got with her. That ultimately didn't work out, but I did get sober and I've stayed sober since. I'm grateful to her for that. Not for leaving me. Though I'm not sure I would've ended up where I am now if she hadn't destroyed my life when she left.

Talking to other addicts is part of the way I stay sober. When I have conversations with people who have struggled with addiction, the connection is deep. When the emotions of the struggle are shared it is relieving, moving, and helpful. I get e-mails all the time from people who are either sober or trying to get sober telling me that hearing people they only knew from TV or music or movies talking to me about addiction made them feel less alone in their fight. I count this as one of the most important reactions to the show. I'm very grateful to provide this help and solace.

PATTON OSWALT—COMEDIAN, WRITER, ACTOR

I wish there was a way to program my head to look at certain foods as if they were crack or like poison.

TOM ARNOLD—COMEDIAN, ACTOR

My mom would come and visit once in a while. When she came, she gave me a dollar. You could go to Kent's grocery and buy ten giant candy bars for a dollar. In the old days, the big ones. Sometimes she wouldn't show up or whatever, but I wanted that dollar because that was my candy bars, it was my sugar. I would put up with that. Whatever, I want to see her. I wanted that dollar.

I'd go right to the store, I'd buy them, I'd come home, I'd line them up on my bed. I'd say, I'm not going to eat them all. I'm going to hide it from my brother and sister, whatever, but I ended up eating them all. That sugar high.

And then my grandmothers were wonderful. They would feed me and watch me eat. I became that guy in the family people liked to watch eat because I ate so much. You feel so loved. That's absolutely my first addiction.

LOUIE ANDERSON—COMEDIAN, WRITER, ACTOR

I could eat twelve pieces of toast, buttered. If you do that slowly, that doesn't seem like a big deal.

You know what I'm talking about. You make four. I have a four-slice toaster. You make four slices and then you butter them, and then you put four more pieces of bread in so you can cut out that time.

Marc

Is there a moment where you're like, I'm not going to have four more?

Louie

Yeah, there's always a moment. This is a whole switch. There's a switch in your brain where you're either in your addiction or you're not. Right now I'm not in my addiction.

MARIA BAMFORD—COMEDIAN, ACTOR

I called a suicide hotline after I could not stop eating, because that's how I stayed in my dorm room by myself. And it was not pleasurable at all, like, it's not fun. I called a suicide hotline, they gave me a number for the Overeaters Anonymous, which is a thing. Just the idea that there were people out there helped me immediately. I stopped doing it.

JEFF GARLIN—COMEDIAN, WRITER, ACTOR

I'm an addict, man. I'm an addict. That's how I approach it. I even go to AA meetings sometimes. Here's the problem with Overeaters Anonymous: A lot of people at OA are very casual. They haven't hit bottom. Whereas you go to an AA meeting, nobody there is not taking it seriously.

What's bottom? Eating until I can't stop throwing up. Not that I'm making myself throw up. Eating a box of Little Debbie cakes and the same night having a half-gallon of ice cream and maybe a bowl of Cap'n Crunch and three or four Pop-Tarts. I used to go to the 7-Eleven by Wrigley Field, buy a bunch of crap, and sit on the hood of my car by the left field wall and just down it. No joy. And the feelings the food was stuffing down, they were stuffed down temporarily, and then, of course, you feel worse. It's any feeling, man. Any feeling. Anything you feel, you want to shove down.

PATTON OSWALT

Let's say you go do an audition or go do a show. The stuff just doesn't go the way you want it to. You go, "Oh fuck, I'm going to go eat." Let's say you go do a show, or do something and it goes spectacular, then you want to go eat as well. You want to go celebrate.

Marc

It's the same with drugs.

Patton

"I deserve it!"

Marc

"I suck, I'm going to drink!"

"I'm the best. Yay, drink!"

ANDY RICHTER—COMEDIAN, WRITER, ACTOR

I have a food thing. I mean I've always been kind of the fat boy. I'm active, but I certainly could lose thirty or forty pounds. That's the main thing for me, is I would love to lose weight, but a lot of that is just stuff like not drinking.

Whenever I've had occasion, for whatever, like a health reason, to not drink, weight just flies off. I had this health thing a few years ago, so I didn't drink for a couple of months. I lost like ten pounds in a week and a half. I don't even really drink that much. I probably have like a glass of vodka four nights a week. That in itself, that's like an extra meal.

The only thing I ever felt out of control with was weed. That was prior to when I actually had health care and could afford antidepressants, and I was kind of self-medicating.

RAY ROMANO—COMEDIAN, WRITER, PRODUCER, ACTOR

I actually have a little history with gambling, back before I had money. I tried to lose money I didn't have. I got close to being bad. It was bad, at one time. But I had no money to lose, thank God. Thank God I got a handle on it before I made money.

NORM MACDONALD—COMEDIAN, WRITER, ACTOR

I went broke a few times when I actually had lots of money. With gambling. And I mean broke. Dead broke.

I don't know what it was. I'm not a psychiatrist, but I do know this. They say gamblers want to lose and stuff, which always seemed odd to me, but I will say the three times that I went broke, for a lot of money, I had a very freeing feeling. I would go to the coffee shop and have a coffee and have nothing. A lot of me is trying to get as ascetic as I can in my life.

Three times I've lost everything that I've ever had. The only time I went to a psychiatrist, it was for gambling. I was like, "How the fuck do I get out of this?" and he's like, "Oh, you gamble to avoid life," but my thing was, isn't that why you do everything in life? To fucking avoid it?

It's painful to think about, because now it would be nice to have the money, but it's just like any escape. I was never a drug or alcohol guy, but when I watch a game and I have a bunch of money on it, then I can understand what's going on. Nothing's ambivalent or anything about it. There's stakes. You know exactly the rules. You're completely involved and you're completely escaped from your life of the real fear. I'd rather fear losing money on a football game than ruminate all fucking night about my upcoming illness and death. My biggest problem is ruminating about death. If I could get over that somehow.

People that know they're going to hit bottom kind of want it, because it's exhausting to be obsessed with something. You are, I guess, trying to do it. Trying to finish it off, finally. If you have $450,000 in the bank and then you lose $400,000, you say, "Fuck it. I don't want the $50,000 to remind me that I had more money."

That's how you do it.

JIM NORTON—COMEDIAN, ACTOR, RADIO HOST

I can't drink and I can't do drugs. It's an absolute. Sex is a really hard one. You can act out by being on the computer, and you read an e-mail that has one trigger word in it or one thing and, all of a sudden, you're acting out.

Half the times I'm acting out, I'm actually doing it for the memory to jerk off to. It's a really weird thing. There's times where I actually missed the activity because I'm just getting through it so I can jerk off thinking about the memory of it. I'm more addicted to masturbating, I think, than I am to actual intercourse. I'm more addicted to the ritual than the actual cumming.

FRED ARMISEN—COMEDIAN, ACTOR, MUSICIAN

When I was in a band, my main goal was to hook up with strangers on tour. I have a suspicion that might have contributed to the fact that our band didn't get as far as it did, because I certainly wasn't about the music.

Through program stuff, I know that there are ways that every day I can try to have a better approach. Today I don't have to worry about my phone or some stranger that I hooked up with. I'm having a good day today.

Marc

You're learning how to not sexually act out and use people in that way?

Fred

Yes. It's hard and I don't assume that it's a pill and everything goes away.

Marc

It's the hardest one, dude. Drugs and booze, gambling, you don't need those things. Food and sex? Kind of need it.

Fred

What's tricky, also, is booze is in certain places, but people are just everywhere.

I'm not delusional about it. I'm not delusional about myself. This struggle that I have, I don't have a choice. This is a struggle. It could be a lot worse. I also could be dead.

Marc

There are worse things than having too many vagina options.

Fred

Yes. I think as long as I understand that there is a struggle, that's what most of it is. I've had some really great days. That's the part where everything else falls away because I know that I've had this much time thinking by myself.

JIM NORTON

I remember one time I went to see a prostitute on Second Avenue. It really shook me. I walked into her place and it was an abandoned apartment. I looked into the bathroom and there's dirty water in the tub. There were fruit flies in garbage. The place is like an old railroad apartment. It was dark, pitch-black, and she was holding a screwdriver.

I gave her $300 and she went to the door. I don't know if she had somebody outside that she gave the money to but then she sat down with a screwdriver. I just felt like something very, very bad is about to happen, something really frightening is about to happen. I sensed that there was something else in the room. I was going to be hurt badly. I just said, "Look, I'm sick. I have to leave."

I let her keep the $300. I was shaking when I left. I don't know why. We have instincts. We have feelings. I saw it calling that night. I was like, "Something really fucking bad just happened." It really threw me as to what danger I was putting myself in.

Marc

That's the liability thing. After a certain point with drugs and drinking, it's not the drugs and drinking that may hurt you. It's the situation you're going to end up in. I think that with prostitution, it's the same thing.

Jim

When you're a complete addict, if you only drink vodka, life gets boring, so you have to drink Seagram's. You have to drink a little bit of this. A little bit of that.

DAVID SEDARIS—WRITER

A couple years ago, I decided to quit smoking. I smoked for thirty years and I've smoked a lot. I wanted to quit. I decided, let's say November I decided to quit. I moved to Tokyo. I went to Tokyo and I rented an apartment for three months. My boyfriend went with me.

If I just decided at home I'm going to quit smoking, and I would sit at my desk the next morning, I would go, oh, this is ridiculous. Give me that cigarette. I was in a whole new apartment, I was in a whole other language. I was a whole new me.

Running away works. I went and quit smoking and I haven't had a cigarette for six years now and I don't even think about it.

I told myself that when I was born, I was allotted a certain number of cigarettes and I guess I smoked them all. If I'd smoked more slowly, I'd still be doing it.

I smoked all my cigarettes, and I took all my drugs too. Other people, they haven't even touched their allotment yet.

I think it helps to have some kind of little story, don't you?

ANDY RICHTER

I quit smoking on September 17, 2001. It was right after 9/11, but that was just coincidental. It had gotten to the point where I'd tried to quit smoking a number of times, and then we quit when my wife got pregnant, because she quit too. She struggled with it a lot. Then I started up again after my son was born. I went to work on a movie in Canada, and started smoking eight-dollar cigarettes up in Canada.

Every winter I was losing my voice twice, three times. I was starting to film this network television show that had my name in the fucking title, and I just really felt like, "I cannot lose my voice. I have to do this." I was just ready. It was such a disgusting, gross habit, and I was not enjoying it. I rarely had that moment of that first cigarette, and going like, ahhhhhhh. I really felt like I was just jerking off with shit lubricant every time I did it.

KAREN KILGARIFF—COMEDIAN, MUSICIAN, WRITER, ACTOR

I don't drink anymore. In 1997, I started having seizures from drinking and, also, I was on speed for a while. Trying to get down to a nice Hollywood fighting weight. After speed and booze, there's no time for eating after all that. These diet pills are like prescription pills, but they were on par with the best cocaine you've ever had. It was like a cocaine high and it lasted for twelve hours.

I was having seizures at night and I didn't know it. I would wake up with a really bitten tongue or I would wake up on the floor and I'd be like, "That's so weird." I once had a dream I was a spinner dolphin and I was just having a seizure basically.

The big climax of that story came when I woke up one morning and I immediately got on the phone and was talking to somebody and I was like, "I keep biting my tongue and my tongue is so bitten." I turned and looked back and the wall of my bedroom had just a huge spray of blood on it. I looked at it and I was just like, "I can't deal with that. There's no way." It looked like a minimurder and I had no capacity to deal. This was literally when I was getting up in the morning and walking into my kitchen and grabbing a bottle of Jameson and taking a huge swig. In my mind, I knew things were getting really bad.

But, at the same time, when you're a comedian and you go out every night and drink there's this weird kind of normal, it kind of normalizes it. Anyway, eventually my friend Kristin came and stayed with me and she woke up one morning and I was having a seizure, like my lips were blue and I was totally out. I woke up one morning to a couple LA firemen sitting on my bed saying, "Do you know your name? Do you know what day it is?"

I'm just wearing a Dodgers T-shirt and no pants and I was just like, "You guys." They were amazing-looking, of course. It was very surreal.

Marc

Who called them?

Karen

Kristin.

Marc

She buzz-killed your seizure party with the firemen?

Karen

Yeah, I was having such a great time and she called The Man. I mean, I think it was one of the worst ones I'd had because I was actually out for a really long time and whatever. That could have been happening for a while and I just didn't know. Anyway, I went to the hospital. It was crazy. There was no liquid in my body. A doctor said to me, "The seizures are just from alcohol withdrawal." I said, "But I've never stopped drinking." Which is really one of the saddest things I've ever said.

I still have seizures to this day. I am on medicine that controls them. I still have them. I personally think the diet pills screwed something up in my system. But it's just all theory. Like, I've gone to a ton of neurologists and all they can say is, "There's no reason that you should be having seizures." But I do.

RACHAEL HARRIS—COMEDIAN, ACTOR

I love alcoholics. They're my favorite people. Everyone that's smoking in the back? I don't smoke, but that's where I want to be.

Maybe Jimmy Carter had some blatant substance abuse problems, and that's why I was so attracted to him. He had humility. Anyone who's really humble, that is exactly the person that I'm the most attracted to. Usually people in recovery that are like, "This is my deal, I'm not perfect, I'm going to make mistakes," and I'm so empathetic to that, and I think it's because of my dad. He was very misunderstood, and I felt like he was always the bad guy with my mother and my stepdad, and rightly so. I understand, but as I got older I realized people aren't all bad.

CRAIG FERGUSON—COMEDIAN, WRITER, ACTOR, TALK SHOW HOST

I was drinking all through high school. I mean, we all kind of did. I think it's ingrained in the Scottish culture. Not for everyone. I hate to give the idea that all Scottish people are as fucked-up as I am. That's not true. There are some fabulously gifted, talented people. I just wasn't. Or maybe I was in an unusual way for someone of my socioeconomic group at that time to be. I had a talent which was completely fucking worthless. There were no comedy clubs. There was no outlet for it, other than as a survival technique. It wasn't really a career choice.

DAVE ANTHONY—COMEDIAN, WRITER, ACTOR

I don't know a good comic who has a father that's not crazy, an alcoholic, or gone. A good comic.

Marc

That is true, though, now that you mention it. I think about the guys I know, their dads are crazy, alcoholic, or gone. The ones whose dads are gone, I think actually if they survive that, do better, because they have a lot more to prove. Children of alcoholics and crazy people have spent a life managing chaos.

Dave

Exactly, and it's not just that. If your father's an alcoholic, or your dad was bipolar, what you did, and what I did, is to use humor to try and make sure that your dad or my dad wouldn't go to that bad place. We thought that we could control it by trying to be funny, we were just trying to make the whole place lighter and happier when we didn't want the dark thing to come in.

And the bad thing is my dad was always shut off when he was sober, and nicer when he was drunk, until he got really drunk. When he was drunk he was the happy drunk, so then how confusing is that? "Oh, you like me when you're drunk, but when you're sober you don't?" Jesus.

Although a few drinks beyond that, he became the Really Drunk Guy who's embarrassing. Just so drunk that we used to drive home from baseball games, we lived in the Bay Area, and so we'd go to a Giants game, and he'd drive on the highway home to Marin, and I would have to tap him to stay awake because he was so hammered.

KURT METZGER—COMEDIAN, WRITER, ACTOR

My dad's dead. I was the last one talking to him of my family. He just drank himself to death in a fucking trailer at the end. He really got sad-alcoholic at the end, man. He wanted to die. I didn't see him when he was yellow or however the fuck they found him, but I was still talking to him. He had gotten so dark with my brother and sister that they stopped talking to him.

I remember telling my brother, "You really should call him, because I don't know what's going on with him, but if he drops dead, you're going to feel bad that you did this thing where you're like, 'I'm not speaking to you.'" I remember my brother weeping when he died. He never called him. So I was the last one to talk to him.

The other thing is my old man, who was always my buddy

growing up, for the most part, more than my mom, he felt bad for himself too much. He really did. My mom just ate him from the inside out like fucking wasp larva, basically. He was trained to be like, "You get married. You never get divorced. You're supposed to have kids. You're not supposed to fuck until you're married." All this shit that I'm sure he didn't want to do. I'm sure he never even wanted kids. But the rules were the rules.

LOUIE ANDERSON

I always tell people that growing up in an alcoholic family is one of the weirdest things because it's like being around nuclear fallout. Later in your life it comes up. It really affects your whole life.

My dad was a fascinating guy that I didn't know. His father was a great inventor. He invented fifty things. He invented some sort of deep fryer thing way back. He was an alcoholic.

He sold all his patents to lawyers. Then him and his wife would go on these cross-country train drunks, and leave the kids.

During one of the trips, there was a murder in my dad's house by a Swedish gang. His parents were gone, and there was a murder. They took all the kids away, including my dad. Because the parents weren't there.

Then my dad got put up for adoption. You know where that term comes from? They put you up in front of the congregation at the church. And people would pick who they wanted. It was good and bad, you know what I mean? Like the kids didn't have a place, so the community was trying to be helpful.

My dad and his sister got split up. He had a sister he was very close to and about his age. He went one place and she went another. It destroyed him. He got adopted by a German family who worked him as a farmhand and he stayed in a different part of the house. He ate different food.

Then at fifteen he went and made them sign a thing. He goes,

"I want to join the army." He says, "I want you to sign this and say I'm old enough to join the army." They did, and he became a bugle player in World War I.

I figured all that out. I think, "Oh my God. My dad had a most miserable thing. He was a better person than his parents were in some grotesque way."

Marc

You've got all this resentment at him for being an alcoholic, and you've got all this shame. All this stuff that you hold him responsible for, and he's a monster in your eyes. It sounds to me that the process of working through this and finding more out about him, allowed you to see him as a person and maybe forgive him.

Louie

I did forgive him.

RACHAEL HARRIS

My stepdad was the type of guy that would come home after work and drink a six-pack of beer, but I would never know he was drunk. That was like a can of Coke. I didn't see horrible ramifications, and he didn't become mean. He might have done that with my mom, like the way that he talked to her or whatever, but it was my mom who was the crazy person, because of his drinking. She was the reactor, that was picking up everything, and she was feeling everything, so we were like, "Man, Mom's the crazy person," when really she wasn't.

The way it trickled down for me was, okay, I'm going to clean the house before any of them get home, make sure everything's in its perfect place. So Mom doesn't come home and say, "What the hell, like what the fuck, why are these dishes in here? Didn't I tell you to clean this up? I work all day!"

Marc

Your stepdad's alcoholism didn't affect you directly, it affected you through your mom trying to deal with his shit.

JASON SEGEL—COMEDIAN, ACTOR, WRITER

If Me Five Years Ago saw Me Now, I would be unrecognizable. I was drinking quite a bit. I got to the point where I felt like I was going to collapse under the weight of it. I felt very trapped.

I felt isolated. I also would very simply wake up in the morning and say, "I am not going to drink today," and by midday I was drinking. It was not a party in any way.

Marc

Did it start as a party?

Jason

My hunch is it always starts as a party.

Marc

Then all of a sudden, "I'd like you to meet the monster. I hope you had a good time at the party, now you're working for this guy."

Jason

Exactly right. You've lost control. I got really lucky in that I had a real moment of clarity where I said to myself, "I want to be the best version of myself." I got really lucky that that happened.

It was a dark day. I had something bad happen. I had not been drinking for a little while, for months. I decided, you know what, I'm going to drink. I didn't have booze in the house for myself at this point. I had a case of rosé for guests. It was summertime. I decided I'll have a glass of rosé. I don't even like rosé. Basically, it turned into a weekend where by the end of it I was surrounded by these empty bottles of rosé. I thought to myself, "This is not for pleasure. I don't like rosé. This is something else going on."

The thing I realized about booze is that I am not going to win. They're not going to stop making booze, I can't drink it all. You know what I mean? For me, it's like fighting Mike Tyson. I realized at that point the best strategy for me is not to get in the ring.

DAX SHEPARD—ACTOR, WRITER, DIRECTOR

I have so many stories that end with "And then I continued to get fucked-up for a year." I think that people tend to think of it as a bottom. I have, like, eleven. I tried to get sober a dozen times and I could put together two months here, three months there. I always got sober for movies. I cared about that. And in between movies is where it got really dangerous.

So, I did this movie *Zathura,* and I knew I had to get sober to do that movie. And so I thought, "Oh, I'm going to go to Hawaii and have this one last vacation." And I chose Hawaii specifically because I was like, "There's no cocaine in Hawaii." It just seems so far from everywhere. That was my assumption. It was hard to find. But I found it. I didn't underestimate the amount of coke. I underestimated my willingness to search it out and find it.

Everyone's a newlywed except for my buddy and me, who are just there to get fucked-up. So we're at a bar, we're drinking with locals. I've already done *Punk'd,* so I'm kind of popular with that crew. The first two days at the bar, it's kind of cool I'm there. The third day, I realize it's worn off. They're going to kill us. But I met a guy who said, "I know where to get coke. Let's go." I go with him and his girlfriend. We're driving. It's raining. This guy's driving way too fast. He's got his shirt off, he's got a beer between his legs. I'm in the process of telling him, "You've got to slow down and turn down the radio," when we go through a left-hand turn, he loses control, we spin, we hit a guardrail. Cars are fucking flying off the road to avoid us. We somehow end up going straight. We drive out of it. He thinks it's great. "I fucking drove out of that, bro!"

We come into the next town. Cop passes us, sees the smashed-up back end. We pull into a gas station. We're getting pulled over. I'm looking at myself in the rearview mirror. I'm in a cutoff T-shirt and a cowboy hat. I don't know anyone in the car. The cops are coming up and I'm like, "I've been in Hawaii three days. This is where we're at."

So they let this guy go. They make the girl drive, who's just as drunk as all of us. We continue on to the drug house. It's not coke. It's crystal meth. I buy it anyway. So me and my buddies smoke crystal meth for three days. I get to the point where I'm like, "I need to get this out of my body. I've been up for three days. I need to go for a jog." I jog on the beach in front of the Hyatt with the roosters going. I came back to the room and sweat for like four hours.

The night before we fly back, I go out. I get so drunk. I had a layover—because this is a bargain flight—between Kauai and LA in San Francisco. And I'm at a bar in the San Francisco airport because I'm so physically sick, I cannot make the flight unless I get at least four Jack and Diets in me. I'm sitting in this bar, in the corner of the bar because I'm so afraid someone from AA is going to see me. Up to that point I had three months.

Here I was. I was about to start this movie. I had just finished *Idiocracy* with one of my heroes, Mike Judge. I was in a movie that came out a month before that was a hit. I was sitting in the corner of this bar, literally hiding, and I had accomplished all these goals I dreamed about for ten years, and I was afraid to be in public at this fucking airport. I was like, "You're doing this wrong. You're afraid to be you, and you've gotten everything you wanted."

PAUL GILMARTIN—COMEDIAN, ACTOR, TELEVISION HOST

I could see on paper that my life was great. I was making great money. I'm on TV. I've got people paying to come see me do stand-up. I got a wife. I got a house. I got my health. On paper, my life is amazing, and I'm thinking about suicide, if not every day, every hour. I had taken the test to get a gun. I had a gun permit. I was starting to hear voices. When I would lay my head down at night, to sleep, I could have sworn I heard people in the backyard saying, "Paul. Paul." One of the reasons I wanted to get a gun, because I thought, there are people in the backyard.

Then eventually I realized, after I stopped drinking for a little bit, the voices went away. I was like, "I think I'm just drinking too much." I went to see a psychiatrist because of these feelings of suicide and he suggested that I stop drinking and using drugs. I thought, "No problem." The psychiatrist said, "I can't gauge where your depression is until you quit, so I need you to quit." I tried to quit, and I found out that I had lost the power of choice. That made me more anxious, so I began to drink more.

I remember being out of town, and I said, "I'm just going to have one drink." Because the usual group of people that would go out drinking couldn't go out. I don't know if you know that feeling, when you can't sit in your hotel room, but you also don't want to go drink at a bar by yourself and feel like a loser, but that was the better choice. Nothing mocks you more than an empty hotel room.

So I went to the bar and said, "I'm just going to have one." I stayed until closing time. It was just me and this other person. I said, "Hey, I think we can get a drink across the street." Because I just didn't want to be alone. This person said, "No, I got to get up for work in the morning." I said, "Please don't leave, I'm so lonely." To a stranger. I don't remember what she said. I think I was just in my head at that point, saying, "Oh my God, you fucking loser."

I'm sure you know this feeling, when you're loaded and you're miserable the other twenty-two hours a day, and you get your buzz on, you're feeling that beautiful sensation of relaxation and excitement. Complete detachment from the world. I want to keep it going.

I couldn't get help because I was like, it's the only thing that makes me feel good. How could I give that up? Then I woke up one morning, and it was like every other morning, my first three thoughts were: you slept too late, you're a lazy piece of shit, your life is passing you by. My stomach would tighten into a knot. I'd think about all the things I had to do that day, dreading them. The only thing I'd look forward to is getting loaded, yet, knowing intellectually that's what's making this spiral. I just said the words out loud, I said, "God help me. I can't do this anymore." I'm not a religious person at all. I was raised Catholic. If anything, that turned me off to it. For some reason that day, I got help, and I've been sober every day since then.

It's a fucking miracle. But it's been a lot of work, and a lot of opening up that trapdoor and looking at what a frightened, insecure, self-centered, self-pitying, impatient, competitive, narcissistic, vindictive little boy I can be on any given day.

ROBIN WILLIAMS—COMEDIAN, ACTOR (1951–2014)

I only drove drunk, that I remember, once. One time. I woke up the next morning asking, "Where's my car?" It turned out the bartender had driven me home. He was a sweet guy and he drove me home. The next day, I couldn't find the car. I thought oh my God, my car's been stolen. Actually, no. They parked it for me in a safe parking lot. It's nice when people take care of you when you're that loaded.

"Hey! Take Mork home!"

I walked home one time from a bar in Toronto and I woke up the next morning with a mitten. I went, "Oh my God, this is a child's mitten." It turned out a waitress had given me her mitten. She had tiny hands and she'd given me her mitten because I'd lost a glove. That's the worst thing. When you wake up going, "What's this? There's a road flare. Is that human? No, it's rabbit blood. Oh thank God."

ROB DELANEY—COMEDIAN, WRITER, ACTOR

I was very lucky. It won't sound lucky at first.

I drove when I was in a blackout. I was over at a friend's house here in LA. Having a good time. A keg party. It started out normal. Other normal people drinking normal amounts of alcohol. And then we tapped a second keg, or rather finished it, so then we moved onto wine, and then we moved onto whatever else was around, and my final drink that I ever drank was in a Solo cup, like a keg cup. I had a bottle of vodka in one hand and a bottle of bourbon in the other and I poured them both in up to the top, which if you drink you know that isn't a drink, it's just gross. That's a red flag. I drank that all the way down and then I was like, "Hey, that wasn't bad," so I made another one and that's when I can remember my consciousness just stopped recording.

The next thing I remember is being in the hospital surrounded by cops and doctors. What I had done is, I had been like, "Well, I'm going to sleep at my friend's house," and everybody had left and I just went to sleep on her floor, then apparently I got up in the middle of the night. This is the first time that I know of that I had done this, but I got up still in a blackout, so I kind of began my new day and the first thing I decided to do was take a car, not my car, at like four in the morning.

I got in the car and I drove it, not anywhere near that party or near where I lived at the time, and I drove it really fast into the Los Angeles Department of Water and Power at the intersection of Pico and Genesee and that was a pretty cataclysmic car accident. There was no one else involved except me, thank goodness. I didn't know that at the time. I did have to ask the cops if I had killed anyone and they told me that I had not. I took out three parking meters, two trees, a lightpost, and then the building and the car.

I was in the building. Half in, half out.

Marc

You don't remember having any sort of anger at the water company? No water problems at home?

Rob

No, it had nothing to do with my bill.

Marc

There was no momentary, "Those fuckers!"

Rob

Water and power! Grr!

Marc

Fuck them! I saw *Chinatown*.

Rob

None of that. I don't even remember. It could have been the kind of a thing where I fell back asleep within my blackout and then drove into it, it could have been an aggravated "fuck that building." I don't know.

I broke both my arms. You can see, there's a pretty big scar on this wrist where they kind of rebuilt it. This longer scar on my arm here is, that's all titanium in there. This was very badly broken. I'm slightly bionic. My legs were not broken but they were kind of torn open, my knees, so they had to sew them up with hundreds of stitches and put me in leg stabilizers so I couldn't bend my knees. They recovered fairly quickly. For the first few days afterward I was in things that did not allow me to bend my knees, which I should tell you is kind of the aha moment. Being wheeled around in a wheelchair in jail by the cops and I couldn't use my arms. They took me to the hospital in an ambulance and did what they needed to do to stabilize me, and then the cops said, "Mind if we take him now?" So they took me to jail.

They said, "You were extremely, unbelievably drunk." They drew my blood and it was a .271, which, you know, a .08 is illegal so that's effectively three and a half times the legal limit. They brought me to jail to book me and all that. When I was in jail I couldn't use my arms on the wheels, I couldn't use my feet on the ground, so occasionally I would slide out of the wheelchair in my bloody hospital gown, which was covered in blood and would come up over my dick and balls and asshole and show that to everybody in jail, which if you've been to jail you know you're not supposed to do that.

Nothing happened. Nobody fucked my ass or anything.

Marc

I guess they draw a line. They're like, "I want him to be able to fight a little."

Rob

I know. That's when I knew. I was like, "This is a problem." When nobody will rape me. It's funny because it was right then that I was like, as they say with drinking and stuff, if you need to go there to stop, that's where you need to go. For me, I'd been trying to quit for years before that.

Marc

Is it a family situation?

Rob

It is, yes. Alcoholism, drug addiction, depression are pretty rampant.

I would have stayed in jail for days but they were like, "We can't take care of you here so we're going to take you home but here, come back on this date to court and then you can come back to jail for a long time."

The next day I went back to my apartment, they took me back, they folded me in half and put me in a cruiser and drove me home, and I remember lying on my bed for a few hours and then I got up to piss and my urine was neon blue. That was terrifying to me because my urine is never neon blue, and I started to cry. I went to blow my nose and a bunch of bits of glass came out, which I later found out were windshield chunks, so then I started to sweat and I took off my hospital gown and there were stickers all over my body, but they were heart monitor anchor things that I had no idea, and I'm peeling them off. I would find more of them a week later.

I found out later from reading the hospital intake thing that the blue stuff, they had infused my bloodstream with something called methylene blue, which is what they flood you with to see if you're hemorrhaging internally. I hadn't been, but they didn't tell me that. They weren't like, "Just FYI, your urine will be the color of Gatorade for the next five pees." That was the worst hangover of my life, that day.

Marc

Peeing blue, covered with stickers, blowing glass out of your nose.

Rob

Then basically I was sentenced. They said I could go to jail for *x* amount of time or I could go to rehab and a sober-living halfway house for four and a half months. I picked that because I didn't want to go to jail, and I genuinely at the time was like, "I've had enough and I really want to get better and not do this anymore, and I don't know quite how to do that," so I definitely threw myself at their mercy.

CRAIG FERGUSON

After I got sober, that's when things began to change. I've been sober now almost twenty years. I've been sober much longer than I ever drank alcohol. It's very difficult for me to define my life by that one thing. That I'm still an alcoholic is beyond doubt, but that doesn't mean to say that alcohol is a problem in my life, because it's not. It fucking could be in a heartbeat, but it's not right now.

Marc

The interesting thing about sobriety is that it's much more difficult to be sober than it is to drink. Really, actually stopping drinking, once you get the hang of it, is the easier part of it. It's fighting that fucking itch and that weird discontentment and that weird neediness. That's the evolution, right?

Craig

Though I subscribe to the notion that alcoholism is a disease, and if treated, you will recover from it, like it's a disease. I think with me it's not a disease. I think with me it's a character description. I'm a personality type. What's your personality type? Alcoholic. Some people are winter. Some people are summer. I'm a fucking alcoholic. It's just what I am. I can't be cured of my personality. I've tried. By drinking.

JASON SEGEL

A month into not drinking, I was driving down the street. I was driving back from San Diego Comic-Con. I was listening to the oldies station. All of a sudden I realized I was singing along to "Rock Around the Clock." I was like, "Whoa, I feel good. I feel pretty happy. I've seen this in movies where people sing in the car in a real happy mood." I've never looked back. It was the best decision I ever made for myself.

ARTIE LANGE—COMEDIAN, WRITER, ACTOR, RADIO HOST

Remember that slogan "Hugs are better than drugs"? You remember that? Bumper stickers. I remember when I first saw that, I thought, "Oh jeez, I don't know if that's true. I never went to the Bronx to get somebody to hug me."

ROBIN WILLIAMS

I'd go from doing *Mork and Mindy* and then coming to do The Comedy Store and then go to The Improv. Then you'd go hang out at clubs and then end up in the hills at some coke dealer's house. (knock knock) "Angel, it's Robin." You haven't gone to sleep. You're like a vampire in a day pass.

If you're famous, most of the time, you get it for free, which is weird. It's like the same thing when you get gift baskets at award shows going, "I don't need this stuff, thank you," but my coke dealers would go, "Here, dude! It's part of our advertising campaign. I got Robin loaded." It's part of the whole thing of a little dust for you and then you'll spread the word to other celebrities and eventually, if they get busted, then they could subpoena you.

KEVIN HART—COMEDIAN, ACTOR

My dad was on drugs when I was a kid. As I got successful he cleaned up. Smart. Smart move by this man. Very smart. When I was a kid he was just in and out of rehab.

My dad was cocaine. My dad was heroin. Weed. That's probably it.

My mom kicked him out when I was young, but he was still in our lives. He was in and out of jail. My dad was a rebel. I love him for it, though. I know what not to do because of what my dad did.

As I got older, me and my brother figured out we got to help Dad. We put him in rehab, it didn't go, he came out, and I think the disappointment on your sons' faces as we look at you, is enough to make you feel like you need to get your shit together. I think that's what did it. You can put a person in all the help you want, at the end of the day if they don't mentally want to do it, they're not going to do it.

For us, it was saying, "You know what, Dad? Do you. Live your life. We can't change you." He had the realization on his own. I'm glad, honestly, that he went through what he did. I don't have a drug itch in my body. I will never touch drugs. Just because of what I saw, but if you take him out of my life, who knows? With all this money I'll fucking be snorting up piles of cocaine. Who knows what I would be doing? I wouldn't know why it was bad or why not to mess with it. Now I have a visual reality of what it could do.

JOHN DARNIELLE—MUSICIAN, WRITER

Speed was my thing for a while. There's very little that wasn't my thing at some point or another, but speed in '85, '86. Back when it was made in bathtubs and back when you would split a quarter into two-eighths and just slam it one at a time. When it became clear that you could get AIDS and die from that, your first AIDS test was remarkably terrifying. That week-long wait that you used to have. Everybody you were going to have to apologize to, everybody you were going to have to call up and go, "I killed you." The terror.

ARTIE LANGE

I was taking fifty pills a day. I went to this one club and I was in full-blown withdrawal when I got there. There were three sold-out shows. I was sweating bad. The manager was like, "What do I gotta do to get you onstage? I need to get you onstage."

"Can you get me a hundred Percocet?"

He says, "I can. How many are you taking a day?"

"Maybe like thirty."

He says, out loud, "You should try heroin. It's better for your liver."

And I said, "Thank you, Doctor."

He got me the Percocet to get me through the show. But then at the end of the night he had four bags of heroin. And it was brown. It was good. He says, "Just snort it."

I go back to my hotel. I did three lines of it. Liberal, generous lines. I put on the TV and there was some movie on. And when my head hit the pillow I said out loud—knowing me—I said out loud, "I'm in trouble."

It was euphoria like I never felt before, going through me. My head hit that pillow, and you know how I could tell heroin's great? People ask, "Why is heroin addictive?" This is my answer: the movie that was on was *Alex & Emma* with Luke Wilson and Kate Hudson, and I never turned it off.

AMAZING JOHNATHAN—COMEDIAN, MAGICIAN

I did a lot of cocaine. I did a lot of it. For a long time. I wasn't one of the guys who quit after John Belushi's party. That's when everybody quit, around that year. Everyone thought, "This is serious. This could kill you." No, I kept going man. That didn't faze me at all. I ended up smoking it. You know what got me off of it? Speed. I couldn't get coke one night, so speed was the only thing left to do. I actually smoked that too. I smoked it like a fiend and I would go in my garage and I would write and write and write.

Then it stopped. I stopped being creative on it and it was like, now I was a normal guy with a habit.

ARTIE LANGE

The thing about heroin to me was you didn't forget your problems. You remembered them but you didn't give a fuck about them. It was great. It was like, "Fuck you, I don't care." Again, the same thing with coke. I finally said, "I can control this. It's all right." First six months, my tolerance wasn't up and it was great. I was able to get a contact that kept me supplied.

My tolerance got built up after six months and then I was like, "Oh my God, I'm not getting high anymore." I couldn't stop withdrawals. Then I started missing shit. Showing up to shit looking bad. Trips on the road were hell because I'm like, "I got to find a contact in Pittsburgh, otherwise I'll die in Pittsburgh from withdrawals or something."

I hired guys to keep me away from drugs and one guy was my security who was getting me drugs. It's all you think about. Fuck pussy, money, a career, friendships, and family. All you think about is the next fucking hit. And avoiding the withdrawals because it's the worst flu times a million.

NATASHA LYONNE—ACTOR

So many people struggle to stick with sobriety. It is not for the faint of heart.

If you are really going to do it. If you are as low-bottom of a case as I was, which was like a real sort of I-hope-to-die junkie, then I wish you good luck and godspeed. I had someone describe it to me as not only do you have to smash down the house, but you have to then take out the Indian burial ground underneath the foundation of the house and then begin to rebuild. That process to me is certainly why I think a lot of people twenty-eight days later can't really hack it because it's not a twenty-eight-day scene.

For me, and the existential angst of my teenage years, I was really getting hooked on the aesthetic appeal of just so many of these heroes. This mass of characters that just seem like I'm walking in line with, like they're my friends. That's part of what's tricky. It's hard to listen to music when you get clean because it just brings up all of that stuff. Like, I want to be the fucking cool guy. You romanticize it. And a series of platitudes certainly don't feel very romantic by comparison. If you have the sort of makeup that leads you to want to shoot up while listening to Lou Reed in the first place, "one day at a time" feels like the most absurd thing I've ever heard in my life as a solution to my fucking problem.

I think it was the hard drugs that really took it to another level. The full-blown addiction. I remember making a very clear decision when I threw in the towel on life. I made an active choice to walk away and be like, listen this is the fucking truth, it's the belly of the beast. It's not about dancing on tables, this is about hanging out with one-legged Tony who has a colostomy bag in his fucking project apartment with the little tiny roaches crawling down the wall. You know, passing the pipe and going in the bathroom to shoot heroin with the girls who are turning tricks and luckily I have residuals.

I think I was sort of like, "What is this about? Fame? Why is that the big end in life?" To be like, "Let me borrow your dress so I can go to your big movie premiere so you can take my picture and then maybe you'll give me a job if I'm skinny enough." Fuck you. I didn't want to do it. There's no there there.

So once that happened is when it really got bad. I made the decision that the best way to get rid of my heroin problem was through crack.

I spent so many years being like, I hate myself and I want to die, that like, I'm going to fucking die, I might as well live a little. I just did so much of that thinking that I'm just relieved now.

The first bunch of years are so just really brutal. I hated myself a lot. My first few years of being clean and functioning, I was just so angry. Like, what the fuck do you mean I have to make my own bed? These basic things that nobody taught me. What do you mean I've got to get there on time?

You have to constantly monitor yourself. "All right, you're doing a good job. You're doing all right. Listen, you brushed your teeth at night too, this is a fucking epic day."

Marc

People who don't have the bug, who don't have the hungry animal inside of them that is never sated, never fed, that demands that you feed it, with the idea that you're going to feel whole and better, there's just no end to that. If you've never had the feeling where your brain locks in on something so hard, whether it's drugs or food or gambling or sex, there is a trigger within people that have addiction where it's like, before you get it, all you can think about is getting it and your brain then locks in on the obsession. Once you get a taste of whatever it is, that fucking animal will not stop eating. It's baffling. You can't explain it to somebody who doesn't have it.

But a lot of people have it.

ROB DELANEY

I can name a few works of art that do effectively communicate it kind of well. I think, honest to God and it's going to sound cheesy, but the film *Trainspotting* has elements of it that show the horror of it. That movie *Requiem for a Dream,* I think when it gets really dark, addresses it.

One of the best ones, and I feel like such a dork for saying this, is in the *Lord of the Rings* movie when the Gollum thing splits into two pieces and argues with himself and one of them is trying to rip it apart. That struck home for me because I felt like I had a physical, alive monster with a voice and feelings and all that shit that lived inside. My rib cage was like a jail cell and it was shaking, rattling at the bars, just saying, "Give me, give me, give me," and it's maddening. That is what it feels like.

I don't feel guilty now if I feel like, "Oh, I'd like to be really high right now," or whatever. I don't feel bad about that, I just kind of let that thought go.

It feels like a chemical equation is being completed. I'm a percentage of what I could be, but add drugs or alcohol, now I'm

100 percent and let's fucking roll. Introduce it and then I'm like, "Here I am." I'm not myself until you put drugs or alcohol into me.

Marc

I think a lot of what I felt when I used drugs is that it made me excited. It turned off the "I'm an idiot," or "I'm fucked," or "I don't want to go out," or "I don't want to do this." It was actually relaxing. I did a lot of coke and it would actually have a calming effect on me to some degree. I'm already intense.

What I started to realize, and this is with depression as well, is that at some point you're going to have to figure out that addiction is a disease and it has a lot of effects. If you feel like you have that, I found it's best to just look at that as its own sickness and some of the symptoms are depression, self-centeredness, complete lack of empathy, or too much empathy. Basically anything in your personality that drives you to say, "I got to get high. I got to eat. I got to go lose all my money. I got to fuck everything."

Anything where the voice inside of you says, "The only way I can feel better is by doing that," introduce yourself to your sickness because that's your guy.

MENTAL HEALTH

"The Wound Is Still There"

It seems there are people who talk about mental health and there are people who really don't talk about it at all. I'm a talker. Or at least I was. I'm not as much as I used to be, which I can see only as an indication that I am getting better. My mental health when I started the podcast was probably the worst it's been my entire life. Some of my feelings were justified; deeper issues exacerbated some of them. There was no doubt I was in psychological and emotional trouble. It was a dark time. I was at the edge of who I thought I was. Nothing was working out and I couldn't see a way out of it.

I've been to therapy for long periods of time at different points in my life, different cities, and different therapists. My experiences have been pretty good. I can look back and say I learned something from all of my therapists and some of them got me through bad times. You pay them to listen, to be there for you. Generally, at the very least, they do that. They hold your feet to your own fire if they are worth their salt.

I became aware that I had anger issues, food issues, substance abuse issues, intimacy issues, self-esteem issues, and an anxiety problem. I was selfish, self-involved, narcissistic at times, emotionally abusive, and full of dread.

I was also smart, funny, and charming. When those are loaded up with issues, it's a pretty good package. It's a living. It was who I was and who I still am.

I've always been on to myself enough to stay alive and not do something so stupid that I'm dead. It was that manifestation of selfish fear that kept me alive. I credit the podcast for getting me fully on to myself. Because I was in such trouble when I started it I really needed to talk to people. I needed to hear them. I needed to engage and grow my empathy. I needed to listen. I needed to see myself in others and also hear of struggles that were harder and deeper than mine. People like Todd Hanson, who spoke in detail about his suicide attempt, or Maria Bamford, who manages an obsessive-compulsive disorder, or Aubrey Plaza, whose anxiety issues led to a stroke. Their stories helped put my own problems in perspective.

After years of talking to people, I can honestly say that I have learned to accept myself for who I am and accept my issues and problems for what they are. If you learn to shut the fuck up and listen and empathize with others, your emotions start to regulate a bit, your problems became manageable, and your issues become tedious to you and maybe you can let them go for a while, or temper them.

Also, the feedback from having conversations about mental health, and how those conversations helped others with mental health issues, helped my mental health. Look, I'm still pretty fucked-up, but I'm not as dangerous to myself or others and I can choose what I want to live with and how much I want to work on change. Sometimes you just have to be okay with who you are.

DAVE ATTELL—COMEDIAN AND ACTOR

I've been to the hospitals for the troops. You go to Walter Reed, which is where they bring them after they go to Germany, the troops that are wounded. You see a lot of guys going through vicious, hardcore rehab. They've lost arms and legs.

They've got a dog there, which I thought was like a Seeing Eye dog, but he's really just there to be their friend. When they're feeling down, he can sense it, and he'll come over to them and they'll use him to lean, to stand up, and to start doing their exercises, and walk. He's like a friend.

I went to the hospital, and this dog that can sense pain would follow me around the whole day. This guy's there with no legs, but the dog's like, "No, that guy's going to make it. This guy? I don't know."

AUBREY PLAZA—COMEDIAN, ACTOR

I do a thing where I listen to my hair. I do a loop and then I scrunch it inside of my ear. I'm usually freaking out when I do that. My therapist said it's a soothing thing, a defense mechanism. I've been doing it since I was a kid. Then I play with my lip. I do both of those things because my parents would always yell at me for doing them. They would just bat my hand away.

LENA DUNHAM—ACTOR, WRITER, DIRECTOR, PRODUCER

I used to be a huge hypochondriac. It's really shifted for me in the last year or so. One time, I was so sure I was pregnant, I told my producer Jenni that I thought I could feel my baby crawling up and down my spine, and she was like, "That's not what babies do." At this point, they're not big crawlers. If you were one month pregnant, your baby wouldn't be doing a little dance. It's not the dancing baby from *Ally McBeal*.

DAVE ATTELL

My mom has a hoarding problem, so I got to scream at her about having three hundred pairs of socks. Then she throws back, "Well, if you had heat in here, I wouldn't need all this." She's not a dirty hoarder. It's all folded neatly and nicely, and it's in boxes. I'm like,

"Who's this for?" She's like, "Oh, I want to give this to . . . ," like, somebody who's already dead. I'm like, "Just get rid of it."

JENNY SLATE—COMEDIAN, WRITER, ACTOR

Sometimes people think that because I'm cheery or whatever, it means that I'm silly or repressed, but honestly, I just think it's the opposite. I am occasionally sad. I'm not paralyzed with fear, but I would say that I feel very lonely often. When there are no people around I feel sad, like a puppy, like a dog looking out the window.

NORM MACDONALD—COMEDIAN, WRITER, ACTOR

The problem with laughing is it will build to a hysteria sometimes that I have to crank a couple of benzos to prevent a panic attack. I start laughing and then it gets out of control, like hysterical. I still have extreme sensitivity to things. Not to life things, but literature or art or something like that. I have incredible sensitivity. I kind of have to stay away from it.

Like paintings. I don't know anything about art. Nothing at all. But I have had experiences that have been so hard on me. Like one time, I was in New York and somebody dragged me to a fucking art museum. I hate art. I was looking at this picture of this girl, and I was falling in love with her. She was so fucking beautiful, this fucking girl in this fucking picture, and then the guide was telling me the fucking thing was drawn in the sixteenth century. Obviously this lady was dead, long dead, and here I am fucking in love with her, and so I'm like, "Ah. Fuck it." It was so hard on me for so many days. It sounds crazy, right?

Marc

Not really. It sounds like that's a very good painting.

Norm

It was an incredible painting, but it would make me cry and I didn't cry at my dad's funeral. Real life stuff seems so prosaic to me that it never really touches me much.

AUBREY PLAZA

I had a pretty serious anxiety issue, and when I was twenty I had a stroke. At the time, my doctors thought it was because of the birth control pill. That has since been negated, and it boils down to migraine-related stress issues.

It was Queens actually where it happened. I was in college. It was the summer before my junior year. It really was a freak thing. I didn't have a headache, nothing was wrong with me. I took the subway in to have lunch with friends in Astoria.

I got into their apartment. I sat down. I was talking about a Hilary Duff concert that I had taken my sister to the night before. Then I looked down at my right arm, and all of a sudden, it was like my brain was telling me that it wasn't my arm. I literally thought, "Whose arm is that that's on my leg?" It was like my arm was just detached from my body. Then the whole right side of my body was paralyzed for a second. I remember I was hitting myself, like hitting my arm to figure out what was going on because it wasn't numb. It was just, like, not there. Then I blacked out for a second, and then the sound got really weird. I regained all my motor skills, but I couldn't talk. I just was making a weird sound. I was going, "Uh," like that. My friends thought I was doing a weird bit, and they were like, "Stop it. What the fuck are you doing?" Then I couldn't talk. I had expressive aphasia because the blood clot was in my left temporal lobe, which is my language center.

The paramedics came. They were asking me questions. I was totally there, and I could understand what they were saying to me and I knew what the answers were, but I just forgot language completely, and I forgot how to write. It was really the craziest thing that's ever happened.

They took me to the Mount Sinai in Queens. I was in the ER for two hours before a doctor even saw me because I looked fine. I was so young, and I looked fine, but I wasn't fine. Finally, when they brought me in, the doctor had me do a really simple thing where she was like, "Put your right hand on your left knee," and I couldn't do it because I was confused. Then they freaked out, and they were like, "Oh my God. She's having a stroke," because it was very obvious that I was having one. If anyone did any simple stroke test on me, they would've known right away.

The second day at the hospital I started talking, and in the middle of the night I remember waking up and shouting, "Aubrey Plaza!" Then I started talking and then they transferred me to the hospital in Delaware, so I could be near my family. I was there for a little bit. There's not much you can do sometimes with strokes. They can keep an eye on it and make sure it doesn't get worse, but your brain has to heal itself.

I could say some words. A lot of them were the wrong words. I remember in the hospital, they would ask me the same questions over and over. "How old are you?" Sometimes I would say sixteen. It was the only number I could get out. I don't know why. Then Joe, my boyfriend at the time, was like, "You're not sixteen. She's nineteen. You know, she's not sixteen." Then he'd be like, "Wait, are you sixteen? What is going on?" Because he didn't know what the fuck was going on. He was like, "If you're sixteen, we have to have a talk." He was freaking out. That was the first time he met my parents. We had been dating for over a year. They came to the ER. They met in the ER.

That gives you an indication of the level of anxiety I have. Because essentially it was stress related.

CHELSEA PERETTI—COMEDIAN, WRITER, ACTOR

I just stare at people with small noses, and I marvel and I think, "God, your life must be so easy." Girls with small noses, I will stare at them and stare at their profile, like, "What an easy laugh and a small nose. Your life must be so easy."

WHITNEY CUMMINGS—COMEDIAN, WRITER, PRODUCER, ACTOR

Being attractive brings up a set of issues with yourself. The more attractive someone is, usually the less attractive they think they are.

For me, I may be an attractive comedian, but I was an ugly model. As a model, I was always the ugliest and the fattest. I would get fired from jobs on the spot. I was told my ribs were too big so I couldn't fit into a dress. It's like I was always the ugly girl but just in a different echelon.

JUDD APATOW—COMEDIAN, DIRECTOR, WRITER, PRODUCER

When someone is laughing, I know they don't dislike me. I don't know if they like me, but I know in that moment they don't dislike me, and that's why I get the need for constant approval, because if you're smiling, I know you don't hate me. I don't know if it's positive, but it's not in the negative.

Steven Spielberg, who I used to work for at Dreamworks, was trying to reach me to let me know he liked *Knocked Up*, and I so wanted a letter from him. Paul Feig got one when we made *Freaks and Geeks,* and I was so jealous that he got a letter from Spielberg saying that he loved *Freaks and Geeks,* and I didn't return the call and I told my assistant, "Can you say Judd's out of town and is it possible that he could write a note just so I could have the letter?" I knew a compliment was coming and I'm so wounded I needed to have it forever.

He sent me the dream letter, the beautiful letter with nothing but kindness. I have it. What happened afterward was I thought to myself, "This is the best you can do. Who else do I want to compliment me? How many of these do I need to feel good about my work and myself?" and how it doesn't last, and the wound is still there.

SUE COSTELLO—COMEDIAN, WRITER, ACTOR

My therapist told me, "I bet you people have been nice to you your whole life and you haven't seen it." Literally it took me like five days to deal with that. Because she was right.

JANEANE GAROFALO—COMEDIAN, WRITER, ACTOR

Some days I'm feeling pretty good. I'm pleased with who I am. There's other days where I literally, I'm a bad match for myself like a terrible Match.com profile. I am the worst person for myself. I'm as down as down can get. I can't even put my finger on why.

Usually it's brought on by something. It can be something I see in the news or something someone says or I overhear. It's going to sound like I'm trying to be so noble and I don't want to come off like I'm being that way. It usually revolves around if I see somebody being bullied or if I see animals being mistreated. Animals do have advocates, but they don't have as many advocates as humans do. They can't speak for themselves, just like with little children. Animals don't have the advocates in place that humans do to a degree. I can see someone in the dog park manhandling their dog and I'm done for the day. I'm so down. I don't know, I can't explain it.

Marc

You feel the pain of the animal. The vulnerability and its inability to help itself.

Janeane

Exactly. If I accidentally channel-surf past *Animal Cops* and just catch a snippet, I'm down for the count for the day.

TERRY GROSS—RADIO HOST

I think one of my gifts is also one of my weaknesses, which is I have an antenna for other people. My friends and my producers might disagree with me about this. I think I have an antenna that picks up on what other people are feeling, but there's something good and bad about that. The bad thing is you're always wondering, "Oh, I think I hurt somebody's feelings. Oh, I think I said the wrong thing. Oh, I think they hate me. Oh, they just moved their mouth in such a way and I think they meant to say something bad and they stopped." It's like reading other people and guessing them and feeling what you think they're feeling.

But that's the thing as an interviewer, you want to be thinking, "What are they thinking now, what are they feeling now? What do they think when they go about their lives? What's their typical life like? What was it like for them when they experienced that trauma?" And that guides me in figuring out what to ask them, but it also makes me very nervous. A little insecure.

BEN STILLER—ACTOR, WRITER, DIRECTOR

To me sometimes there are days when I really have trouble making a phone call. Do you ever have that feeling where you just say, "I don't know if I can really get it up to just engage with somebody I don't know"?

LOUIS CK—COMEDIAN, WRITER, DIRECTOR, PRODUCER, ACTOR

I went to Times Square to buy a trumpet. That's where all the music stores are. I just wanted to buy a trumpet to learn how to play trumpet. I went into Sam Ash or one of those places and there's all these student trumpets for, like, a hundred dollars. The guy started showing me: "Here's a nickel-plated, beautiful trumpet. It's got a flawed bell because it was hurt, but they repaired it." It was like fourteen hundred dollars. I didn't have any of that kind of money, but I went to an ATM and I took out everything I had in the bank and I bought this fucking fourteen-hundred-dollar trumpet without having any ability. I'd never even blown into a trumpet before.

Then I was walking through Times Square with this fucking thing in my hands just freaking out and feeling bad and I ducked into what they used to have then, the peep shows. Next thing I know I'm in a peep show booth, those little upright coffins, looking at a chick, a tired fucking Latvian girl probably, through the window of this peep show and jacking off. It's like a two-foot-by-two-foot room. I jerk off and I came on the trumpet case, which was standing between my legs. Once I came and I looked at this cum on the trumpet case, on this beautiful brass-buckled trumpet case, I realized if I had come to this peep show first I could have saved fourteen hundred dollars. I wouldn't have a fucking trumpet now, which I never really learned how to play. It was an important thing for me to realize that.

I went to a therapist for a while and he started dragging me through my past. It was exhausting. I couldn't do it. I also didn't see an end to it. I started saying to him, "I don't want to do this anymore. Can you just give me some advice? Can we just boil it down to how the fuck do I get out of my own way?" He told me, "All right, well, when you do things that you regret all the time, like eating bad food or jacking off in a weird, shameful situation you wish you hadn't, sexual compulsion behavior, eating compulsions," he said, "the issue isn't the food or the sexual objects, it's anxiety. You're having anxiety and you're doing these things to try to deal with your anxiety. Maybe if you tell yourself that in the moment it might help you."

That was an enormous help. That's sort of what I told myself with the trumpet, which is every time I'm starting to have a thing that I'm not in control of. Like I want to buy a motorcycle. This happened the other day. I want to buy a Triumph Bonneville motorcycle. I have no business buying a motorcycle. I pored over the Web site. I started reading reviews of Triumphs and trying to talk myself into it. It's okay to spend eight thousand dollars on a motorcycle. I'm practiced now at stopping and going, "Why are you looking at that? It's got nothing to do with motorcycles. You're anxious. Something's irritating you." Just the act of doing that cuts you off. Calms you down.

Jacking off is a great way to get rid of anxiety. It's not sexual, and knowing that is very helpful. There's something going on inside of me and it doesn't even have to be that it's deep-seated in who I am. Fuck it. It's just anxiety. You're feeling bad. Take a fucking breath.

BRUCE SPRINGSTEEN—MUSICIAN, SONGWRITER, AUTHOR

I had a classic thing happen to me in New York City where I got caught in a classic New York City con game.

Guy came up to me on the street. Said he was from South Africa. Came into town, taxi driver picked him up, got dropped off. Lost a briefcase. It's at Madison Square Garden. It's filled with money. And I'm going, "Oh, how can I help you?" This leads to a variety of other circumstances where I finally end up on a street corner with a guy who says, "I've got a gun in my pocket." I finally realized, "I'm caught in something here."

I ended up walking away anyway, but I said, "Hey, why am I the guy, that out of the thousands of people on the street that day, somebody looked at me and said, 'That's my man!'" I said, "Okay, I'm putting something out here that's great sometimes but not so great in everyday life." I'm kind of stupid this way.

MARC

William Burroughs said, "You can't beat the mark inside."

BRUCE

No, you can't. You can't, and it took me a long time to realize that a part of me was that person and then to start to build the boundaries that not only were good for me but were good for the people that were around me because I wasn't doing them any service either. That was kind of the beginning. It was an adult thing to do.

You've got to learn the no word.

You've got to learn how to say, "No, I can't."

For me that was really hard because I had heard "No, I can't" so often when I was a child. I said, "I'm not going to say no to anybody. When I grow up, I'm not going there."

JUDD APATOW

I've had therapists who've said, "Everything that happened to you happened in the first three years of your life." It may just be the way your mom looked at you. I don't know if that's true.

I do know that in every situation that I walk into, it doesn't matter whether things are going well for me in life or careerwise or not, I feel like the weirdo. I feel like the awkward guy picking up my kids from school. I feel that way on the set of my own movies. I never feel like I own the moment. I just feel like a punch could come from any direction, even if I'm everyone's boss.

When I'm at a party or somewhere, there's a part of me that wishes I could run out and sit in my room and watch *The Merv Griffin Show* alone.

Marc

Why are we so afraid of joy?

Judd

That's the question. I've thought about it a lot. I think it's because we think right behind joy is a knife that will cut our throats. If we really feel it, it's almost like a laugh. Your chin goes up, and your throat is exposed. If I laugh too loud, someone will slit my throat. That's the terror of joy. If I enjoy this as completely as I want to, it's going to hurt when it goes wrong. The mistake is it hurts already. Shutting yourself down is what really hurts. It doesn't actually make sense, and you have to think about it all the time to know that's what's happening. That I'm not actually enjoying this.

You're not present because you're waiting for a punch. That's how I feel. I feel like I have my dukes up all day long looking for someone who's going to punch me, and here's the thing, no one ever punches me.

JEN KIRKMAN—COMEDIAN, WRITER

I have to go to Australia on Friday and I'm convinced I'm going to die because I get anxiety attacks on airplanes. Being there, I feel like I'm going to be like, "I'm in Australia. I can't leave. I can't just get on a plane." I get agoraphobic that way. Panicked. Because I know I can't control it and I'm not afraid like the plane's going to crash or I'm dying or anything. I just don't like being in situations that I don't decide to be in. I have to go.

Marc

That's why you don't want to have children.

Jen

Yes. I'm working on so much shit that by the time I grow up and get my shit together I'll be like, "Oh, I can't wait to enjoy this adulthood a little bit."

I feel like if I was listening to me, I'd be like, "I cannot stand this girl right now."

Marc

The thing about talking about this kind of stuff in an honest way is that not many people do it. There will be judgers, but there will also be people that are like, "Oh my God. No one ever says that. I feel exactly that way." Conquering my fear of flying taught me a lot about conquering fears in life because it is really the core of that panic disorder. Because if you're afraid of flying, you get onto that machine and you've got to fly somewhere. You have absolutely no control over any of it. It becomes a metaphor for life. You don't know how to fly a plane; if something was to go wrong, there was nothing you can do. Literally, either you choose to live in the panic; which 99 percent of the time will turn out to be a waste of fucking time and energy, or you fucking let go and say, "You know, it's out of my hands."

JUDD APATOW

I enjoy therapy, but I know that I don't do as much work by myself as I should to keep present. I've always known that if I meditated for fifteen minutes in the morning and fifteen minutes at the end of the day, my life would be completely transformed. I've never done it once. I can go ninety seconds, and I will feel better even on ninety seconds, but I won't do it. The part of me that won't allow me to do it is the part that wants to watch *The Merv Griffin Show*.

Marc

The part waiting for the punch, waiting for the knife.

Judd

I'm protecting myself. I'm saying to myself, "If you meditate, you're going to think about how none of this shit makes sense." I guess a Buddhist would say, "No, if you meditate long enough you would know that it all makes sense," but there's a part of you that's like, "No, it doesn't because no one said life was fair."

You're going to look into the dark abyss in your quiet meditation and realize there's nothing fucking there.

BOB ODENKIRK—ACTOR, WRITER, DIRECTOR, COMEDIAN

I am pretty crazy too. I've got a lot of rage. Frustration, rage. It's one of the things I've been facing up to, and I've always known this as true. So many things about yourself that you someday have to confront are things that you always knew. Then the day comes, and you're like, "Argh! Damn it! I thought I wouldn't have to!"

KEN JEONG—COMEDIAN, ACTOR, LICENSED PHYSICIAN

My dad told me I was a perfect person except for my anger, whether it was chemical or Korean. He goes, "Ken, you're a good guy. You're perfect except for you have temper." He would always tell me that even when I was eight years old.

One of my best friends does a great impression of me being mad. I'll be like, "THIS IS HORRIBLE! THIS IS HORRIBLE! THIS IS FUCKED-UP! I'm sorry, man, I'm so sorry."

That is me in a nutshell. I'm the self-aware angry guy.

In med school I was really angry because I didn't know if this was the right path for me. I think anger comes out of feeling trapped in life. I don't know. This is based on my own experience. When you feel like you don't have any other options, or this is your only way out. Maybe it's out of anxiety or frustration, but I remember being very mad in med school a lot because I felt like, "Is this really the path for me?"

DAVE ANTHONY—COMEDIAN, WRITER, ACTOR

Do you know what emotional geography is? Maybe it's just a fucking term I made up. My feelings until I was about thirty-two—until I got therapy and got my shit worked out—were only anger. Just different levels of anger. There was no happiness. I basically had no other feelings. Some people are happy, and then "I'm okay," and then "I'm mad." For me it was like, "I'm really not angry," "I'm kind of angry," "I'm very angry." That was my range.

Marc

Have you ever had that anger where you're trying to behave and own your anger, so you just shut down completely and tear yourself up on the inside?

Dave

Are you kidding? I call that "my twenties."

I was living in New York and I took a trip out here with my girlfriend at the time, and we were driving. National parks, nature, I love that shit. We were driving to this place called Red Rock outside of Las Vegas, and you have to get there when the sun's setting because that's when the rocks are red. I misjudged the drive and so it was clear we were going to miss it by forty-five minutes. I will not say a word for like an hour and a half. I was fucking mad, for like an hour and a half, and she did nothing wrong and she thinks that I'm now going to kill her or something.

Then we get there and I'm still mad. We miss the sunset, then we go to Las Vegas, and then I'm like, "Well, I'm over being angry," and she's like, "Okay, well now I'm in a different place." You don't just turn it off for other people. That's my whole fucking life. That's what I always did. I'm like a psycho, and then I'm like, "Okay, I'm not angry anymore," and she's like, "Well, now I am, lunatic." That's everything, that's my whole deal. When you get to a point where you realize how taxing it is and how exhausting it is, you don't want to do it anymore.

Marc

And realize how much of it you make up.

Dave

You make up all of it, it's all bullshit, because it's all conversations in your head that haven't happened. I went through a period where I had to realize it was all conversations in my head. It's that thing where you're having this argument in your head, and then the person knocks on the door and walks in, and you're like, "What the fuck about Japan?" and they're like, "I don't know what's happening." "We've been talking about Japan for an hour!" I see people do it and I'm like, "You're having a conversation in your head." Once I realized I was doing it, I made a conscious effort to stop it. Once you stop it, you go, "Oh, this is so easy to not do it." It is a choice.

The other thing was me being a victim. The classic time I remember I was at the gym, I was jogging, and there was some sort of poster about Nepal, and I was like, "Fuck, it would be so great to just go to Nepal and just check out that country and just see the Buddhist monks and just the mountains and everything," and then I get to, "I'd probably get kidnapped by Muslim terrorists and they would hold me hostage and then they'd eventually just cut off my head." Then I just stopped and I was like, "What the fuck just happened? Seriously I just took the most awesome fantasy and turned it into me getting my head cut off!" So crazy.

That was the minute when I was like, "Oh my God, I'm a victim." It goes all the way back to your childhood of bullshit and it goes piling on top of itself and it became me.

BRUCE SPRINGSTEEN

I built a thing where I would survive alone. I didn't trust anybody after my parents left and after I had some very close people who died on me. I said, "Whoa, this world will kick your ass and turn you inside out. I don't trust anything or anybody that I haven't built myself."

So you go about building, building, building, building, building, building, building and you keep the world at large at bay. That's how you live. You believe not only that's how you live now, that's how you can live forever. Then you reach a point where you realize, yes, you have built yourself a fortress and you are locked inside. All by your little, lonely self. That's when you realize, "I've got to go outside. I've got to go outside. But I don't like it outside. I don't like what's outside. I don't trust any of the people outside. I only trust myself, when I'm doing what I do. I don't trust the world at all. The world is dangerous and scary."

But you've got to go. You've got to go.

MARGARET CHO—COMEDIAN, WRITER, ACTOR

It all has to do with eating disorders, which has been my major problem, which is why I was an alcoholic and why I took drugs and everything. It's because I have a crazy eating disorder. I think because my mother's anorexic, and I was brought up with it. If you felt fat or if you got a little fat, you were almost unlovable and invisible and a worthless person. When I get right down to all of my issues, that's still that, I think that is the deepest one.

MARIA BAMFORD—COMEDIAN, ACTOR

I think it is genetic because I have an aunt who is bulimic. It's not my fault.

NIKKI GLASER—COMEDIAN, TELEVISION HOST

The very end of high school, things were changing. I was about to go to college. I got nervous because a boy liked me. For the first time ever, a guy that I liked, liked me, and I got nervous about it. I was excited, and I just didn't eat for a day because I was nervous, just nerves.

The next day, someone was like, "You look great." It must have shown right away, and I was like, wait, I just didn't eat as much yesterday. I'll just keep doing that, and that's what just started it. I lost so much weight in a month, I started not being able to stand up, and then I would have to just stand for a couple seconds to catch myself so I wouldn't pass out. It started getting really scary.

Everyone was like, "You don't look good," and I'm like, "I'm not trying to look hot, that's not the thing." At first that was the thing and then you can't stop, and you're like, well, this is not the thing because I do not look good. That's my problem with women's wear, is that our jeans are all so tight. Men are now wearing tighter jeans, so you're getting a sense of it. When you are a little bit heavier than you usually are, you feel it everywhere. That's why it's so nice to wear boyfriend jeans. For a woman, it's so great, because you don't feel fat every fucking day that you're a little bit bloated or whatever.

MELANIE LYNSKEY—ACTOR

My mother had a lot of eating issues when I was growing up, and that's a tough thing to be around. It's really an intense thing to see someone not like their own body. And then also to have a lot of weirdness around what you're eating, when you're eating. It's so hard to get rid of it. And I think that's why now I'm like, "I'm going to eat a fucking cookie." Once I stopped being so obsessive about my thinking about eating—and my eating—just the freedom from that was overwhelming. It feels really nice to not think about food all the time.

I weigh a lot more than I used to because I don't think about food all the time. I used to be very skinny, but you would never know because I hated my body and walked around in big clothes. What's the point? You can never escape it. You're with yourself all the time. And also, you have to eat. It's the most inescapable thing to have an issue with.

I was bulimic for ten years. I was never a binge-y bulimic. I was too ashamed to binge eat. But I had such a strict diet and then if I ate anything over it, I would get rid of it. I was just obsessive about my eating. I got in a relationship when I was twenty-one and I really opened up to this person. He said to me, "That's so violent. What a violent thing to do to yourself." And I never really thought about it like that. I remember when I was twelve years old and I read about it, I was like, "Oh, great idea." He started crying and said, "That breaks my heart that you would do that to yourself. It breaks my heart that you can't experience something delicious." We'd go out to dinner and I would eat a salad with no dressing. That's all I would eat.

He started—it sounds weird and controlling—he would make me eat something and not let me know what he was putting in it. He would make something and say, "Stay out of the kitchen," and I would eat it and I wasn't allowed to go to the bathroom. I started eating pasta and things with oil on them and I freaked out for a few months. And then I was like, "Oh, I'm not getting really fat. Food is delicious. And I feel fucking happy. This is nice." Then I relapsed for a while, for a few years. I guess when I was around twenty-five I was just done. I still had a lot of feelings about my body, but it just got better and better. Sometimes I look at myself and think, "Well, that's kind of sexy. So round and bouncy." It's like, what's wrong with that? I don't know why I was denying that for so long. I was so excited to see all my ribs? Really? Not everyone's supposed to look like that. It's beautiful when everyone looks different.

WILL FORTE—COMEDIAN, ACTOR, WRITER

Definitely there is some OCD in my system. For a long time, I just thought that, "Oh, that just affects the things that are very clear." Like checking the stove, checking the faucets before I go out, making sure the doors are locked.

Then, after a while, you realize, "Oh, these things are also present in other parts of my life." Then, as you get older, you realize, "Oh, this OCD stuff affects how I am in relationships." Like leaving a party, it takes me forever to say good-bye because I want that closure on every person. I need to say good-bye to them. I want the happy ending of a movie in every conversation that I've had. It's a sickness, a polite sickness.

Marc

If you leave a party, and you're like, "Oh, I didn't say good-bye," you got to go back, run back in? "Sorry, sorry, sorry."

Will

No, but in my head, I'll go like, "I'm going to send that person a text tomorrow and say, 'Sorry I didn't get to say good-bye,'" or something like that.

Marc

Well, that's a good OCD.

Will

It can be, but not when you're in a relationship with somebody, and you're taking up time with these obsessions. A lot of times, these will be people that maybe I'm not super good friends with. Even if I am good friends with them. They're not going to care if I say good-bye. I'll see them again. They'll say, "Oh, you left early. I didn't get to say bye." They don't care.

Sometimes I'll put myself in a position of, "Oh, if that person left this party without saying bye to me, would it bother me?" No, not at all, so why would I think they would care if I did the same thing?

So in a relationship, all this energy will be devoted to spending time worrying about making sure others are happy that aren't as important as the girlfriend should be to me.

I'll go out of my way to do favors for people that I don't know very well. Somebody will say, "Oh, will you send a poster to my brother?" I spent a half hour, maybe an hour dealing with getting the tube for the poster, this and that. I have this script I've had to write forever, then I'm behind on that. Eventually, that's going to come out of time that I would spend with my family at Christmas.

MARIA BAMFORD

I had Unwanted Thoughts Syndrome where I had dark thoughts of things like unwanted sexual violence. It sort of started when I was about nine or ten years old. That's a real syndrome. It is a real type of OCD. A lot of people have it.

You have one weird thought. This is a common one: people with a postpartum depression thing sometimes think of hitting or killing the baby. Then they go, "Oh my God. I can't believe that. Oh, Jesus! That's a crazy thought." And then they move on to something else. Somebody who's more sensitive or more agitated would go, "Oh my God. I can never think of that again. Maybe that means something. Am I going to kill my baby?" Then they can't stop thinking about it, and the obsession is, "I'm going to kill my baby." The compulsion is whatever you're doing to make yourself not think about of it, or, like, starting to avoid your baby.

I would think of whatever the taboo thing for me was, which could be killing my family, killing my friends, sexually assaulting people, kids, animals, that type of thing, and then I would start avoiding and avoiding and avoiding. I would be just by myself, which is the safest place to be so I don't hurt anybody. I realized I was not having close friendships.

WILL FORTE

People would tell me before, "Oh, you're kind of OCD." I'd say, "No, whatever." The moment that I actually said, "Yeah, I am," was such a relief. Part of the burden was lifted.

I went to therapy once. I hadn't gone in years. I went through this breakup several years ago, and I finally went to therapy for the first time. It wasn't even the talking to somebody about stuff. It was the act of giving up part of myself to say, "Oh, yeah. I need somebody else to help me with this. I can't do everything myself," that was a freeing thing.

MARIA BAMFORD

I love twelve-step groups because there was a rigid structure where you talk to people, there's certain ways you share, there's certain ways you talk, it was just like Dale Carnegie. Then you have fellowship and it ends. It's not like an unending sort of "Oh, we're just going to hang out" thing.

SIR PATRICK STEWART—ACTOR

I had an idyllic first four and a half, five years of my life. Born in 1940, I was probably conceived on my father's last night in England, or last night as a civilian.

For the first four years, I lived with my mother and my brother and we had a happy, idyllic life. This big man suddenly showed up when I was going on five and changed everything for us. I have talked publicly for a number of years now about the violence in my home. My father proved to be a weekend alcoholic. The weekends were dangerous times. Not always. Sometimes he would come back from the pub or the club or wherever he had been in a good mood and that was lovely. We could all have a good night's sleep. Sometimes he would be ill-tempered and it could lead to blows and police. He never struck me or my brother. Just my mother.

When I became active in the world of domestic violence issues, I became aware that in fact my father had been severely "shell-shocked" in 1940, during the retreat from France, and returned home clearly a victim of PTSD, which was never treated. In fact there was no treatment for it. "Be a man. Pull yourself together and be a man." That's all the help he would've been given. When I talked to an expert on PTSD and I told him about my father's behavior, he said, "All these are classic symptoms of PTSD." I resolved then to do for the memory of my father what I've been doing for the memory of my mother, and I joined another organization called Combat Stress, which specializes in providing care for veterans who suffer from PTSD.

Marc

I can't imagine the unburdening to let go of some of that anger.

Patrick

Yes, and that was most important because anger is a bad thing to hold on to but yet it also left me feeling that I should find some way of making it up to him. I told these public stories about what he did and how he behaved for many years. I can now put it in context. My father was sick. He was ill and didn't know what he was doing. Had no control over what he was doing. That doesn't mean to say that I condone the violence. Violence is never the solution to anything. This is why a fairly recent movement in this area is saying domestic violence is not a woman's issue, it's a man's issue.

Marc

Also, it's weird with domestic violence because there's this weird stigma around it that other people aren't supposed to get involved.

Patrick

Exactly. It's humiliating and embarrassing for everyone. That was one of the things I struggled with as a child, was the sense of shame I carried with me because when fights arose in my house and there would be yelling and so forth, things being thrown. We lived in a community where people were cheek by jowl. Everyone would hear that. In fact, we had a wonderful neighbor. Her name was Lizzy Dixon. Lizzy worked in a weaving shed all her life. She was a big, powerful woman. I do quite clearly remember one night, her throwing our front door open. We never locked our doors.

My father was in one of his rages and she stood in front of him, raising her fist in his face and saying, "Come on now, Alf Stewart. You try it on me. Let's see how far you get with that. Come on! Have a go at me." She would've flattened him. There's no doubt about that.

Great, great woman. I wish I could meet her again to say thank you to her, because she often stepped in and stopped things from getting worse.

BARRY CRIMMINS—COMEDIAN, WRITER, ACTIVIST

I had PTSD because when I was very young, the babysitter's father was coming over and raping me for a few months. It took me until I was about thirty-eight to really deal with that and face it and whatever. I was in shock most of my life. To protect myself. If people got too close to me, I wouldn't give them anything.

I always knew, but I never knew exactly. Then someone came forward, and then there was another person who knew about it, so it's corroborated. We knew who the guy was. He died in a New York state prison. For raping little boys. Serving his third or fourth term.

My parents would go out. They've been through the Depression and World War II, and they go out on a Friday night, like, "We beat the Nazis. Let's go." This guy would come over. I was like five years old, and it was life threatening. Getting asphyxiated because I was getting my face shoved in a pillow, so that was what I had to get back, to figure out. It's funny how this stuff sticks with you because, really, the main thing I do is try to help people. Helping others, it's promoted my healing more than anything, like AA or whatever.

You think you're fine for years. Well, like a month and a half ago, there was a story in the paper about a little girl in India who was about three years old who had died from being raped. Then I was just sitting in my living room by myself, and I just thought, "That poor kid. Imagine, raped to death." Then the light came on, like, "Holy shit. I almost got raped to death a bunch of times." You know you got a couple choppy weeks after that, and that isn't being some wimp. This stuff is serious, and you gotta wrestle every wolf-man that knocks at the door and get through it. You can't go around things, you have to go through them, but that doesn't mean it's my whole identity or whatever. I'm like a million other things.

The day I found out who the rapist was, I get a call from a social worker. She knows the guy. She says the name. "Oh my God. That's who it is," I said. "Well, where is he?"

She said, "Well, he died in prison. I was involved in that case. He died in prison last year."

The first thing I felt was pity for the guy. Some people get really mad at me about that, but I just thought like, "What a complete waste of a life." I tried to find out from New York State where he was buried so I could go put flowers on his grave to say, "I didn't become you. I didn't become what I resisted."

Marc

As opposed to pissing on it.

Barry

Yeah. Well, that's what everybody wants you to do. But I became a human rights activist and not someone that offends human rights.

JACK GALLAGHER—COMEDIAN, PLAYWRIGHT

My mom died after a long illness. She was sick for a long time with a mental illness, and she died. I had a sister who died when she was very young, forty, and my mom never got over it. It just sent her into this little pit of despair, where she was depressed and never got over it. It was really sad, she was such a vibrant person; then when Sharon died, she just lost it.

My mom died, and then nineteen days later, my father died unexpectedly. Like out of nowhere, and when he died, he left nine hours of audiotape talking about his life, which my younger brother got him to do. We knew he was making the tapes, we didn't know what was on them. When he died, I got the tapes.

The beginning ones are funny. They start, "My name is John Gallagher." At the end he's like, "Goddammit, pain-in-the-ass son of a bitch, if I ever see him again." Got really honest, and he talked about a lot of stuff you don't want your dad to talk about.

He had a nervous breakdown, and I remember the nervous breakdown because I was like eleven. I remember them taking him out of the house in his robe, shaking, and saying to my mom, "Where's Dad going?" She said, "He just needs to see a doctor." We were Irish Catholic, you didn't talk about that.

I remember walking up to his bedroom, my mom saying, "Your dad's sick." The door was shut. "Don't bother your dad." The door was shut for days, and I remember putting my ear against the door. Then I remember just thinking, "Fuck it." Opening the door, and I'll tell you, I remember this like it was yesterday, there was a little light coming in from the bottom of his shade, and my dad was lying in his bed, curled up in the fetal position, shaking. I shut the door and I thought, "Fuck." I pretended it didn't happen, then a couple days later, they took him away.

My dad became one of my really good friends as we got older, and I would talk to him on the phone every day. I'd call him every day because he was a good guy, and when I got past the point of him being my father I realized he was just this frail guy who didn't know what the fuck he was doing. He had five kids. He was trying to keep his head above water. He didn't have a college education, he hustled, and he was a good guy, and we never were hungry.

I didn't give him any fucking credit for it until I started thinking, "This is fucking hard to do." Then he became my friend, then he passed away and I missed him. Why did I expect my parents to know what they were doing? Because I don't.

BRUCE SPRINGSTEEN

I always look at my dad as, of course, he had anger and frustration and humiliation, but he was also just a guy that was lost in the wilderness. He'd never undertaken that project to find your course and steer it toward something. Of course, what I was doing looked ridiculous to him, as it might to a parent looking at their kid who's spending ten hours in the day just whacking on the guitar in their room.

All of those things sort of contributed to, I think, what he would have felt was an unsuccessful life, which is not necessarily how I look upon it right now. I mean, he had three children. He raised solid citizens and my mother was a fabulous partner and there was actually a lot of joy in his life. I think he was too at sea himself to appreciate it.

On top of it, he was truly mentally ill, and that cast a shadow over everything. He certainly didn't know it and really neither did the rest of us until we were probably into our twenties and he was in his forties.

Your parents, you love them regardless. I was just more inter-ested in who he was, what that had to do with me, and also how I could be of service and helpful, once I realized that I was going to be the parent and he was going to be the child.

It happened when he got very ill and he needed to be taken care of. My mother's relationship to him was limited as to how disci-plined she could be, so it kind of fell on me to get to California. I had to get him medicated, I had to get him to the doctors. All of which he resisted, resisted, resisted, but he become a danger to him-self and to others. He was paranoid schizophrenic, which is what they called it at the time.

It was pretty intense because you're hearing voices and you're becoming very manic. You're going for days without sleep and en-gaged in very manic behavior. At some point he became a risk to himself and to my mom and to the citizenry at large, so I had to go out and try to assist him in getting better, which we were able to do after quite a big battle.

He had to get treatment and the correct medication, and it

improved his life greatly toward the last fifteen, twenty years of his life.

ALLIE BROSH—WRITER, ILLUSTRATOR

I was actually really relieved when I first became depressed because that was the first break I'd had from anxiety. When I'm really depressed, I don't have enough energy in me to be anxious.

TODD HANSON—COMEDIAN, WRITER, ACTOR

I often say if you're not at least a little bit depressed you're just not fucking paying attention. I don't mean just about some political injustice, I mean just about the human condition in general. Just what goes on every day in the world. Man's inhumanity to man, or more likely women, it's just horrifying. If you pay attention to what's happening, it's pretty bad. But there's beautiful things too, like this moment between you and me, so there's some things to make up for it.

A friend of mine was going through a hard time, she calls me up, she's like, "I need a friend right now. Can I come over?" She comes over and we're talking about one of the worst things that I've personally gone through and at the time somebody came up to me and said, "Todd, you're looking at the world so negatively. Look at the positive things in the world. Listen to the birds in the trees. Can you hear the birds in the trees? The birds are singing. Listen to the birds singing." And I said to the guy, "I appreciate what you're trying to do, but when I hear those birds singing, I'm not hearing the happy twittering of happy little creatures. I'm hearing the screams of territorial animals that are either competing for mates or competing for some sort of feeding territory against other competitors which will starve them out if they don't win, and in the kill-or-be-killed, eat-or-be-eaten caldron of murder that constitutes the natural world, that's what I hear when I hear the birds in the trees."

So I started relating this to my friend and my friend said, "Yeah, but you were in a really bad space at that time so you were hallucinating, you were hearing something that wasn't there, you were hearing these frightening cries of the birds instead of happy songs." And I said, "Well, I was definitely in a depressed state, but I wasn't hearing sounds that weren't there. I was hearing the real sounds of the birds." And she's like, "But you were wrong because when birds sing they're happy." And I said, "Well, technically they're singing because of territorial—" And she just cuts me off and she says, "Todd. Don't ruin birds for me." And I said, "You're right, fair enough. I'm not going to ruin birds for you. Go ahead and think they're happy."

PATRICK STICKLES—MUSICIAN

I have moments of incredible joy. The fact of the matter is you just make the decision to be an openhearted person in general. You decide to be openhearted and you say, "I will be sensitive and I will accept all the stimuli of life and I will allow my emotions to be triggered accordingly." When you do that, you open yourself up to very great pain and people can hurt you very, very badly if you make yourself vulnerable before them like that.

At the same time that openheartedness will also allow you to have the greatest joys in life and feel the most love and the most real transcendent happiness. You have to accept that. You can't let in just the good stuff. If you want to really, really love the world you have to accept the things about the world that you hate. Not accept them like "just the way it is and it's fine," but don't shut yourself off to those experiences, because in so doing, you're going to also shut yourself off to all the wonderful things in life.

Yes, I'm able to be very, very hurt. Psychologically damaged by certain things that other people would just shrug off, but I think that that gives me a greater ability to stop and smell the roses sometimes.

ROB DELANEY—COMEDIAN, WRITER, ACTOR

I've dealt with depression, and it became very serious after I stopped drinking and doing drugs. About a year into sobriety I had my first experience with super unipolar suicidal depression.

Marc

Unipolar? What the fuck is unipolar?

Rob

Not bipolar. Bipolar would be like manic depression. When you're unipolar you're like, "Please let me be bipolar. I'd do anything." You'd kill for another pole.

Marc

Another pole, except for the one you want to hang yourself from.

Rob

Exactly. That was my experience. Those things can go hand in hand, but I found even though I was going to therapy, talk therapy, I was exercising, I had started to get a job, I was just really trying to truly be responsible, but it's just like the bottom fell out and I very much wanted to die. Fantasized exclusively about suicide, so people who cared about me said, "Maybe you should try medication," and I thought, "No, I would never do that. Only a weakling would do that." You know, you fix it, you can get out of it yourself.

What I tried to do is take myself out of myself. Like you, for example, if you were like, "Hey, Rob, I'm feeling XYZ and I'd like to blow my brains out," I would do anything within my power to help you, whereas I wouldn't do that for myself, which is crazy. I really tried to think of myself like, "All right, don't be you." I tried to be as objective as possible and I tried to understand that the things that my brain was telling me were crazy, so I did get on medication and the fact of the matter is, it made me able to feel every emotion rather than just one nightmare, the "blow your brains out" one. Now I can still feel sad or upset, but I can also get happy, proud, horny, hungry. Those are the other poles. The horny pole.

The thing is I think people might not understand is that real super-clinical depression isn't just a mood, it's like a feeling. Your penis shuts off. I mean, I didn't use it for a month. Before, I was like, "What's the problem?" A beautiful woman could be like, "What do you think of these?" And these are her naked breasts she's shoving in my face. I'd be like, "Get them out of my face."

Didn't eat at all, had diarrhea all the time, and couldn't sleep at all. The physical symptoms were bananas.

Since then I've had jobs, great big corporate jobs, relationships, been physically healthy. You'd be like, "Hey, Rob, I could hire him to do this thing or accomplish this task or talk to him in a cogent fashion about an issue." As opposed to, say, "He could fill that corner with diarrhea and tears."

PATRICK STICKLES

I lived a certain way throughout my entire life and kind of just had the vaguest of feelings that I was a weird freak. I knew I was a freak in some way and somehow other from society. I didn't really understand how. I knew it had made trouble for me and would continue to make trouble for me throughout my life. When I got to be about twenty-six years old, I came to understand that I was a manic-depressive.

It's kind of a skeleton in my family's closet. I think I might be the first one to come out of that closet. Looking at just the history of my own life and the people that I was close to, I entered into a phase where it just became too clear to ignore. I was like, "Oh, shoot, I've been really depressed."

I always knew that I was depressed and I'd been on antidepressants for many years at that point, but I was like, "Gee, this is wild, because last week I was the saddest, mopeyest guy in the world and now I stay up all night every night and I never stop talking. Isn't that a little strange that just so recently I was this way and now I'm this way?"

It came to be too much to ignore and then I was like, "Okay, so I'm a manic-depressive. This is going to be a hell of a ride. Let's do it." At the height of my mania I ripped my entire life apart and I did everything that I could to destroy every institution in my life and several of them I destroyed irreparably. I could look back on it now as saying it was my mania that gave me the strength to destroy these walls I had built up around myself and get myself out of situations that were toxic to me, when in my depression I would be too chicken shit to do the work of it and endure the trauma of dismantling my life in that way. To look back on it now, I could have done things a lot differently and a lot of people would have been a lot happier, including and especially myself.

Anyway, the point is that it was, like, kind of a game to me at that point and I was just invulnerable and everything I was doing seemed to be brilliant to me. Then people were trying to warn me, "If you really think this is what you're going through, you're going to pay for this at some point." I was like, "You don't know what the hell you're talking about." I felt like I could fly.

They were right. In March of last year I hit the wall for real and basically didn't get out of bed until December. Even when I was able to do that, I got out of bed but I could barely talk. In the trauma of going through this and the terror of not knowing what's going on in your brain, I listened to a lot of the wrong people and I took a lot of treatment for it that I've come to see now was a very big mistake.

The goal of these doctors when dealing with a manic-depressive person is they feel like this person is potentially dangerous, so we've got to find the part of their brain that makes them dangerous and turn it off. They did it. They turned that part of my brain off in a big way. With drugs.

They didn't electrocute me like they did to try and cure the homosexuality of the teenage Lou Reed. I asked for the meds. I was the decider ultimately, but I was so desperate for any kind of solution and they told me that they had one. What they didn't tell me was that when they turn off the part of your brain that makes you this dangerous person, they turn off everything else about you that makes you who you are. They take your sexuality away from you. They take away your ability to generate abstractions.

The depression that I went through last year was the worst thing that I ever experienced by far. The thing that was really terrifying about it was not that I looked into the future and felt, like, an un-speakable dread because I had felt that dread my entire life. I felt the dread but I lacked the ability to articulate it.

When I was younger and I would get depressed I was still able to make my art and stuff. I could write a little poem and I could get a little bit of the bad stuff out. Encourage myself a little bit. In taking away the part of me that made all those problems for every-body when I was manic . . .

They killed the poet in me.

They took away my ability to make the unique connections that I can make. I'm not saying that I have this one-in-a-billion brain or anything. But people have a neuro-network, they have stored all this information and make connections between them. My brain was just like the dustiest old library. Maybe there's all this infor-mation in there, but on the medication, it's all in a big pile and it's all under a foot of dust and it's useless.

BRUCE SPRINGSTEEN

People always talk about how women have a body clock, but I think that men have one too. When they get into their early thirties and mid-thirties, you start thinking about, "Okay, where's the rest of my life? And why don't I have one? Shouldn't I have one? Haven't I figured out all the big problems?"

That's when you realize, when it finally lands on you, you realize, "Oh my God, I'm back to zero in this area and this has nothing to do with the craft that I have, with this fortress I have built for myself for thirty some years. In this other area, I'm completely naked in the desert. There is no fortress. It doesn't exist." Suddenly, when you realize that, you realize how adrift you are and you realize that life plays a nasty little joke on you in that you can become quite mature and quite successful and quite developed in one area and become completely retarded in another part of your personality.

DAVE FOLEY—COMEDIAN, WRITER, ACTOR

I see crazy eyes now and I'm out of it immediately. I can tell if someone's crazy from like two or three blocks away. I grew up with a father who has borderline personality disorder. The more you try, the more they hate you.

I've grown up watching my dad treat my mom like shit, then being like a young man who considers himself a feminist. I was the one to prove that men could be something different from what my father was. All this dynamic feeding into me, just going, "Okay, I can take it. All right, just one more day. All right, if I just figure this out, then she'll be happy and she'll love me and we'll both be happy." That transitions to "Okay, one more day and if I can just figure this out, I can leave and she won't kill herself and I won't be responsible for her killing herself." Then it gets sicker and sicker, you know?

I remember driving in my car on the way to work one day and it was actually a Barenaked Ladies song that came on my stereo, a Steven Page song called, "Break Your Heart." This song comes on and I suddenly just burst out in tears as I'm driving and I have to pull off the road and just sit at the side of the road just weeping and that's where I go, "Okay, this is a sign, I think that I'm not happy." I think I'm so unhappy I can't drive safely. I got us into therapy and that eventually led to things starting to improve, which of course led to her taking off with the kids.

ROB DELANEY

When I was in the throes of suicidal depression, I didn't pray for myself but I did sort of say, "This is so fucking horrible that if I get better from this I really hope that I get the opportunity to help other people through this." I think there's a selfishness, not a disgusting, evil-based selfishness, that comes with suicidal thoughts and stuff, but there's a selfishness that is egotism and you think, "All my problems are so much worse." It's like egotism in reverse, so to speak, and you think that you're so special and important and your problems are so unique, that you're among the one one-thousandth of a percent of people who should do this. I don't buy that. I don't think anybody's special-good or special-bad, and I think we're sort of all in it together.

I remember when I was in the halfway house a kid slit his wrists. He didn't die, but we had to take him to the hospital. They had me go with him because I had been there for a little while and I was kind of his big brother. I remember being in the emergency room with people in the middle of the night in LA, so people come in with crazy gunshots and everything, and just being like, "This is what I feel like inside." So it was like equilibrium. It was like a normal person slipping into the Dead Sea for a floaty bath.

Life is going to kick your fucking face in and you're going to get depressed, you're going to get upset, you're going to get sad, and that's okay. When you get to that you can transcend it and be like, "Oh, I don't have to be miserable." Horrible things are happening everywhere all the time, and there's a statistical likelihood that I will die of stomach cancer or in a car accident, let's enjoy ourselves while we've got it. I realized as I said it, this might not sound uplifting, but I believe it. Life is super hard. Once we achieve peace with that knowledge, then happiness can then be possible.

KURT METZGER—COMEDIAN, WRITER, ACTOR

My grandmother killed herself—my mom's mom—in a pretty fucked-up way. A really fucked-up way.

She cut her own throat. By the way, getting the full story of this, I had to piece it together, because my mom and my aunts will never tell me this shit.

Apparently, my mom's like twelve, my grandmother cut her own throat in the kitchen. My mom comes home from school. Her mom's gone. There's just a pool of blood in the kitchen, which she and her sister had to clean up. Then I think my grandfather just married this other woman and felt like a good guy because he got the kids a new mom or some shit. You know, some miserable fucking 1950s, 1960s shit.

BOB SAGET—COMEDIAN, ACTOR, WRITER

I was at The Comedy Store the night a comic killed himself. Steve Lubetkin. He was a friend of mine, like an actual friend of mine. I don't like it when I see those kind of things from friends. I become the narcissist. It's like, what right does he have to upset me by killing himself when I value life? I just, I get really, really angry. I don't care how nuts they are. Take your goddamned medication, get a family member, and fucking stay alive.

PAUL GILMARTIN—COMEDIAN, ACTOR, TELEVISION HOST

I come from a long line of Irish-Catholic alcoholics that were high functioning. Then one day we try to kill ourselves.

My dad tried to kill himself when he was in his sixties. He was an insurance executive. Literally, had the Don Draper office, you know, with the bar. Didn't show up for a business meeting, and he had tried to open his wrists in a New York hotel. This was in '92, and they committed him to Bellevue. The psychiatrist would only let him out of Bellevue if he would check himself directly into rehab. Christmas Eve of '92, we picked my dad up at O'Hare Airport and drove him to a rehab.

Here's the degree of denial in my family, there was only a pay phone in the hallway at Bellevue, so we're trying to get ahold of my dad. You're basically trying to get other mental patients to pick up the phone and go find somebody they don't know. After two days, we managed to get ahold of my dad. I said, "Dad, it's Paul. How are you?" My dad goes, "Oh, fine!"

ALLIE BROSH

On New Year's Eve, my sister drove her car in front of a train, and that's how it ended.

Marc

Had she been suicidal before?

Allie

She had. She had made a couple attempts. The way my mom referred to it was, like, practice suicides where she would do something, but it was clear that she wanted to have an out just in case she changed her mind.

We always sort of feared it, but it never felt like it was really gonna happen.

She kept going off of the medication. She had a really hard time accepting that she needed the medication because she didn't like to see herself as somebody sick.

She had recently tried to change up her medications, and it just wasn't working. It was a couple months where she was just totally—didn't have any emotional variation whatsoever, just felt bored and detached all the time. I talked to her on the phone a few times because I've also been suicidally depressed. We were able to talk a little bit about it, but I didn't feel like anything I could've said really would've helped much at that point.

It just brought up a lot of weird stuff. I was pretty horribly depressed at that time period as well, so I was having a hard time figuring out my emotions around it. It brings up this whole thing where my parents knew that I had been suicidal at some point. Suddenly, there was this weird conversation when I first got home for the funeral. My dad gripped me by my shoulders and looked at me in the face, just crying, saying, "You can't kill yourself. You can't do this. You're all we have left." There was also this pressure. It's sort of a fucked-up moment because my immediate thought was, "Well, fuck! Now what am I going to use to comfort myself when things get bad? Now I'm not allowed to! Now there's this weird thing of my dad's sobbing face holding me by the shoulders."

There have only been a few—maybe just the one time where I really, seriously considered doing it. Other times, it's just comforting to me.

AMAZING JOHNATHAN—COMEDIAN, MAGICIAN

I never think about suicide ever, but I was just kind of contemplating, like when I got divorced, I was sitting there with a gun in my mouth. It wasn't loaded, but I just wanted to feel the drama.

ALLIE BROSH

The way that I work through things is that I just talk them to death. Like when I'm stuck psychologically at a point where I just kept replaying the scene of what my sister's last moments must have been like—just over and over and over, obsessively for days and weeks.

My brain immediately goes to the most morbid, horrifying way that it could've played out, and repeats that scene. I'm obviously stuck at some point and I need to move past it.

One interesting thing I found out is that when people were expressing sympathy to me—I get all these e-mails and stuff, messages, and phone calls from people, being like, "I'm so sorry that this happened." I noticed myself feeling almost guilty, like I don't deserve this. I don't deserve your pity. I don't deserve this. I looked back at my sister and my relationship. We weren't especially close growing up. I mean, we had resolved our differences pretty much, at this point, but from an outside perspective, I felt like, "Oh, I shouldn't be as sad as I'm feeling because we were a little bit distant." I was feeling all this genuine grief but I wouldn't let myself experience it because it was like, "You don't deserve to feel that. You weren't close enough to her to feel that," so I didn't let myself go with it. I was just stuck until I could talk it out and realize that that's what's happening, like, "No, I really am feeling these things. I really did love her." That was one of the interesting things that happened. I didn't expect myself to react that way.

I couldn't cry actually. I didn't cry until maybe two weeks after it had happened. I was so depressed and so emotionally dead inside that I couldn't. It was really frustrating to me because I saw myself not crying. I felt awful inside. For not crying. I said, "This is not a normal—this is what a psychopath would be like if they were having this experience."

Finally, at the funeral, I was able to cry and it felt really good to have it come out. It came out all at once. It just hit me like—I was going to say, "like a train," but that's inappropriate.

When you're really depressed, you don't feel like you can take anything beyond the particular brand of misery that you're already experiencing, and 2013 was just sort of a fuck of a year for me. I also had a personal cancer scare, major surgery. Just a ton of stuff happened. I got in this almost victim mind-set of "I'm experiencing this horrible thing and then everything is happening on top of it. That shouldn't happen. That's not fair," but there's no universal justice system, right? There's nothing governing whether that can happen or not.

Marc

Do you want me to confirm?

Allie

Yeah, sure.

Marc

No, there is no universal system. You're just another person.

Allie

Yeah, just another person, so there's nothing like, "Oh, well clearly you've had it pretty hard, so we're going to go easy on you for a little while." There's none of that.

Looking back, it's like, "Wow! I'm pretty resilient." If I can make it through all that and still—it makes me a little bit less anxious and scared about the future because I've seen like, "Okay, I can make it through this cluster-fuck of a year."

It was horrible, but I know that I can get through it. Now that I'm experiencing this reprieve of relative normalcy, it's a good thing to have, because I can see that I've made it through that horrible stretch to this little island of safety where I am now.

I go through this cycle roughly every two to four years where I look back at myself from two or four years ago, and it's just, "Oh my God! What was I doing?" I'm so ashamed of that person from years ago. I live with this constant suspicion that I'm going to feel that way looking back at now, in two years, four years from now. Maybe that's one reason why I don't want to be wrong. I don't want to be like, "Oh, I did a good job," and then be wrong in four years. I want to be like, "Oh, I called it. I called it." I'm not saying it's logical. It's not.

Marc

It's anxiety. It's dread.

It's fear of judgment.

It's fear of not being cool.

It's all that stuff that you grew up with.

You don't want to all of a sudden feel happy and then be told— by who, I don't know—that you were wrong.

Allie

It's like a preemptive defense mechanism.

Marc

But don't you think—through your writing—that there is some self-acceptance now?

Allie

Yeah, oh there definitely is some degree of it. I feel more comfortable with myself. I feel like I have ironed out a little bit more of who I am. I'm definitely not there yet, but I know I feel more comfortable being in my head.

TODD HANSON

In January 2009, I had no intention of ever coming out of the hotel I checked into. It was what the doctors call an intent to die suicide attempt as opposed to a cry for help, cry for attention, whatever. You don't want anyone to stop you from pulling it off.

I didn't want anyone to find me, I lived with my roommate at the time, one of my dearest friends. I didn't want him to deal with it. I figured, in an anonymous hotel, a maid comes in, freaks out for two seconds, they call the paramedics or the cops, whoever deals with it, and that's it. I left a note for the cops.

It was a day that wasn't so much a day as it was years and years and I've been sad my whole life and I'd had enough. I brought my pajamas and a robe for some reason, I don't know why, and I brought a pad of paper and a pen and a canister of pills and a bottle of scotch whiskey. Because I had read that you need another central nervous system depressant like alcohol to ensure that the pills work. I took sixty pills. I read on the Internet that six combined with being drunk would be enough, so I took sixty. Maybe I'm the first person to point out that he discovered a factual error on the Internet, but apparently that information wasn't correct or maybe nobody really knows. I talked to the doctors and they were like, "We don't know why it didn't work."

I'm not an alcoholic, I'm not even a big drinker. I'm not one of those people that responds much to alcohol. I drank the booze rather methodically out of a tall water glass. It took two and a half tall water glasses to finish the bottle and it was really weird; I was drinking it like water and it was just going down. It was weird my body did not reject the alcohol. Even though normally I can't have more than three drinks without being sick. I drank half the bottle and then I took the entire mouthful of pills and then I drank the other half of the bottle and laid down and went to sleep.

I left two notes. I left a note for my family and friends and loved ones. It was short. Then I left another informational note for the cops. The note to the cops was a red flag to them because it wasn't a sentimental thing, like, I'm looking for help, it was, like, please call the following people. It was just numbers of people that they would need.

The other note was very short and just said that I've been very lucky to have received so much love from so many people and I was really grateful and I didn't mean to hurt anybody but I couldn't deal with it anymore and I had this sickness for twenty years and I was sorry. But that it wasn't anybody else's fault because they'd all been way nicer to me than most people get and certainly more than anybody deserves or anyone has any right to expect. I felt very privileged and so I didn't want to send that love into a bad place, but of course I did. What else could you do? I don't know. It didn't make sense is what I'm trying to say.

I went to sleep and then I hear a maid banging on the door and I'm like, shit, I set this up on purpose. They said that the maid would not come at the normal time, but now they're interrupting the thing. What if I get discovered? What I didn't understand was that it was actually more than twenty-four hours later, the maid had not come by mistake, it was the next day, and nobody knows why I was alive at that time. I wasn't supposed to be. I shouldn't have been but I was.

I didn't know that it was the next day and I just felt like, fuck, this is going to interrupt it, and I tried to talk my way out of it so as not to be discovered. I tried to hide the notes, but I was on so many benzos that I was barely coherent. Anyway they eventually found me at my house, so I don't know if the hotel threw me out and I was like, "Fuck, where do I go now?" I just wanted to lie down and let the pills finish.

My neighbor April saw me on the street and apparently I had been trying to open the door but couldn't work the key because I was so sedated that I could barely stand and I could barely talk normally. And she's like, "You okay?" And I'm like, "Yeah, I'm fine." So she said, "All right," and she left. Then she thought about it and she came back and I was still fumbling with the key and then she said she noticed that my shoes were on the wrong feet and that I had a bloody nose. I don't know if I fell, I must have tried to throw my clothes on real quick before I answered the door at the hotel, I don't know. But I don't remember having the wrong shoes on my feet or hurting my face. Maybe I fell down while I was staggering home.

Eventually, my roommate figured it out because he. . . .

He noticed that the cat food was on the floor open where the cats could get it and that's what. . . .

That's what made him figure it out.

That's the other thing the note to the cops said. It said, "Please, my cat's at home, but. . . ."

You know despite this self-serving nature of the other note— "it's not your fault, don't be hurt by this, it's really all for the best"— the fact is, I left the cat food on the floor for the cats to eat so that when nobody fed them they'd have some food before somebody discovered them or whatever. But I did abandon the cats. Writing on the note "find my cats at home," I abandoned them and these little guys depended on me, and I abandoned everybody else. I said thank you for all the love they've shown me, but I didn't show it back. I abandoned them, and that's why now I know it was the wrong thing to do.

But when I woke up I did not think that. I was very upset that I had been found and was not in the hotel.

The way I look at it, I didn't choose to come into the world the first time, I found myself in that circumstance because my parents had sex, and it was the same way this time at age forty. I think of it as a second birthday. That's what I call it with my friends or whatever because I didn't choose it any more than I chose the first one, it was not anything I would have opted to do, but I found myself in that situation and so many people showed a lot of love. And I thought, well, I can't disrespect that, it's too special of a thing and it's too rare of a thing in the world to take what little of it there is and transmute it into pain by abandoning all those people trying to tell you they love you.

I mean, when I finally checked out of the hospital, I had nothing. I had not really changed my mind about anything. I wasn't really wrong about the circumstances that were going on at the time. Everything that was going wrong was in fact going wrong and continued to go wrong, but I had two things. The first thing was I had decided all these people's love was worth preserving and therefore I had a will to live. But I didn't have a desire to do anything. I had no idea what the future would hold. That whole first year all I did practically was sit on this couch every night and I had my cell phone and I would just call and if I didn't get anyone on the line I'd leave a message and call the next number, and if I didn't get anyone on the line I'd leave a whole bunch of messages and then somebody would call me back. I would lie here on this couch holding the phone like a teddy bear, waiting for it to ring, and if somebody called back, then I'd cry on the phone with them, and if nobody called back, then I'd cry alone, and it was like that for a long time.

All those people coming to see me, they were all trying to cheer me up and I was just arguing with them. They were all like, it's going to be okay and I'm like, you don't understand, it's actually not. But they were right and I was wrong. A component of mental health is a slight inability to see things accurately. You see people who are mentally healthy consistently have a slightly higher opinion of themselves than they're actually worth or they think that their life is a little bit better, or they think some looming disaster isn't as bad as it really is.

I just wanted to say I'm sorry to all those people. It's a selfish thing to do to take people's love and not give it back, and if you abandon them, then all of the investment of love that they gave you, you've just transmuted into pain and it's not fair to them. Not only do I thank all those people, but I also apologize to them. I have said this to all of them many times and they're sick and tired of hearing it, to be honest, but I just thought it was important to say not only thank you but I'm sorry.

And it will not happen again.

FAILURE

"An Uppercut Right to My Feelings"

I knew what I wanted. I wanted to be a great, relevant comic. It was black or white, life or death, success or failure, mostly failure in my mind. I was only as good as my last set, and I never got the break I wanted. I just knew I didn't have it and wasn't getting it despite the fact that I worked obsessively hard. It was never enough compared to _____. I was desperate and angry all the time. I lived in a failure state of mind all the time. I was sinking.

With a failure state of mind you are susceptible to massive resentment, jealousy, bitterness, self-hatred, creative paralysis, anxiety, and dread. Most of these are just fuel for the fire of failure. They were also the engine of my creativity. They were my themes. They drove me. I thought they were all the keys to my success. The bitterness started to erode my ability to create. Bitterness is just amplified self-pity, and self-pity in any form is not entertaining, but I insisted that all people must feel the same way I did.

I used to think people who didn't fail were somehow shallow sellouts who just knew how to sell themselves. I still think that is partially true, but what I have learned from talking to people is that those who work really hard and harness their talent, if they have it, can find a way. People I talked to, like Danny McBride, Terry Gross, and John Oliver, are all tremendously talented, all incredibly hard workers, and all well experienced in enduring soul-crushing failures. I also learned that acknowledging your victories, even minor instances, is important. Success or failure as a general description or overview of a creative life is ludicrous.

When I started the podcast I had failed. I was in my mid-forties. My comedy career hadn't panned out. I had no real prospects in my mind. I was broke and coming out of a second childless marriage. I thought I was the victim for a while, but then started to see my part in my position in life. I had to accept it and try to move on. I had to really let it all go in my heart and just start the podcast with no expectations and no income and keep working. I believed I wasn't ever going to be a relevant comic and that all my opportunities were behind me. I was old and had missed my window. It wasn't until I let go of expectations and let the humility settle in as opposed to anger, self-pity, and the idea of failure that I became grounded in my body and a fucking grown-up.

Oddly I still talk about all the themes that once hobbled me but know that I can walk and have some hindsight. They are a cautionary tale or a struggle that can be won. Without failure, I would not have any success.

JASON SEGEL—COMEDIAN, ACTOR, WRITER

If the criteria of success is that if you don't make it, you're a failure, then a lot of people are walking around feeling shitty.

AMAZING JOHNATHAN—COMEDIAN, MAGICIAN

The school talent show stopped me from being a real magician. The talent show at my high school went so horribly wrong that the next day in school, the kids didn't tease me. Kids are cruel about that stuff, but it was so bad they didn't say a word. They avoided me.

I did six tricks, and all six tricks went wrong. I mean, the girl in the sword box had a leg cramp, and she said, "I have to get out! I have to get out of this." She got out of the sword box halfway through the trick and knocked all the sides off. Two mirrors smashed.

I killed my dove. I produced a dove and it ran. It got out of my hand and was running and I chased it and it stopped real fast. I couldn't stop that fast. I ran right over it, squashed it with my foot.

Then, oh, I exposed the levitation. You could see the steel bar holding the girl up in the air the whole entire time. It was supposed to be hidden until I got right in front of it.

This was going to be my big thing. This was going to get me chicks in high school. This was going to be what made me from an idiot to a champ.

Then the final thing was the guillotine. I said, "That can't go wrong," because the blade falls. It penetrates the neck and doesn't cut the head off. That's the trick. Then they shut the lights off. Well, they shut the lights off just as the blade started to drop, so you never saw it penetrate the guy's neck. It just blacked out. That was it. That was all done to Elton John's "Funeral for a Friend." I'm dressed like a dick from *Godspell* with those rainbow suspenders and the heart on my forehead. I thought that was so cool. I had my hair permed like Doug Henning. I just tanked, man. I went to Toronto and got so shitfaced after that night. I said, "I'll never do magic again." I never did. Never did a serious magic show after that.

JON BENJAMIN—COMEDIAN, WRITER, DIRECTOR, ACTOR

I've done phone pranks that have gone awry. One involved the FBI.

My friend Charlie, he lived in Boston, in the South End, and I would occasionally stay at his apartment when I didn't have other places to live. The gist of it was, we were watching TV, we were getting high. My mom is a ballet teacher, and me and Charlie grew up in the same town where his sister lived. He was telling me that his sister's kids are going to go to this other ballet school that was in Worcester. It was kind of a rival to my mom's.

So I jokingly said, "Let's call her. Give me Didi's number, I'm going to call your sister and tell her not to do that." So I called their phone. It was a machine, and the message came on, and I left this message in an old lady voice or something, like, "This is Diane, from the Charlotte Klein Dance School. After reviewing your daughter's application, we don't feel she's ready for the Charlotte Klein program. Perhaps you should try Performing Arts School in Worcester." My mother's school.

Whatever. It was dumb. That was it. Hung up. I don't even think Charlie laughed. He was just watching porn or something.

Three weeks later, I got a call from Charlie saying, "This is all fucked! I went to Worcester, and we are fucked! You're fucked!"

"What are you talking about?"

"Your message!"

"What do you mean?"

His sister was a lawyer who worked for his father, who was also a lawyer. He was a big divorce attorney in Worcester. The sister was working on a really ugly divorce case, where the mother of the woman was harassing Charlie's sister. The mom was a mean angry person. So they took the joke message that I left to be the mother of the woman involved in the case, and they took that as a threat on Didi's daughter's life because, according to the message, she knows where the kid goes to ballet school.

Apparently, in the three weeks before Charlie's call, they had called the FBI, they pay like eight grand to do voice match from the machine, the tape of me, going "This is Diane, from the Charlotte Klein. . . ." I don't know how they jumped to that conclusion. I must have sounded just like that woman, and that woman was making this veiled threat about "I know where your daughter goes to ballet school."

Marc

How did it get resolved?

Jon

Oh, never.

Charlie's father called me up and he was like, "You psycho fucking idiot! You will never make a cent! I'm going to sue you! You'll never make a cent for the rest of your fucking life, you psycho! How could you do that?" I was like, "I . . . I didn't even . . . How was I . . ."

Charlie, apparently, completely sold me down the river. When he got home, it was like that scene from *The Godfather*. The father is pacing.

Charlie is like, "What's going on?"

They're like, "This is bad."

"What's happening?"

"This woman is trying to kill Didi's daughter."

They told him about the tape, and the message, and Charlie's like, "That was Jon Benjamin."

Immediately. "That was my friend Jon Benjamin."

BIG JAY OAKERSON—COMEDIAN

I was driving strippers and escorts to bachelor parties. A friend of mine said his girlfriend's dad works for this company.

"Yeah, he just goes and drives the girls and you stand there and collect the money for them and then you leave."

I thought it was going to be the best job ever, but it's a very dangerous job. You get a bunch of drunk guys around like one vagina, it gets hostile pretty quick and they're all jockeying for position. The thing is, on the phone you can't call a company like that and say flat out, "Do these girls fuck if you pay them?" They'll always be like, "You know, they have fun." When you get there you never know what's going to happen.

You walk in, nine times out of ten, these guys have an expectation like, "Well, how much does it cost to fuck the girl?" Then I got to go, "Ahh, she doesn't really do that." They're like, "What?" They get angry and they start getting aggressive.

Marc

You would go bring one girl to a place and there'd be five guys who want to fuck her?

Jay

Oh man, I wish those numbers were right.

No, it was one or two girls and there'd be fifteen to twenty guys.

I thought everyone would be docile like myself and they'd be excited there was pussy in the room and they'd be too nervous to try to do anything else and they'd leave.

I had a gun pulled on me. The first time I ever got confident in a physical confrontation in one of these shows, a guy pulled a gun on me in Atlantic City. It was two girls and they were getting changed back into their clothes. It was after the show. An old Italian guy is banging on the door trying to get in. He wasn't a scary-looking guy at all. I walked out of the room and I told the guy, "You can't go in. The show's over. It's all done." He says, "No, I'm going to go in. I paid for this." I was like, "No, no, what you paid for is over. The show's done." He says, "Well, I paid for it so I say I can go in there." Very confident I say, "Well, I'm saying you can't go in there, so what are we going to do?"

He pulled out a gun and put it right between my eyes. Loaded, cocked, I have no idea, but he put it right between my eyes. I remember the first thought in my mind was "I don't give a shit about these two girls at all. They're just animal drug addicts. Why do I have a gun in my face?" I used to be afraid of rain when I was a kid. I'm a mama's boy and I cry more than I should and now I'm trying to be here and be like a badass to protect these two animals. They don't give a fuck if I get shot for them. They'll go out there and fight the guy themselves. This is better than their home life, what they're living right now.

Marc

What did you do?

Jay

I said nothing and then he laughed and put the gun down by his side and walked away. I love telling stories like that and your friends always say, "Dude, he just walked away and put the gun down by his side. I would have fucking tackled—" I'm like, "Would you have? I'm happy he didn't shoot me in the face." I feel like I won.

"Oh, dude. Man. He turned his back on you? You could have—" "Could have what?" I was proud of myself for not shitting my pants when he did that. Proud of myself. That was one of the scares, gun in my face.

Another time I had to drive two miles down a dirt road. The boss called me up and he really presented it to me very bluntly. He says, "You're going to drive this black girl and this Puerto Rican girl to a racist biker party." I thought he was kidding. Do you care about these girls' safety at all, because what am I going to do?

We met the guys at a liquor store because they said we wouldn't find the place. This was in South Jersey. Right when we're driving down that road, I always assume we're in agreement. I always think these girls aren't, like, ballsy and they're afraid too, but they're never afraid. We drive two miles down this dirt road, and as I'm driving on the road, I'm looking at the girls. I thought we were all in agreement that we're going to leave. We're going to wait for them to get far enough ahead where we can just turn around and we can bug out of here. The girls just wanted to go in and make the money. They really didn't care. They kept saying, "We've got a job to do." Like they were doing noble work. "Hey no, we signed up for this. We're not going AWOL."

I had to go in first to call the boss, and when I walked in, everything was confirmed. There was a bed. There were guns all over the bed. It was the biker version of when you come to a party and someone's like, "Put your coats on the bed." There were guns all over.

I called my boss. He says, "How is it?" I was like, "Nah." He goes, "Is it scary?" I was like, "Yeah." The bikers were all around me, so I can't say that there are guns. He says, "Are there are guns?" I'm like, "Uh-huh." He says, "Are they holding them on you?" I say, "Not yet." He says, "I talked to them on the phone, they're good dudes," and just hung up.

They actually didn't cause much of a problem with me. There was an internal biker problem. It scared the shit out of me. The girls went into the bathroom to change into their stripper clothes and a lady came out in a robe from a bedroom, clearing her eyes like she didn't know that there was, like, a very loud biker bachelor party happening in the next room. Just confused by the whole thing. Tries to go to the bathroom and the strippers, they have the class of nothing, so they were like, "Bitch, we're in here." She got mad and started a big fight.

Then her husband, I guess, her old man, he came out of the bedroom in tighty-whiteys and nothing else. Real scrawny, feathered hair, and he starts arguing and I guess one of the bikers was his brother and they went over and started fistfighting right in front of me. My jaw was on the floor. I was very visible at this point. All these bikers are like, this guy's not going to do anything. I was terrified. They pulled out a gun and the brother in the tighty-whiteys ran through the screen of the back door. Right through it. Just took the screen right out and jumped over the deck and took off into the woods. The brother shot into the woods like nine times.

For the hour I was there, he never came back. I don't know if he was dead or hiding, but either way, that was the least of my concerns. At least it wasn't me they shot at. Now I could try to brown-nose up to him like, "Your brother's kind of a dick, huh? What a weirdo. Stay out there in the woods, jerk-off!" I was trying to be on their team.

Then, I never confirmed if it was a joke or not, but they were in earshot of me. I guess they didn't know that and the girls were changing back into their clothes and I heard one guy say, "What do you want to do with this fat kid when we fuck these chicks?" I yelled out the words "Thirty seconds" to the bathroom. "Thirty seconds!" Then I went and started the car and we got the fuck out of there. They didn't come after us. I guess they were preoccupied, thank God.

It was a forty-five-minute drive back to Philly, and all three of us were teary-eyed. I was crying. They were yelling that I'm the worst bouncer and I knew it.

I know, I'm awful.

DANNY MCBRIDE—ACTOR, WRITER, PRODUCER

I went through a really bad breakup with a girl I'd been dating since college. She moved to Los Angeles with me. Then she started wearing slinkier clothes, and everything just went downhill really fast. When you move here as a young kid, you're right out of film school, you're twenty-one years old, and there are guys who are twenty-eight and have some real money, and you're still living on $25 a week.

Marc

And you realize that you're just there to provide them with new girlfriends.

Danny

Exactly. I can remember still today when I found out that it was over with. I was working at the Crocodile Café in Burbank, which is no longer there, and I went to the manager and just told him, "I don't think I can do my shift today. I don't know. My girlfriend just broke up with me." I'm sitting there like, "Don't cry," and I start crying in front of this guy who doesn't give a shit, and he's just looking at me. He's like, "All right, just get yourself together. Go take some time off." He puts his hand up. I assume that he's going in for a hug, but he wasn't. He was going for a handshake, and I'm hugging him, crying, with my apron from Crocodile Café on.

I remember just walking back to my apartment with my apron wrapped up and my white polo shirt with my name tag. I'm just like, "Fuck LA. I hate this out here. This is the worst." I hit rock bottom with that, definitely.

Something even worse happened with her, which was when I got back on my feet in Glendale, starting a new life with me and two of my other buddies. I got a job, I got things going. Then I get this phone call. One of my roommates answered the phone and it's the ex. He was not supposed to give the phone to me. That was a solid rule, but he smiles. "Hey, the phone's for you." This had been about six months since we broke up. She is on the phone and she's crying.

She's like, "Danny, you got to come get me. The guy that I'm seeing just threw me down the stairs and beat me up. You got to come pick me up." I don't want to be with her, but I still am tortured over this. I'm like, "Okay, I'm all in." I get my two roommates, and I'm like, "We got to go over there and kick this guy's ass. We're going to go save her." We get the golf clubs out of my roommate's car and we're driving to Burbank. I remember "Satisfaction" was playing. We could have no hesitation. We have to pull up and smoke this fucking guy.

We roll up to where she's at. We're looking for this street. It's in Burbank. We pull up, and she's just standing there on the corner with this dude who's six five. He's a personal trainer. He's this huge muscle-bound dude, and all of us just stay in the car. We're just like, "Okay, come on. You can just come on in this car. Just get in here." She goes to the car and he doesn't let her in. He grabs her back, and so I'm in this weird position where it's like, "Fuck, I guess I got to get out," so I get out of the car and none of my roommates come out. They just hand me the golf club through the window, so I'm just standing there with the golf club. I'm just like, "Come on, man. We got to let her get into the car now, man."

The guy just looks at me and he's like, "What the hell are you going to do with that golf club, huh?" He comes up into my face. I'm like, "I can't believe you'd hit a girl, man. What's wrong with you?" He's like, "What are you going to do with that golf club?" It's this big challenge. He had challenged me, so I had to do something with it, so I fucking swing back and crack him in his knees as hard as I can and I just hit him with the shaft. It literally just breaks, and he's just standing there looking at me. I'm holding just the handle of the golf club. Eventually, I just try to chase it with, "Aw man, how messed up are you that you would hit a girl." Needless to say, that dude just fucking pounds on me. I'm getting the shit beat out of me. My roommates are still sitting in the car watching it all. The ex-girlfriend gets in there and she's hitting him and finally I'm trying to get everyone in the car.

The dude just walks over to the passenger seat. My buddy is sitting there with the most useful weapon, which is a baseball bat. Just sitting there, shaking in the passenger seat. The guy just comes over, opens up the door, and just grabs the baseball bat out of his hand and then just starts going to town on my car, and it's just like, Jesus Christ, this whole thing failed. So we get her in the car and get out of there. Then on the way home, it's just like, "Who the fuck are you dating? What is this? What's happened?"

We get back to the apartment. That's when she tells us that this guy knows where we live and all this stuff, so we're screwed. We found out that this guy has a criminal record and he's coming for us. I'm trying to calm my roommates down. They're pissed, like, "Why the fuck are you getting us involved with this shit?" I'm like, "It's going to be fine. This guy's not going to mess with us. He has his own deal with her. We were just picking her up."

No bueno.

Next thing we know we look out our window, there are six SUVs circling the front of our place. We're in this really weird apartment complex that was backed up to the LA River. Apparently they had been on a date before, so he knew where our house was from across the river. They're trying to find out where we are.

My roommates are gone. They're out to their car. I just grab a handful of stuff and a kitchen knife and I'm moving through this fucking apartment complex. We're the only white guys that live at this apartment complex. It's all Asian families. They're all eating dinner and I'm crawling around with this knife looking for my roommates and end up getting into the parking garage. I get to my car, but my roommates' cars are still there, and I was like, "Fuck, these guys, they haven't got out. This is my responsibility. I got to go back for them."

I'm looking for them. We all run into each other, scaring the shit out of each other. We got in the cars and literally left and never went back to that apartment for six months. We were paying rent there. All of our stuff was there, but we were so fucking scared, we just never came back there until we had to move because our lease was up. Even to that day, we were tiptoeing in, in disguise, trying to take things out.

TOM SCHARPLING—COMEDIAN, WRITER, RADIO AND PODCAST HOST

I was at Luna Lounge with my friend, and at that point I was working in a music store. My friend was writing for MTV, writing commercials. And there's young Marc Maron onstage. I was already feeling not good about where I was in life, and you were telling some story up onstage there, and then you said, "That's like the difference between someone who works at a music store versus a guy who's working up at MTV."

Literally, I was next to my friend, and it was that dynamic. I was like, "Oh, this is not good. I am not in a good place at all. Now people onstage are making fun of the hole I'm in, like using it as a demarcation point where I'm actually at in my life. My friend is literally working at MTV now, writing up there." That kind of spurred me, I was like, "I have to change things."

BIG JAY OAKERSON

I wasn't getting enough work with the strippers, so I asked the boss, "Can you give me a little more?" He says, "Well, by day we send out people to kids' birthday parties dressed up like characters, like Elmo." He goes, "Would you want to do that?" I was like, "Sure."

The costumes were awful. He bought like these generic ones. Not the real characters. It was like a brown Winnie-the-Pooh. The first one I ever did, I was Elmo, but the outfit had no feet coverings so it was just my Nikes sticking out. It was sweltering hot, there's no AC, and these outfits are like a burlap sack, a costume made out of carpet. Rug art. You know like the hook art? It's like that. I'm profusely sweating and miserable and the mom kept yelling for me to do the hokeypokey. That's the only kids' song she ever heard of. She kept screaming that and called me motherfucker. There were children everywhere. No one cares at all.

The guy gave me a tape of the hokeypokey and a costume and I don't really know what in the hell I'm supposed to do. I don't know if I'm supposed to talk. I'm familiar with Elmo. Not super familiar, but I just didn't know if it was just dancing the whole time or playing with the kids or do I play a game with them. I had no preparation. He just told me, "Go be Elmo for an hour."

I have a bag and an audiocassette tape.

The moment it started to feel good was like the little girl whose birthday it was, some of those kids were really shy, but she was affectionate. She hugged me and she said, "I love you, Elmo." I thought she was a pretty cool child. It was pretty neat. I had younger siblings, so I'm good with kids.

Then the punk kids in the neighborhood showed up, fucking destroyed everything that I just built with this little girl. They started telling everybody that I'm not the real Elmo. One kid called out my sneakers, which really stung, because I was like, "Maybe this girl won't notice I'm wearing Nikes." He says, "If he's the real Elmo, why's he wearing Nikes?" Then he started looking through the mouth. He's obnoxiously looking right at my face through this little thin screen and then when he realized that I was white he lifted the sleeve of the outfit and screamed, "Elmo's white!" Like Paul Revere'd it, to the left and to the right. People really stopped what they were doing. Everything was sort of like the record scratching, everyone turning around. Like everyone was shocked that I was white. The kids didn't like me anymore. It was so weird. I got awkward.

Then the kid goes, "Let's see if Elmo has nuts." I lost him in my vision because I had about a six-inch range and I remember my plan was just to start spinning in circles and I would see him, and then I wouldn't and I'd try to go the other way. I tried to keep him in front of me and he kicked me from behind. He got behind me and fucking put a foot deep in my ball bag.

Because it was so hot I wasn't wearing pants. I just wore my underwear underneath. It was the most flush shot I've ever taken. I went down. The mom just kept yelling at me to get up and it was hell. I felt that the stripper things were going to be the worst, but I've been equally scared at those kids' parties.

LOUIS CK—COMEDIAN, WRITER, DIRECTOR, PRODUCER, ACTOR

In the late 1980s, you could do ten sets a night at all the comedy clubs and they were fifty bucks each. I had a motorcycle then. A Honda Super Sport 750. I used to go on the FDR Drive doing literally a hundred miles an hour so I could get to shows quicker. I'd do two shows at the Boston Comedy Club in the Village, one at The Cellar, two at The Village Gate, and then I'd run screaming uptown to do Catch a Rising Star and The Comic Strip. We'd get fifty bucks a show. Pockets full of cash.

I remember one night I had done ten shows and I was like twenty-three years old. I parked my bike at my garage in the Village and my pockets were bulging with cash that I had made. You know, fifty bucks a show, ten shows. That's five hundred dollars. Five hundred bucks for a night's work, twenty-three years old. Then I'm walking to my Bleeker Street Village apartment.

I thought, "I have the greatest life in the world. I don't even care if I don't become famous or anything. This is the balls. I have the world by the fucking balls." I had that thought that night.

The next night I was going down Second Avenue doing about seventy miles an hour and a car went through a red light going perpendicular. I never even touched my brakes. I just plowed right into this car. I flew over the car. I lost my sight, but I was still cognizant. The bike was in pieces. My sight came back and the bike was in pieces in front of me. I heard a woman scream. It was a nightmare. I got strapped to a board and taken to a hospital. After lots of CAT scans and tests and shit this doctor came to me in a hallway. He said, "You're fine. You're stupid, don't ride motorcycles anymore, but you're fine. Take it easy for a while."

I hopped off of this table and I thought I'm just going to go home. The threshold to which you need to be hospitalized is still pretty high, but I really fucked myself up. I could barely walk. I hadn't broken anything, but my whole body had bruises all over the side of it that grew as the weeks went by. For two weeks I was in bed. I was a fucking wreck and my motorcycle was gone. I slept that night and I just felt really terrible. I think I peed myself. It was just a really bad, humiliating experience. Then I looked in the mirror the next day and I was balding. I saw it for the first time that I was losing my hair.

Within that week Catch a Rising Star closed. Catch and The Improv went down like one-two. They both closed and things started getting really bad. Things immediately started getting bad and the 1990s came and all the clubs started closing and I couldn't make a living anymore and I couldn't pay my rent. That night was a huge, instant turning point. Everything from that night on in my life went badly for like three, four years.

STEPHEN TOBOLOWSKY—ACTOR

I was in graduate school and I was a versatile actor. I always played the old men. I was playing, like, an eighty-year-old man in this play and I was spraying my hair with streaks and tips as opposed to wearing a gray wig so I wouldn't look like a huge transvestite. The last day of the show, I went back to my little apartment and I washed my hair, and as I'm washing my hair, huge clumps of hair started coming out in my hand. I mean, gigantic clumps, like I was around radiation or something.

I don't remember if I cried, but I felt like I cried for a month. I felt like it was the end of all my dreams. This is the end of me being a star in show business, this is it. From that moment on, in the shower that afternoon, I could look and I could see I was going to be one of those guys that looked like I was balding. I was devastated. I didn't know what I would do, and I think I was in kind of a denial, really, for months.

I didn't see a woman after that that didn't look up to the hairline and go, "Oh, okay, bad DNA. Okay, we'll move on." Every casting director smiled at me and then the little eyes kept going up, saying, "Okay, maybe a professor or teacher down the line." It just happened that I didn't quit, I guess.

DANNY MCBRIDE

I substitute taught for a while. When I moved back to Virginia, I was bartending at night and substituting in the daytime. I was making an honest living. The first day I was a substitute teacher, I was in there and I was just feeling weird.

The first group of kids came in. I had written my name on the chalkboard, doing the shit that I remember people would do when

I was in school. I just started unraveling with the first kids. I was introducing myself, and then all of a sudden, I found myself having to justify to these kids why I was a substitute teacher and just tell them, "I got real plans. This is a fucking stop on the block for me. I'm on my way back out to LA after I save up some money." These kids are just looking at me, like, "We don't give a shit. We're not even listening." These were probably ninth or tenth graders.

I needed to justify it. "Hey, this isn't my full-time thing." All they cared about was like, "Mr. McBride, you smoke weed?" All they cared about was if I smoked weed and what kind of car I drove. "What kind of car are you driving?" I'm like, "A Hyundai Elantra." They're like, "Pssh."

TERRY GROSS—RADIO HOST

I taught in the toughest inner-city junior high school in Buffalo, New York. Eighth grade. This would have been 1972.

I wanted to be the teacher who I wanted to have when I was in junior high, so I foolishly went to school dressed in my purple corduroy pants and work boots. How am I doing?

It was terrible, it was so stupid. I probably did my fair share of weeping the first day. It got worse as things went on, because it just fell apart. The first day they're testing you. Then they realize how weak you are, how bad at this you are. I couldn't keep the students in the classroom, I couldn't teach them a lesson, I couldn't do anything.

Marc

You were a teacher with a personality of a substitute.

Terry

I was a child. I was twenty-two. I was shorter than they were, and I didn't know how to be the authority figure.

I got fired in six weeks.

People say there's no way of firing teachers. Well, they fired me. I'm living proof.

This is a really chaotic, violent school and one day one of the students took out a knife and dropped it just to see, what is Ms. Gross going to do?

Marc

What did Ms. Gross do?

Terry

Ms. Gross watched. Ms. Gross acted like she was in a movie and she went oh, a kid just dropped a knife, I don't know what to do. I felt like they've written this really interesting movie and they cast me in it and they forgot to give me the script. I had no idea what to do.

Thank God I got fired. The principal observed me and the administration graded me. They're like, "Okay, you're from New York City, so we're going to give you a high grade in culture." And they gave me below average in dignity and self-respect. What the hell does that mean? Who is measuring this?

But what gets respect in inner-city schools was not something that I had. In other words, you have to be tough, you have to be the authority, you have to draw the line, you have to meet certain challenges. I'm the opposite, I'm shy and introverted and use self-deprecating humor. How does that go over when you're teaching? Not good.

BILL BURR—COMEDIAN AND ACTOR

I live in this old building. There's no insulation in it whatsoever. I've been sitting on my couch late at night and feeling like I'm the only person in the world. All of a sudden you hear somebody clear their throat and they sound like they're on the couch with you, like the place is fucking haunted. They're literally across the courtyard. I don't know if it's the acoustics. I don't know what it is. Everything's fucking loud as hell in there.

We live above this old guy, the classic old guy you don't want to be. Living alone, no pets, blinds pulled. You don't even know what the fuck he does. He's always really sarcastic. If you drop something because there's gravity, you just hear him muffled downstairs, "Do it again!" He's doing that. "Keep it up!" He does that. I think it's funny. If he says, "Do it again," I do it again. I don't give a shit. My girlfriend, maybe because it's a guy, she feels bullied by him. Two months ago she tells me, "You really need to go down there and talk to this guy." What am I going to do? I'm going to go down there and what's going to come of this? I don't want to do this shit.

Two or three days ago it's the end of Christmas. I'm dragging my Christmas tree down. It's like ten in the fucking morning. Legally I can start building a house at 7:00 A.M. I'm bringing a tree down. He comes out and sarcastic as hell to the point I didn't even get it, but he just had this bizarre look on his face and yells, "Beautiful morning, isn't it?" Yelled that. I was looking at him like, "What the fuck? Is this guy out of his mind?" I realized he's being sarcastic. He heard the tree coming down. I'm like, "Whatever."

I go in the house. My girl's like, "He was yelling again. Go down there and talk to him." I'm like, "Fine. You want me to talk to him." I go down there to talk to the guy. As I start walking up his walk he's sitting there. I see this little kind of look of fear on his face. I didn't go down there to have an argument. I was just like, "Listen, man, you're always yelling up there. What is the problem?" He goes, "It sounds like she dropped a brick!" He just starts screaming at me. I say, "Look, we have hardwood floors. I came down here to work it out." He says, "What does that mean? What is that, some sort of hip, new saying?" I swear to God.

I kept my cool. I kept saying, "Dude, I'm just coming down here to blah, blah, blah, blah, blah." He just kept yelling at me. At one point he made a reference to my bad guitar playing. As sarcastic as hell, he says, "How's your band? Ha, ha, ha." Laughs.

I swear to God, if there is an afterlife I want kudos on this because I immediately wanted to be like, "How's your fucking life? Really. Is this what you dreamed of? Huh? Who's your last roommate, fucking Larry Fine? You fucking asshole." But I have a line. I don't yell at old people. I don't.

"How's your guitar?"

It really hurt my feelings because that was outside the realm of comedy. I don't have musician walls built up. He got in. He fucking gave me an uppercut right to my feelings.

TOM SCHARPLING

There was a point where the toilet was leaking, and I'm just like, "I can fix that. I'm not going to call a guy at $150. I'm just gonna learn about this, do it," and I did it, and I was way too proud of myself.

Then another toilet started doing it, like a year later. I tried to fix it. It was something different, and I'm just like, "Oh, boy. I've hit the ceiling." The bar was very low on my ability to fix a toilet. I couldn't. "I can't get this chain. It's still running. Oh, come on. I thought I had this aced. Fine. What's the guy's number?"

STEPHEN TOBOLOWSKY

I think a thing that helped me a lot, and it's a weird thing to say, was sports. I loved sports a lot. The thing that helped me as a character actor is that I was a very poor basketball player and a very poor football player, but I knew from sports what it meant to be on a team. That sometimes you score, sometimes you play defense, sometimes you throw the ball out of bounds, but you have different roles to do.

Marc

Also, in sports sometimes you lose. My biggest regret in life is I was not taught some sort of reasonable sense of competition. For me, losing or being rejected is life threatening. If you like sports or you played sports, even if you weren't good at it, I think the most important lesson is that losing is not the end.

Stephen

I think it was, and I believe it was Eugene O'Neill who said, "I hope always to have the courage to push on to greater failures." I think it is important to understand that failure is not part of the bad stuff. Failure is actually a building block of the good stuff, if you have the courage to keep going.

But it can break you.

JOHN OLIVER—COMEDIAN, WRITER, ACTOR, TELEVISION HOST

There are moments in sports, especially when you're a kid, that really hurt. I remember missing a penalty when I was twelve years old in a local competition and it probably took me three years to get over it. I just felt like at that point it was the worst thing that had ever happened to me, even though it wasn't.

A penalty shot is all built around individual failure. You are the person who has lost it in that single moment, that single kick of the ball. It absolutely broke me.

My only redemption for that was that years and years later, at the Edinburgh Festival, there was this charity football match that I played in, and I had to take a penalty, and I scored it, and I nearly burst into tears. There was an internal closure. No one knew, and they were probably concerned as to why in this equally meaningless game there was a guy who doesn't cry, visibly on the edge of tears.

I scored another goal in that game and we won, and my dad was watching. My dad always wanted me to be a footballer more than he wanted me to be anything else. And as a joke I took my shirt off. Sometimes footballers do that celebration, so I took my shirt off and I ran up into the crowd and gave it to my dad as kind of a joke, and he was actually moved. I've never really seen him moved much in his life, and I think he realized, this is as close as I could give him to the son that he wanted.

I went as hard into sport as I could, but I wasn't good enough. I can't even believe I'm saying that out loud now, but I wasn't good enough. I was never going to make my career as a professional footballer.

Marc

Exactly what year did you realize that?

John

Probably about three years ago.

TOM SCHARPLING

I mean the fear of success is not the thing for me. I think the fear of failure is almost all of it for me. I feel that looming. I've always thought it's like, the amount of geniuses that are out there, there's like five of them, maybe. Like Paul Thomas Anderson, that guy is on a different plane than all of us.

Then there's the bottom 20 percent that's like the Rupert Pupkins of the world that are just completely talentless and they have to learn that when the cards get dealt, that, "Okay, it wasn't for me."

That middle stretch, all that separates the people is just how hard you work and if you kind of keep your head in the game.

I was just like, "I can do okay in that mix. I know I'm not a genius, but I'm pretty sure I'm not like Rupert Pupkin, like I know I'm not a fraud." It's like if I do the best that I can do, then that takes care of a certain amount of it. I've always kind of operated with that in mind.

BOB ODENKIRK—ACTOR, WRITER, DIRECTOR, COMEDIAN

The things that I've focused on and tried to do, even some of the ones that failed, I feel proud of them. I feel proud of the work I put into them, and the fact that I brought a certain personal vision to that.

The pride that I take in that, and the amount that I let that define me, is a little cockeyed, because it just doesn't really matter what you do. It's just what you do. You can only get a certain amount of appreciation from the public, or from the industry or your peers, and that's wonderful, but it doesn't sort of really satisfy anybody. You should pursue your goals, you should want people's respect, you should want to respect your own work, but that isn't who you are. Who you are is not what you do, and it's not the accolades you get, it's not the pride you take in your work, it is not your work.

The hardest part is realizing like, "Wow! Just so much of me is wrapped up in who I am."

Marc
What do you feel when you're actually able to detach from all of that?

Bob
Emptiness. Utter emptiness. Right? Complete loneliness and emptiness. I do think having a family and having kids is a really, really deeply rewarding thing, but I don't think it's the sole hole-filler. It is not. You absolutely are on your own, man. I don't care if you have kids and you are a wonderful dad and mom, that's great and you should be happy, but you still have your own journey and you have to fill that hole yourself and figure it out.

I think one of the big things I've done in the last year is just allow myself to just change. Just really stop getting on the same treadmill every day, it just isn't getting anywhere. Whatever that is, do some things with yourself, with your day, that just are not what you've always done. Whatever that thing is, just move on from it.

CHELSEA PERETTI—COMEDIAN, WRITER, ACTOR

When I was young, I used to tell everyone everything, and then as I got older, I'm like, "Okay, I'm going to keep more to myself." If I used to have a project in the works, I never would tell anyone about it. I used to be like, "If it doesn't go, I don't want anyone to ask me about it at a party." I really had this fantasy for a while of printing up a bullet point list of what's going on in my career so when I go to parties I have these little slips that I can just hand to people.

If I meet a confident person, I'm just searching for where they're not confident so I can relate to them. Are they human? If someone just seems really together and confident, I'm like, "Come on."

TOM SCHARPLING

Once in a while, my father would say, "Look, if you would have been a garbageman and that's what you wanted to do, that would have made me happier than anything as long as it's what you wanted." Look, I'm not putting down garbagemen, but I kind of had a skill set that was making itself pretty clear at an early age, and it should have taken garbageman off that list.

DAVE ANTHONY—COMEDIAN, WRITER, ACTOR

I'm a self-sabotager because my father was an alcoholic and he wanted me to succeed and the way to get back at him is never succeed.

In San Francisco, one of the club owners was like, "You're the next Jon Stewart, I'm going to give you the fucking keys to the city here, I'm going to give you all this time onstage, blah blah blah," and I moved to New York. That's the kind of shit I did, like, "Hey, you know what? We're going to set you up." Thanks, see ya.

Marc

You say the sabotage is to disappoint, I really think it's to protect ourselves, I think that our parents were so emotionally inconsistent, that the risk was actually to get into the situation where they either said we were doing a good job or they took it away from us. I feel like we're programmed to sort of make sure that we don't just do a great job. Then the risk is that the old man is going to go, "Yeah, it's not as good as I can do," or some version of that. "Oh, you think you're good?"

Dave

What's crazy about my dad is, he's still alive, he's really, really drinking now, but over the years I would just think, "Well, he doesn't really give a shit about my stand-up career," but I would find out he would tell other people that he thought I was awesome, and the comedy was great, and he'd watch this and watch that, never a word to me. "Hey, how about some acknowledgment? This is why I can't succeed!" It's crazy-making.

And here's the worst part, I found this out like two years ago. I was at my sister's and we always talk about my dad when we get together and she was like, "Don't you remember wit training?" and I was like, "What?" and she said, "We had wit training." When my parents were divorced, we would go over there on Sundays, he would sit us down at the end of the night and give us wit training. He would throw out something and we were supposed to be funny back, and my sister would just sit there and I would engage with it because I just wanted my daddy's love. Yeah, so I had wit training. How creepy is that?

SUE COSTELLO—COMEDIAN, WRITER, ACTOR

I have a fundamental belief that a lot of people have an aversion to love and to niceness. We take ourselves down, the self-sabotage. That is the key to life, I think. I think the key to life is realizing you are going to get fucked over, because as kids we're all vulnerable. I don't ever want to feel vulnerable again. I don't ever want to be hurt again. Well, part of the maturation process is to understand it is going to happen, so suit up.

TOM SCHARPLING

I liked Pink Floyd when I was fifteen. Then there was a point where I had no use for it. I liked all the Syd Barrett stuff, but then something happened and I just started getting fascinated. There was this weird stretch with them where Syd Barrett freaks out and—maybe it's a career thing for me, I'm just relating—but those guys were like in the wilderness for years. The guy that wrote the songs is gone, and now they are just kind of looking at each other like, "I think we're going to keep this thing going." They are writing songs that are vaguely like his. They have to start over, and they are doing all these things like *Atom Heart Mother* and *Ummagumma* and these weird albums.

It's kind of fascinating to see them have to learn how to be a band publicly. They are failing wildly sometimes in front of everybody. I think maybe I relate to that part of it. I feel like I'm that right now. I feel like I'm in my *Atom Heart Mother* phase of my career where I kind of had a job that paid for a long time, and now I kind of don't. I'm figuring out what my future is going to be. I'm hoping I come up with *Dark Side of the Moon* at some point.

I started listening to *Wish You Were Here*. I think it might be the most depressing album. If you think about it like this, I can probably make a case it's the most depressing album ever. Their lead singer flakes out, they go like four years struggling to succeed, and then they come up with *Dark Side of the Moon*. It's beyond any-one's wildest expectations. It succeeds. They're enormous now, big-ger than they ever were with Syd Barrett. Then, the album after that, *Wish You Were Here*, is about how it's all just worthless. They are just like, "This is all garbage. Everything we fought for is mean-ingless. We're all miserable."

Just imagine you hit the lottery twice. They hit the lottery the second time, and they are playing these sold-out shows across the world and everything. They look in the mirror and are like, "This is all just garbage. Our lives are garbage." They write this album about how fame is worthless and meaningless. "Have a Ci-gar." These songs about how it's all corrupt and it's a joke. No one actually knows who we are. That's the most depressing thing ever. To get all the success, they got everything they wanted, and then they realized it was just nothing.

WILL FERRELL—COMEDIAN, ACTOR, WRITER, PRODUCER

I had lunch with my dad one day when I said, "Hey, I'm going to try to go for this comedy thing. Do you have any advice?" And he gave me some of the best advice, which doesn't sound like great advice, but he said, "Well, if it was all based on talent I wouldn't worry about you. I've watched you now on these shows and I think there's really something there. But you have to remember there's a lot of luck and if you get to a certain point, three years, four years, five years, and you just feel like it's too hard, don't worry about quit-ting and don't feel like you failed. It's okay to pick up and do something different."

For some reason, that took the pressure off. I'm like, "Oh, okay. Well, this is like the lottery. I'll just give it a shot and if it doesn't work I'm not going to feel bad about it." Of course I desperately wanted to succeed like anyone else, but that weird piece of advice, if it was written on a piece of paper, would be the most uninspira-tional thing. But it's practical. It came from a guy who's been a musician for thirty, forty years and all of a sudden it just was like, "Oh, okay, well this is a crapshoot anyway. Let's just relax and try not to squeeze the bat too hard and just have fun and throw it away." I kind of tried to use that as my approach.

SUCCESS

"Bawling Your Eyes Out on a Used Futon for a Good Reason"

Despite several years of conversations on the podcast with very talented and successful people, talk of success comes up much less frequently than discussion of failure. I guess it makes sense. People are often driven by their failures, sometimes entirely defined by them. Success is fleeting and elliptical.

And yet the joy people exude when they talk about moments of success is undeniable and infectious. Whether it's Michael Keaton telling me how he created Beetlejuice, or Tom Kenny telling me how he landed on the voice that became SpongeBob, or Julia Louis-Dreyfus telling me how she stood up to a studio trying to prevent her from getting her role on *Seinfeld,* everyone lights up when they tell a good story about things working out.

Defining success for myself was always challenging. It was never really about getting rich. I never thought about how to make a lot of money. I just wanted to be paid for being a comic. I wanted to be known for it. I wanted to be relevant. I didn't even learn to consider my own success, outside of a joke working onstage or getting a radio job or landing a deal to make a show, until a few years ago. I guess I just assumed if I worked hard or at least kept working, I would be successful. Ultimately I found success. Not in the way that I ever imagined and not entirely about money, though that helps.

The bottom line is, I don't really think about money, never have. I don't spend much. I like knowing I have it because in this business you never know when or if you'll make more, and no one wants to be broke. Especially as you get older. You never know what life events will rob you of your savings either.

I had no idea what would happen when I started the podcast. There was no way to make money. Neither my producer nor I were "business" people. Over the years we figured it out and learned how to build a business out of thin air with voices moving through it. From doing the show, other opportunities evolved. I wrote a book; I produced, wrote, and starred in a TV show; I sold out theaters as a comic; millions of people listened to the podcast. I am a success on all those levels. All my dreams have come true.

When you're talking to other people who work in entertainment, you're bound to hear great stories like this, about the moments when it all went right. Sometimes it was the starting point for a long and prosperous career. Other times it's an anomaly, a brief moment of clarity in an otherwise fragmented life. They don't necessarily have any larger meaning, other than marking a time when the person telling the story felt everything was okay.

These are stories about making it, in spite of what seemed like a stacked deck. These are personal triumphs amidst professional chaos. These are the things that happen when everything lines up in that once-in-a-lifetime way.

CHRIS HAYES—JOURNALIST, WRITER, NEWS ANCHOR

The difference between doing a thing because it will get recognition, and doing a thing because it expresses something or fulfills you, it is so hard to do in a media landscape that is, in a very literal fashion, built upon the endorphin rush of the ping of recognition.

Really early on, when I first started doing journalism, freelance writing, when I was in Chicago, I would write articles, and they would be in the alternative weekly. Then, poof, they'd be gone.

The first day that I had a byline was in the winter, and I got on the bus, and rode it south on Clark Street, knowing that the van that dropped off the free paper came from downtown. I went south until I hit a bookstore that I knew was south enough to have it, and I got it there fresh off the press, and grabbed it and saw my byline. I still remember that moment. Amazing moment.

What I came to realize is that it was going to be a path to misery for me if the way I valued the work was the reaction it got, because sometimes it would get a reaction, sometimes it just dissipated. I realized it in that moment. Now I have lost sight of that a million times since.

Marc

You fall victim to that because now you're making a show that's out in the world, and you're like, "Did it go viral?" Or "Did anyone pick up on that?" "Did it get traction?"

Chris

As opposed to, "Did we make a thing that was good?" A good thing in the world that I'm proud of, as a thing. As a real thing.

"WEIRD AL" YANKOVIC—MUSICIAN, ACTOR

It really surprised me that people have said they're fans of mine. I mean, I've become friends with people like Ben Folds and I got to direct his video as well. Just the people who even knew I existed.

In 1984 when I first started out, I met Paul McCartney at a party and I weaseled my way up to him because I was like, "Oh, this is my chance to meet a Beatle." And he knew who I was! He turned to Linda and said, "Honey, it's 'Weird Al'!" Like, what? No, my brain cannot handle this. It was crazy.

He knew who I was, and then people were taking pictures of us together, and I was like, "This is the best day of my life."

JULIA LOUIS-DREYFUS—ACTOR, PRODUCER

I got an overall deal at Warner Brothers Television.

I developed a script there for me to star in. Got paid to develop it. The script came in, and it wasn't what I had envisioned and it didn't seem fixable to me. I said, "I don't want to do it, I can't do it." I had a window. Legally there was a window, in which I could pull out of this thing. Then about three days later, these four *Seinfeld Chronicles* scripts come to me from Larry David. I read them, and think, "Oh my God, this sounds really good. I got this."

I went in. I hung out with Jerry. Then Warner Brothers threatened to sue me. They thought I had done something illegal or unethical. They were suspicious of the fact that I pulled out of my deal with them, and then so quickly on the heels of that, became involved with this gig.

I was terrified. I was nothing. I was this little person and this was a huge studio and they were threatening. They said they wanted their money back. It was a lot of money. Seventy-five grand. That's a lot of money, particularly back then, it was huge. I thought, "But I didn't do anything wrong. I didn't break our contract." One of my attorneys said, "You've got to just give it back." But if I do that, doesn't it imply that I've done something wrong? I didn't do anything wrong. Right?

I called Gary David Goldberg, who was the creator of *Family Ties* and *Spin City*. He's subsequently passed away, but he was a mentor of mine, and a very good friend. I told him that Warner Brothers was threatening to sue, and what should I do, and I was so scared, and I'm being told by lawyers to give the money back.

He said, "You know what? I don't respond well to bullying. Keep the money."

I took his advice and I never heard from Warner Brothers. Nothing. Is that wild?

They had no legal grounds. They were just being dicks and I called their bluff. It was a great thing, actually. It was a good lesson. "I don't respond well to bullying."

Marc

Okay, the prank you did on the phone, that was funny.

JON BENJAMIN—COMEDIAN, WRITER, DIRECTOR, ACTOR
Wait, it was funny?

Marc

It was irritating. Here's my reaction to that prank: I'm an idiot. Why'd I even fall for that?

Jon

No, see, I take it differently. I take it like I included you. The kid who no one liked, I included.

Marc

Okay, yes. Why, thank you.

So you call Jon's cell phone and you get a message like, "Hey, this is Jon. If you need to reach me, my new cell phone number is . . ." and he gives a cell phone number. Then you're in your car, you're risking your life calling anyway. Then you call the number that he leaves after you remember it while you're driving, and it's the same number.

Jon

That one is working like a charm.

I get a lot of that. "Why? Why did you waste my fucking time?"

SACHA BARON COHEN—COMEDIAN, WRITER, PRODUCER, ACTOR

When we were making *Brüno*, we wanted to finish the movie in this arena. A normal romantic comedy has the guy propose to the girl in a stadium full of sports fans, and they kiss, it's on the video screen. We thought, all right, let's do that. Let's have all the sports fans, but let's do it in an Ultimate Fighting arena and let me make out with a guy. We wrote in the script, we're going to do this and it's going to turn into a riot. We knew it would be a security issue.

I thought, how do I get out of here? We're going to have two thousand rednecks, we want to have a riot, but how do we get out of here?

Basically, I'm told by my lawyer beforehand—I've got this great lawyer who is this gay southern man. He's a genius in the First Amendment. He lives in India. He's got fifteen lawyers working for him and whenever we're in trouble we call up and they're like, "Okay, in the case of *Smith versus the State of Arkansas*, it is very clear that the indemnity. . . ." We call them up and it's really good for us. He has these fifteen guys. All Constitutional, First Amendment law. They say, "All right. There are twelve things you need to know. None of these laws can you break."

The big one was, he said, "Whatever you do, don't incite a riot, because that's a federal offense." If you're crossing a state line to incite a riot, then that's punishable by a minimum of, I think, three years, and it's a federal offense. That's what the Chicago Seven were up for actually.

I said, "There's a problem, because I am crossing a state line in order to incite a riot at the end," because I thought it would be a great thing for the movie.

We went through all the nudity laws and the decency laws. We had to let people know that there would be nudity. As a result I had this poster printed which had girls in bikinis, really hot girls in bikinis, going, "There will be nudity at Ultimate Fighting."

Obviously, when they got there it was male nudity. Then there were about fifteen stipulations of, I can kiss him on the mouth, I can kiss him on the nipple, but I can't put a finger in his rectum. He can place an open palm on my ass cheek, but the moment it gets within two centimeters of the rectum you're done. Basically, Arkansas ended up being one of the only places in America we could get away with it, because the indecency laws were framed wrongly. They put the punctuation in the wrong place. Essentially we thought we could win in a court case. Making out with a guy and being almost naked was okay.

We had two thousand people the next night. We couldn't put barbed wire on the top, but because we had to have some way of stopping people from jumping in, so I put faked barbed wire on the top of the ring, so that people psychologically wouldn't want to jump it. We had all the chairs stuck down with metal, basically. Unsuspecting audience.

We had the police there. There were about fifteen cops there. Basically, the cops said, "Listen. If you break any of these laws we're arresting you." It was a bit like the end of *The Blues Brothers*. I had the cops there. They were going to get me if I broke the law.

In the end it really worked. We changed the scene a tiny bit. I realized that there was a problem with the scene. Because I attacked him, the crowd booed me. This time I said, "You know what? I'm going to turn my back to face the crowd and you're going to punch me in the head." He did it, and it was great. Because he was playing unfairly, the crowd was on my side. I then hit him. He hit me. He was tougher. I had some blood, and then the crowd was on my side. They were fully behind me. They were ready for me to really hurt him, and that's when I kissed him. That's when they freaked out, but they couldn't jump over.

I'm kissing and making out, and all the time I'm thinking of all the legal laws. Okay, I can stroke his ass. He goes to put a finger in my ass, I'm like, "Whoa, whoa. Pull it away." Then at one point I see a chair flying in. It's a metal chair flying in and I'm thinking, "What the fuck? How did this happen?" What happened is somebody had got a knife in and was sawing through the chains. They were so committed to hurting me. Eventually, I'm lying on my back and I'm thinking, "If I hold my costar tightly I can move from left to right and dodge the chairs." Eventually, after two chairs, I hear, "Go, go, go." The rule was, once you hear, "Go, go, go," you have to go. So we went. But we got it. We finished the movie.

DAVE HILL—COMEDIAN, MUSICIAN, WRITER, ACTOR, RADIO HOST

I had this idea, that I was just joking around, thinking of the worst place for me to do comedy. Me, specifically, because I don't do a lot of crowd work, I'm not very likable. Where it would go really badly? I thought, prison's probably the worst place for me, and for most people.

I called Sing Sing, because I wanted it to be like maximum security, because if I'm going to do it, I should do it, right? I set up the show, and I thought, "This is really funny." I thought, "If it goes well, that's great, and if it goes badly, that might be even better." It was just fun to talk about with my friends, and then about a week before the show, I was like, "Wait a minute, this is an awful idea. This is like a horrible prank I'm playing on myself. This is going to go awfully. This is not going to be fun for me, I'm not going to walk out of there."

I was about to go to my computer and e-mail and cancel, and the administrative person, she ended up beating me to the punch, was like, "Hey, we're just checking to see if you're still all set for next week. The inmates are really excited, we can't wait."

I put it on my Myspace page, because I thought that would be really funny. The administration contacted me, and were like, "Hey, why do you have this on your Myspace page? You know people can't just come to this show." I was like, "Yeah, I know, I just wanted to have it on my page." They're like, "All right." I was like, "Shit, I guess I got to go now, they're expecting me."

I had sent a photo, they wanted to make a flyer to hang around the prison, and I intentionally sent literally the gayest-looking photo I had of myself, because I thought that would be really funny. To have this photo of me around prison, I was like, "Oh my God."

I said to them, "I want it to go well, I think I know what to expect a little bit, but can you give me some information?" She's like, "Yeah, so far about two hundred and fifty inmates have signed up to attend your show. They're all maximum security, violent felons, and they really like jokes about being in jail, and their favorite comedians are, like, the Wayans Brothers, Cedric the Entertainer." Basically, she's like, "They will no doubt be your toughest crowd." She put that in quotes, and then put a smiley face emoticon, just to, like, fuck with me or something. I was like, "Oh, man." I was just really dreading this.

I'd never done this before, really written a set specifically for an audience. I just usually go out and do the thing, and hope people like it, but this I was like, "I'm going to make an exception."

I read up on prison, and learned some lingo, and wrote like a fifteen-minute stand-up set, all based on prison jokes. I ended up bringing two other comedians, Laura Krafft and Carl Arnheiter, and my friend Clark.

I wanted the inmates to respect me right away. I came out guns blazing.

"I heard a good thing to do is just beat the shit out of somebody as soon as you get there, so everyone respects you. As soon as I pulled in here today, I punched my friend Carl in the face." They got a big kick out of that. It's not the greatest joke, but they were thrilled. Because they were like, "This is the biggest pussy we've seen in twenty years."

I found this out after the show, my friend Carl was in the back, and a guard came over to him. On the way in, they had warned us, they're just like, "Look, if anything happens, the superintendent"—now they call the warden the superintendent—"he told me to tell you that we're here to help you out, not bail you out. You're on your own, whatever happens."

I'm like, "Whatever happens? If I get attacked, you're not . . . ?"

They're like, "We're not calming them down, if they heckle you."

Then apparently before the show, this guard comes over to Carl, and is like, "Hey, just to give you the heads-up, these guys can be really harsh. He better come on really strong, because if they're not into it, he's going to know right away."

So I came out with my guitar, and just started playing guitar solos first thing, like heavy metal guitar solos really loud. Like at an area rock concert, and I was baiting them to clap for me and stuff, and Carl said the guard walked over to him, and he was like, "He's got them. I know these guys, they like him. He's got them already." I did that, and then I told my fifteen minutes of prison jokes, most of which were all like based on whether or not I would be a prison bitch. They loved it. It was just hacky, like, "I had my first cavity search today, and blah, blah, blah."

There's a thing called a fifi, which is an artificial pussy they make out of a garbage bag, or a rubber glove, whatever. It's fairly elaborate. It's a thing you make and keep under your pillow or whatever.

Before the show, I was able to hang out with a few inmates, and I asked them for lingo that I could pepper my set with. Then I said, "Can I ask you something? Is there a thing called a fifi, is that a thing?"

They're like, "What the fuck did you just say?"

I was like, "Oh, man. A fifi. I'm sorry."

They're like, "Yeah, but how the fuck do you know that?"

"It's on the Internet."

The guy's like, "You guys, get over here, you're not going to believe what he just said."

They're like, "What?"

"He's asking me about a fifi, and he says it's all on the Internet."

I was like, "If I talk about that, will these guys think it's funny?"

They're like, "Oh my God, they'll love that."

I talked about that stuff a lot.

I had a blast, man. I got a standing ovation, and we walked out, like through the cell blocks, and they were all screaming, "Dave! Dave!" Clapping. And we got outside, and they were all hanging out the bars, like the end of *Shawshank Redemption* or something.

I was just basking in it. I was like, taking all this time. And one of the guards was like, "These guys really respect you if they say anything to you. They just usually ignore people when they walk out of here. You've made friends here today." I was really psyched.

This is the twist I wasn't expecting: Afterward, I noticed my anxiety level had dropped significantly. Not because I thought I was a badass all of a sudden, or like I'd done a good deed or something. I think my buildup of being so freaked out to do this, and then having a really great time, I knocked something loose.

BERT KREISCHER—COMEDIAN, ACTOR, TELEVISION HOST

This Will Smith deal came out of nowhere.

I was right out of college. I was this number one party animal. I would just go up onstage and fucking tell jokes about eating acid, and drinking and smoking weed, doing coke, real party shit. These kids would love it.

This one kid knew a guy that worked at *Time Out New York,* and he told him, "You've got to write an article about this guy. He's the number one party animal in the county. He's becoming a comedian. He's getting big!" This guy wrote an article, it came out Monday.

Barry Katz called me on Tuesday and he says, "I understand

you're working the door at my club? Do you have any scripts or anything?" I give him a script I'd written, and I go up and do eight minutes. He didn't watch a second of it. I knew it because it was a small club and you could see.

He says, "I think you're very talented. Keep working here." Then left. I'm working out at the gym on Friday morning and he goes, "How would you like to go up in front of David Tochterman tonight?" He's a casting director and a development guy. He discovered everyone. He discovered Brett Butler, Roseanne. He was working with Will Smith at the time. Barry said, "He read the article and he's really interested."

I murder this Friday night. David Tochterman approaches me in the bathroom and says "I think you're amazing. I want to do a deal." Then Saturday he calls and he's like, "Hey, you want to go hang out with Will today?"

"What?"

"Will wants to meet you. We're going to do a television deal."

"Fuck!"

He gives me an address and it's the Beat Factory or the Hit Factory up on the Upper West Side. Recording studio. He's recording *Willenium*.

Katz goes up there with me. I walk in, and it's a huge dance studio, like a ballerina studio with mirrors everywhere, and there's two folding chairs in the center of the room. The person walking in says, "It's just him, he just wants to talk to him."

So Barry leaves. "I'll be out in the lobby."

He goes out in the lobby and I sit down in the fucking folding chair and all of the sudden Will walks in. Like, Will Smith. He's a big guy, like six two, he's in great shape. Doing movies, getting ready for *Ali*. Sits down on a folding chair right across from me and he's like, "Tell me about yourself."

I just fucking, like, start spewing like a crack head, just "hey-heyhey you're from Philly, my family grew up in Philly, they grew up in the Main Line."

We're laughing and we're talking, and then all of a sudden he says, "Hey, what are you doing tonight?"

"Nothin'."

"Well, come into the studio, let's meet the guys. Then why don't you and me just go see a movie?"

"Okay."

After I leave, I call my dad. I had just gotten a cell phone.

He asks, "How did it go?"

"Good."

"Yeah?"

"Yeah, we're going to the movies tonight."

"Who?"

"Me and Will Smith."

"What?"

"Yeah."

"Where?"

"At Planet Hollywood. That's where Will said we'd go to the movies."

He says, "What the fuck?" Then he says, "Oh, buddy. I'm sorry."

"What?"

He says, "He's gonna queer ya."

"What?!?"

"He's a Mo Dicker, he's a Mo Dicker, he's gonna queer ya."

"What?!?!?"

"This is how Hollywood works. He wants to fuck you."

I said "Dad, he doesn't want to fuck me."

"What's more likely: that he wants to do a television deal with a guy that works the door at a comedy club and wants to go see a movie with you? Or he just wants to fuck you?"

I'm like, "Aw, man, I'm getting fucked tonight."

I remember going back to my house, thinking, "How do I get out of this?" Like now I don't want to go to the movies. I don't want to do any of this.

Then I think, "Fuck it. I guess I'm going to go up and play my cards, up until we go all in and see how it all works." Maybe I can show him some of my flaws that he's not interested in. Turn him off in some way.

I go up to Planet Hollywood. I walk into the front to the lady. I say, "Is Will Smith here?"

She's like, "Excuse me?"

"Will Smith?"

"Oh, in the back."

I walk to the back and it's the fucking mannequin of *Men in Black*. It's like a mannequin of Will Smith, it's not real Will Smith.

I come back. I go, "No, I'm looking for the man Will Smith." I remember her looking at me like, "You think celebrities come to Planet Hollywood in New York to have dinner?"

"He told me to meet him here."

She says, "Well, he's not here right now, maybe he's showing up later."

I just sit.

I'm sitting in the waiting area at the front door and all of a sudden up these stairs comes a six-seven 350-pound black guy named Charlie Mack and he just looks around and says, "You Bert?"

"Yeah."

"Downstairs."

"Okay."

Now I'm like, "Great, I've got to fuck this guy too. Fucking six-seven Charlie Mack." I walk downstairs, there's nine other black guys. It's got a table in it, with nothing on it and a curtain and it's nine black guys and Charlie Mack.

"Great. Now I've gotta fuck these nine, Charlie Mack, Will Smith. I'm sure Jazzy Jeff's showing up. I'm fucking Jazzy Jeff too."

I just stand and no one talks to me. No one makes eye contact with me. No one engages me. I'm just standing against this curtain, thinking, "This is how it goes down." Like that's all that's going through my head. Panicking. Started as a TV deal, and now these guys are going to play leaky submarine with me all night. All of a sudden Will comes down with Jazzy Jeff and I'm like, "Okay. This is how it goes down."

He says, "This is the guy." Everyone is like, "Oh, okay."

He says, "Bert, are you ready?"

I say, "Yeah, I guess." Like, let's do this.

The curtain opens behind me and there's a private theater behind me. Like there is a real private theater in Planet Hollywood behind me with huge couches. They all start walking and I see them and I'm like, "What the? There's a fucking movie theater?"

Will was like, "What did you think was happening?"

I was like, "Nothing at all."

We sit, we watch *American Pie,* and then I start recognizing all the guys in the room. It's Kool Moe Dee, it's Biz Markie, Big Daddy Kane. I'm thinking "I could have fucked Kool Moe Dee? I could have fucked Biz Markie? My list of gay interactions would have been through the roof!"

We watched *American Pie.* We were drinking and having a great time and Will was like, "What did you think of the movie?"

"It was awesome!"

He was like, "What was the best part?"

"The part where I didn't fuck twelve black guys!"

That was the best day of my life.

ANNA KENDRICK—ACTOR, SINGER

When I got cast in *Up in the Air,* I thought it was a mistake. My agents said, "We think you're going to get an offer on Monday." I said, "Guys, you were not in that room with me, it did not go well." I thought they didn't like me. I was like, "Okay, great." Driving home from Santa Monica like, "That's solved."

Marc

The long ride after the bad audition.

Anna

Exactly, so brutal. Doing it again in your head like, "Oh God, why didn't I play it like this?"

My agents told me on a Friday, "We think you're going to get an offer on Monday." I was like, "I don't think you're correct." Then they called me again and said, "Yeah, it's happening."

The first week I was just like, "What am I doing? This is crazy." I didn't meet George Clooney until we were on set together. The first thing that we shot together, we were doing kind of a walk and talk, and we were standing waiting to go and he says, "Do you get nervous? I get nervous." I was like, "Oh my God!" That was the smallest thing but just opened up my whole world.

He probably does that for everybody when he can tell they're thinking, "What am I doing here? I don't belong here." Just a couple of words from him and you're like, "Oh my God, he's a person, and I'm a person, we're the same."

Looking back on it, there were times he could tell that I was in my head, overthinking. There was a day when I was really in my head about a scene and he was throwing Nerf footballs around, like intentionally kind of hitting me and stuff. I was genuinely like, "Bro, I'm trying to get in the scene and stuff." But he knows you need to snap out of it a little bit.

There was a day when we were shooting the scene where I'm sitting across from the computer screen and I'm firing a guy over the computer screen for the first time. It's an older guy. George was sitting next to me and he sat there next to me all day because I couldn't move, I was stuck. It was such a complicated, heavy scene. They were moving camera equipment and stuff and I was sitting there and he sat next to me.

I remember asking, "Can you run lines with me?" He immediately did the scene with me and I didn't realize until later: he's a fucking movie star, he could have just fucked off and called his agent, whatever. Let alone run a scene with me that he's not even in. He's there but he ran the other guy's lines with me. That kind of generosity, somehow I think about all the time. If he can be that generous, everybody should be able to do that.

JONAH HILL—ACTOR, WRITER, PRODUCER

The day I shot my scene in *The 40-Year-Old Virgin,* it was probably I would say the most important day of my life. Definitely one of them.

I was friendly with Seth Rogen and met Judd Apatow in the audition for that movie. I met Seth in a movie theater before then. I just sat behind him, and Jason Schwartzman was a mutual friend of ours, so we talked about Jason and how great of a guy he is, which he is. So we were friendly and then I got that part and it was one line. And the whole bit was about an eBay store with Catherine Keener and it didn't make sense because I want to buy a skateboard and she said you can't, I'm like, I don't get it, and that was the whole scene.

Now, it was pouring rain that day when I got there. This sounds like I'm trying to be overly cinematic or something. But it was pouring rain and they couldn't shoot the scene they were trying to shoot outside, so we had a whole day to shoot this one fucking line scene and so Judd was just like, "Start." I noticed everyone was improvising, so I just was like this is an opportunity to show someone who I think is really, really amazing and look up to so much that maybe I could improvise with these other people here. And I got to improvise that scene for a whole day. We found those random goldfish boots and it turned into me talking shit to Keener, Catherine Keener, who by the way is the greatest person in the world. Seth and Judd would call me over the months that they were test-screening the movie for audiences and say, "There's no logical reason for this scene to even be in the movie. Like, all we want to do is cut it out, but it keeps getting really big laughs."

So that was a moment for me that really, I think—you would

have to ask them—but I think it made Judd want to continue working with me. I am really grateful to him in every way.

JASON SCHWARTZMAN—ACTOR, WRITER, MUSICIAN

When I was seventeen years old, I was in the middle of making a record, I was going into my senior year of high school and my grandfather, Carmine, who had passed away, had written a score for a movie. My uncle, to celebrate it, was going to have the score played live in Napa. He was inviting lots of people from San Francisco. It was a charity type of event, I believe. Not totally sure. I wasn't supposed to go. Anyway my mom was going and last minute she's like, you've got to come, it was my father's music. You've got to hear my father's music.

I rented a tuxedo and we went up and at this party there was a woman named Davia there who was a local casting director in San Francisco. Because she's from San Francisco, she knew my cousins. They were friends and they were talking at this party and my cousin said, "What are you up to?" and she said, "I'm the San Francisco wing of the casting for this movie *Rushmore*." My cousin said, "What's it about?" She said it's about an eccentric fifteen-year-old who writes plays and has a crush on an older woman. She said, "That's funny, it sounds kind of like my cousin Jason. He's right over there."

I had rented a tuxedo with tails. I had a hat, a cane maybe. I was just like a clown. A classic type of clown person. She invited me over and said, "This is Davia," and then she walked away. Davia started telling me that she was casting for this movie and would I like to audition. I said, "Well, I'm a drummer, I'm not an actor." She said, "Well, but Sofia said that you were in her play and that you might have some things in common with this character." But also I had a little bit of drummer mentality in full effect at this time, which is "Are you sure you don't want to talk to the lead singer?"

She says, "No, no, I think you should audition."

I said, "I'm not an actor, I never auditioned. It's silly that I would even do this."

She says, "What's your address? We'll send you the script." This was on a weekend.

I got home and on Monday this manila envelope arrived with *Rushmore.* I remember reading it, thinking, holy shit, this is everything that I love. At that time I hadn't really seen a lot of movies that were what I was into. I had never seen a movie that got me the way music did. That kind of fuzzy feeling. It was everything that I think about. I really connected to it.

I go in to audition and Wes Anderson was sitting in there. He's twenty-seven. I remember instantly seeing he had Converse sandals, which I had never seen before, and started talking about those. It was 1997. In 1996, *Pinkerton* came out. The Weezer record. That was a huge record when it came out. *Pinkerton* was it for me. So I started talking to Wes about *Pinkerton* for twenty minutes. It took my mind totally off the audition and then he said, "Shall we read it?" and I think I might have said, "Let's not. This was so good, it was so nice meeting you, let's just leave it at that."

He said, "No, let's read." Anyway we read it, and because it was my first audition, I didn't know if it was good or bad. Then we started to improvise and then he said, "Why don't you stick around for a little bit, I'm going to read some other people." Then he actually had me come in and be Bill Murray and audition people to play Bill Murray's kids.

I went home, my mom asked, "How'd it go?"

I was like, "I think it was good. I spent a few hours there."

"A few hours? That's good."

Then I guess it got narrowed down to me and a few other people. Because I was unknown, I had to do a screen test. I did a screen test and I got the part. It all happened pretty quickly. They were saying, "Yeah, you're going to be in this movie with Bill Murray."

It just felt like a dream. I started my senior year of high school thinking I was going to finish my record, which I did. But I did not expect to be in Houston with Bill Murray at the start of the school year.

MICHAEL KEATON—ACTOR, COMEDIAN, PRODUCER, DIRECTOR

David Geffen came to me and said, "I want you to meet this guy named Tim Burton." Tim had done this thing called *Frankenweenie* that people really took notice of, and they said this guy's got something. He's a comer.

He created something else. I forget. Oh, he did *Pee-wee's Big Adventure.*

I met him about this movie he was working on, and I didn't really understand what he was talking about. I didn't understand his concept. He was trying to explain a character he had thought of, and he had this script that a guy gave him called *Beetlejuice,* but he couldn't really describe the guy.

It was a fine meeting and I told David, "You know, I don't know how to do this and I don't know what it is. He was a really nice guy, but I don't know how to do it." They said, "No, no, no. Just hang in there."

They talked me into meeting again. Still didn't get it. He had the conceit of the thing, but it wasn't even a guy. It was a concept of something. After two or three meetings or something, I said, "I really like this guy. He's really imaginative, but I don't know."

Then he said something that took hold. It was something like, "He probably lives in all times. He's from no time. He's from every time. He's lived in all time periods or something." I don't know why that stuck with me. I thought, "Maybe I should think about this." I said to him, "Okay, you know what, let me at least go home and think about it."

I had this idea. I called the wardrobe department, I forget what studio, and I said, "Hey, would you do me a favor? Can I get clothes from every time period, all kinds of different things?" I got a rack of them.

I'm home by myself, and I'm thinking about this, and I start to do this walk and this voice and I thought, "You know what? I'd like to have teeth." You can't tell, but the teeth were not only fucked-up. They were a tiny bit larger. I want to put these things in that were a tiny bit larger. Because there was something about him being goofy that made it even more dangerous. If you run into some guy who's nuts and then he's kind of goofy too, that's getting really scary. I wanted him to be kind of dangerous but funny, and I thought, "You know what? I'm just going to pull everything out here."

I walk around my house and I said, "I'm going to create a walk." I look at these different pieces and put that little hat on that said GUIDE on it. I thought, oh, this is kind of out there. Guide to what?

Then I talked to Tim and I said, "I want hair." He should be like, every day, he gets up and sticks his hand in a socket and just goes "tzzzzzzt." That's how he works. I said, "Let's make hair that sticks out." Tim must have said something that made me get this idea of mold. So this great makeup artist and I started to put together mold. I said, "I want mold down my neck." I had never done it all together until the first day of shooting. I didn't know if it was going to work.

I showed up on the set, and this is really interesting. The crew saw me, and I have no idea why, because they didn't know what I was going to do. I wasn't even sure what I was going to do and if I could make it work. They started going, "Juice. Juice. Juice. Juice." It was this really funny thing.

I just fully committed. I said, "This is going to die or this is going to work," and Tim's so great because when he saw it, he went, "Yes." And then he explained to me, "Your head's going to shrink. It's going to spin around." I said, "Okay, now I get what this guy's doing. I get it." I mean, I started really getting it, and that's when I went, "Oh, man, this is out there."

It rocked, and it was so fun. There was nothing that's ever been like it. There's just nothing comparable.

A little bit of time goes by after *Beetlejuice,* and Tim comes to me and says, "I want to talk to you about something." This was gutsy on his part. He said, "I'm doing *Batman.* Would you read the script? I don't want to talk about it too much, but just read it. I want to talk to you after."

I'm reading it, and I didn't have a concept of what *Batman* was. Tim said, "Read this one," which was the Frank Miller thing, *Dark Knight Returns.* I went, "Whoa, this is interesting. The look and the colors." But I thought, "This ain't going to work."

I read it and I said, "Let's go have coffee." I said, "You want me to just talk to you about what I think?" I think this is going to be over in ten, fifteen minutes, because he's going to say, "Well, I don't know about that." But everything I said, his head was nodding.

I said, "This guy's ridiculously depressed. He's a vigilante. He's got these issues. It's so obvious. And nobody's going to make that movie."

He says, "That's what I want to do. That's exactly what I want to do."

I thought, "Oh, really? Oh. Whoa." So we started doing it and he just had such a clear take on it.

That movie really changed everything. If you look at the colors and the look of those kinds of big movies now. It was like an opera.

MEL BROOKS—COMEDIAN, WRITER, DIRECTOR, PRODUCER, ACTOR, MUSICIAN

I'm ready to do *Blazing Saddles,* and there's too much hubris and too much arrogance in me then, really. I admit it. Not now. Now I'm humble.

I asked John Wayne to play The Waco Kid, and he read it. He loved *The Producers,* so he said sure, I'm glad to read it. He read it, and he gave it to me back, and he said, "I can't do this. My fans wouldn't allow it, but I swear to God, Mel, I'll be the first one on line to see it. It's hysterical."

Then I had a brilliant idea. I'd just seen a movie called *They Shoot Horses, Don't They?* with a guy who was supposed to be a comic, and he was brilliant, and he won the Academy Award. Gig Young, who later went crazy, shot himself, shot his young wife.

I asked him to do it, and he said fine. We got on the set. We rehearsed for a week or two. We're shooting his first scene. He's upside down in the jail. I say action. The black sheriff comes over, Cleavon Little. Cleavon says, "Are we awake?" and he says, "Are we black?" Then he starts spitting a little green stuff, and I said to my assistant director, "This fucking guy is incredible. Look, he's playing a recovered alcoholic. Look!"

Then it became *The Exorcist*. He never stopped. He's spewing green stuff all over Cleavon, all over the jail, just a lot of green stuff is spewing. He was having the DTs or something. He had cleaned up for one day to come in and do the part, and they took him away in an ambulance, and I was crushed.

Then I go right to the phone. As soon as the ambulance took him away, I went to my office, said, "Oh my God," and I called Gene Wilder. I told him what happened. He was hysterical. He said, "You're kidding!" I said, "No, I thought I was getting Academy Award acting, and I was just getting green vomit!"

Gene said, "All right. Relax." I was half crying, half laughing. Gene Wilder says, "I'll see you at noon tomorrow." He was in New York, and he flew out.

He was the only one to do it. What a bounce. I got Gene Wilder to play the part, my buddy and my soul mate, and the true genius of my career.

I lucked out.

TOM KENNY—COMEDIAN, ACTOR

I had done a show called *Rocko's Modern Life* in the early 1990s. That was my first cartoon. Steve Hillenburg, who created Sponge-Bob later, was artistic director on that show.

A couple years later when it came time for him to pitch his own animated show, he remembered me well, and remembered a voice that I had done in a *Rocko's Modern Life* episode that was almost like a throwaway two-line voice.

It was based on—and Nickelodeon does not like it when I tell this story, so here's the story—I was in an audition for on-camera commercial stuff. It's the worst. You think you have little control over your destiny in show business doing what we do. When you're the commercial guy and you show up trying to look like preppy dad or priest or chef. You walk into a room and there's eighty guys that look vaguely like you. It's really horrible, debilitating.

I finally told my agent I can't do that anymore. Send me out for voice-overs. I think maybe I have an aptitude for that. I never really did much of it. They said, "What makes you think you can do that?" I say, "I don't have proof, but I will drive anywhere. I will do any voice-over audition for anything." I think that's a pretty good path for me and a good basket to put my eggs in. That turned out to be, luckily for me, true.

I was in the same studio where they were auditioning for a TV commercial that involved Christmas elves, like a holiday commercial. It was all these little people hanging around. A lot of them had their own elf costumes because that's what they do. If you're a fat guy with a white beard, you go out for the Santa stuff. If you're a little person with curly-toed shoes you go out for those auditions.

There was one guy at the audition. He was in a different part of the corridor. He was hanging with a couple of his buds and was just the most bitter, ticked-off little person in an elf outfit you've ever seen.

"If it wasn't for the Christmas shit I wouldn't fucking work! This is the only time of the year that I fucking work! It pisses me off. It's like I'm glad to have it, knock on wood, but motherfucker!"

I was like, "Wow."

I told Steve Hillenburg that story. Years, years go by and he remembered that story. I totally forgot the story. He said, "Remember that guy?"

That's where SpongeBob came from. So he's sort of a munchkin without the negativity.

Someday I'm going to run into that guy. He's going to be standing outside my house like Mark David Chapman. "Hey, Kenny! I got a bone to pick with you!"

ROB MCELHENNY—ACTOR, WRITER, DIRECTOR, PRODUCER

I was living in this garage in West Hollywood. Behind someone's house.

I just had this idea for a short film about two incredibly self-centered almost sociopaths. I wrote this scene where one of them comes over to the other one's house for sugar for this coffee that he had made. It's a guy he kind of knows but doesn't really know that well. While he's there he says, "I just found out I have cancer." The other guy, all he's trying to do is just get the sugar and get out of the room. The last thing he wants to hear is that this guy's got cancer. I thought, that's really fucking dark and that's a really dramatic scene. I wonder if I told if from the guy's point of view who's just trying to get out of the room, could we make it really funny?

I just wrote it and then I thought it was kind of funny, so I wrote a script for it that night. I just worked all night until I wrote this script. I thought it would be funny if there was a third character when this guy comes out of that scene with the sugar. When he gets home to his roommate he says, "Hey, by the way, did you know that Charlie has cancer?" The third roommate, the guy's roommate, realized that Charlie didn't tell him, and why wouldn't he confide in him when he confided in you? He becomes obsessed with the fact that you must be better friends with Charlie. I thought, "Well, that's an interesting dynamic." Something I hadn't seen before.

I thought that was a level of neurosis I hadn't seen in a comedy before, where the characters were just total assholes, like completely the antithesis of what a network note would be, which is to try to make them more likable.

I wanted to make something where, as writers, you're almost actively trying to get people to root against them. I brought it to Glenn Howerton and Charlie Day. They're my friends and they thought it was really funny. They got it and we just started making it. Nobody really understood why it was funny, but I knew Glenn and Charlie would. Then we got a couple of cameras together and learned Final Cut and figured it out from there.

It was a short film. We never thought of it as a TV show. It was just a short film, and I did it mostly because I wanted to see it all the way through to the end. I just wanted to have it be a DVD in my hand at the end and I fully realized that. *Charlie Has Cancer* was the name of it.

We made that and then we thought, "This is pretty funny, but let's do another one." We think this may be a TV series, and we know the first thing that people are going to ask is, "Well, okay. This is episode one. What's episode two?" More important, "We see that you executed this, could you execute this again?" So we did a second episode. That was about me falling in love with a beautiful transgender woman.

We had both of them and that's what we went out with. We shopped it. We had an agent set up two days of pitching and we went to all the networks. We didn't go to places like CBS or ABC where we knew it wouldn't quite work.

We went to FOX. We went to FX, Comedy Central, HBO, Showtime. VH-1 was doing original content then, MTV. Everybody liked it except for FOX. FOX just sat there stone-faced and I think they were just run by morons at the time. They were looking for this exact kind of show, like, they told me, "This is the kind of show we're looking for," and then they just didn't get it at all. They did not get it.

Most of the places said, "Well, we have conditions. We want to buy it, but we have some conditions." We were like, "Well, what are the conditions?" They're like, "Well, we want to bring in a director and we want to bring in a show runner." Our feeling was, "Well, do you like it?"

"Yeah."

"Well then, why do you want to change it?"

"Well, it's not that we want to change it. We want to make sure that you can continue it."

I'm like, "But we just did two of them. If you liked it and we did two of them, why would you not believe that we could do a third and a fourth?"

FX was the only one that said, "Do whatever you want."

We had our own conditions, which was we're not going to do it unless I'm the show runner and Charlie and Glenn are executive producers, and we write the show and we act in the show. Then FX commissioned a pilot. I didn't quit my job at the restaurant, so I was waiting tables while I was shooting. I had just seen so many things fall apart.

I only quit after we got picked up for the first season. Once we got picked up for the first season, I felt more comfortable then.

JIMMY FALLON—COMEDIAN, WRITER, ACTOR, PRODUCER, TALK SHOW HOST

I met Lorne Michaels on the Paramount lot and I waited in the waiting room for three hours. He has an office on the Paramount lot, which is a really cool studio lot.

Three hours later I walk in, everything's white. I walk into a totally white room, so clearly I died or something happened. He's got his feet up on the desk, he was chilling. He says, "Jimmy, do you ever wear wigs?"

At the time my hair was kind of spiked up and I say, "Oh, I just do this myself to my hair."

He says, "No, I'm saying for different characters because we want you for the show."

The rest was like slow motion. I just said, "Sure, do you want me to wear wigs? I'm going to work so hard for you, I'm telling you I won't let you down. I will be a good cast choice. I'm going to really work hard."

I left there and I had just planned my trip back to New York, back to my family, back to my friends, I mean, it was crazy.

Marc

It was just one question, do you ever wear wigs?

Jimmy

Yeah.

LORNE MICHAELS—PRODUCER, WRITER, COMEDIAN, ACTOR

It isn't that you're looking for something. It's that you recognize it when you see it. When I saw *Bottle Rocket,* I wanted to meet the guys who did it. You meet people you think have something. You don't know, but they're moving around in your head. Sometimes there's a spot. Sometimes there's not.

KRISTEN WIIG—ACTOR, WRITER, PRODUCER

I was at The Groundlings and I was in the main company. I think I was only in there for a couple months. As far as the SNL people coming to see the show, yes. You knew that would happen. My manager made my demo reel and sent it to the show and I had my audition. They flew me out to New York.

I auditioned twice. Target Lady was a character I did. That's a Groundlings one. Aunt Linda, she was a movie critic on Update, she was one of the characters. A few impressions. I just tried to show my range of voice I think, a lot, so I tried to do different accents.

They flew me to New York. Never been more nervous in my life, because I don't do stand-up. That talking to the audience thing is something I didn't do a lot. If I was in character, I could monologue for twenty minutes.

I heard that you get five minutes. No more than five. I thought at five minutes they're going to turn all the lights off and everyone is going to go home, so I bought a stopwatch when I got to New York. I practiced in my room and I tried to get it exactly five minutes.

Lorne was at the audition. Paula Pell, Marci Klein . . . I don't know if I can remember who else was there. And you can't really see because it's dark and . . . It's *SNL*. You're walking into a huge church and giving a sermon to people that you've never seen before and have their arms crossed.

I did my audition and then I never heard anything. They did tell me I was going to meet with Lorne. And I knew Will Forte and I knew Jason Sudeikis, and they were like, "Oh my God, you're going to meet with Lorne. That's it. He meets you and then that's the meeting when he tells you you're hired. This is amazing!"

In my mind I was like, "Okay, well, great. I guess I have a job."

I go to meet with him and I'm sitting in his office and I'm nervous and he's talking about Chevy Chase, something, and then he's like, "You know, we don't have room for you right now."

I said, "Okay."

And he proceeded to talk and I didn't really hear anything and I didn't want to cry and I was like, "Okay."

That was it.

I did cry afterward. I cried, but it also felt like, "Okay, if that wasn't meant to be my path, great." And then, a month and a half later, I got a call from them again saying, "We want you to audition again."

In my mind I'm thinking, "Oh my God, I did everything I had in that five minutes. I don't have anything else."

They said, "You can repeat some stuff, but new stuff would be great."

"Sure. Okay."

So I went out and then I auditioned again and I felt great about it, and some of the people came to my room after and said it was great and funny, and I was like, "Okay," and then the season started. I went back to LA and the season started and I was like, "Well. I'm not on the show, because I'm watching it, so I guess I didn't get it."

Then, after the third show, they called me, and they said, "You're hired. We want you to come out for the fourth show, watch it, and then you start that next week."

I had to pack up my life, and I was like, "Okay, I'm on *SNL*." I've never been more nervous, intimidated, scared. I've never lived in New York City before. I've been there for the audition, and I was just like, "Where do I live? How do I get around?" It just kind of started.

JASON SUDEIKIS—ACTOR, WRITER

I got asked if I wanted to be hired as a writer on *SNL*.

I met Lorne in his office. He offered me water. I said no. I then gave myself the little life lesson. From then on it was like, "Oh, say yes to the water." Just say yes because you'll get dry mouth. This guy may never give you anything again, drink his fucking water. It's probably great water.

Then we had a great moment where Horatio—or was it Tina? I forget who it was, it was a person that was someone I looked up to and I can't believe I'm in the same room on this floor with them and they're talking to me and giving me advice. "Don't worry, it's just kind of a cool meeting, he's just going to make sure you're not crazy. He won't ask you anything about the show, so don't think it's anything like that." I'm like, "Okay, good. Thank God."

Literally five minutes in, we're talking and then he asks, "So what era did you grow up with?"

I'm like, "What do you mean?"

"Of the show, what era?"

And I just went fucking blank, I was like, "Horatio said you wouldn't ask me a thing about the show," in my head, and I'm just kind of staring. The answer is Dana Carvey, Phil Hartman, those years.

I was like, "Oh, gosh." The first person that came to my mind was Eddie Murphy, one of my absolute all-time favorites, top three performers ever. But I know he didn't hire Eddie Murphy. Swallowed that and then the other one. I was like, just, "Well, you know, we grew up with the best of John Belushi videotape," and just kind of stumbling forth. He just kind of smiled and he goes, "No, no, that's okay. I didn't watch the show when I didn't work on it either." Which is so great, such a bailout.

He was very patient and understanding of my situation. I think he knew I wanted to perform.

I wrote for thirty-seven episodes. There was always sort of a sign indicating that there's a chance I would be a performer, but I had to have that talk with him. I was kind of like, "I don't think I can write here, I don't think I'm giving you all I can give and you're not getting everything out of me." That's like what I would say to a coach. I'd go in there and say, "You've got to give me the green light. I'm not going to shoot every time, but I've got to know that you trust me to." It's one of those kinds of conversations.

He called on a Friday. My friend Katie was an assistant for him at the time and I had a voice mail, like old-school screened calls. I was lying in bed, it was, like, twelve thirty on an off week. In the afternoon, I'm not even up.

"Hey, Sudeikis, it's Katie. I've got Lorne for you, give us a call." I was like, "That's a first." So get up, took a shower. Called my wife at the time and I might have left a message because she didn't answer. I say, "Hey, I might be calling you back here soon with some info. It's going to be something. It's either going to be you're fired or . . . It's not going to be, 'How you doing?'"

Then I call Lorne.

"Hi. Lorne, how are you doing?"

"So we want to move you into the cast."

It's always "we," "the show." It's always the Royal We, it's fantastic. I actually appreciate that sentiment.

"Great, when?"

"Monday. When it comes time to write, just write something you think you can score on."

I was like, "Okay, great."

I said, "Thank you"—and then hanging up—"for changing my life."

I called Kate and then called my buddies and we went and got day drunk and hit golf balls at Chelsea Piers.

My first show, it was like, "I'm in the cast, holy shit." Went home that night, tried to fall asleep until 6:00 A.M. Couldn't. Had to get up. Went over to my television and the used futon that I had bought because I thought I was going to be out of there in a few weeks, two years before. Watched the opening credits, listened to Don Pardo say my name, and bawled my fucking eyes out. That's how it went down.

Marc

It's nice to be bawling your eyes out on a used futon for a good reason.

WILL FORTE—COMEDIAN, WRITER, ACTOR

I was doing a Groundlings show one night and all of a sudden there's a whisper that I hear "Oh, Lorne Michaels is in the audience." I was under contract at *That '70s Show* and we had just found out we got picked up for two years. I had a great show that night because there was no way I could do *SNL* even if Lorne liked me. All these other performers are probably nervous about it and I was loose as a goose.

I had a good show that night and then he asked me to audition. I hadn't even thought that would ever be something that I could do. Then the production company of *That '70s Show* said, "Oh, you've got to go audition!" I wanted them to say, "Oh no, you can't go audition," because I was terrified of it.

I finally just thought, "Okay, I've got to go audition." It was as terrifying as I thought.

For my audition, I did this sketch I used to do at the Groundlings. It's about this gold man who panhandles. Basically, the guy is dressed all in gold and if you give a dollar or something they'll do the robotic movement. So a robber comes, takes all his money and he is very sad and then a little kid comes by and asks his dad, "Why is this gold man so sad?"

"Well, I don't know but if you give him a dollar, maybe he will tell you. And if you give him two dollars, maybe he'll tell you in song."

So the kid puts two dollars in and I sing this really uplifting song about the tough life of a gold man. At the end, I sing, "Well, it's because I got a little secret: I sell cock for my face paint. I sell cock for my face paint!" The rest of the song is just the words "cock" and "face paint" basically. "I sell cock for my face paint. Cock! Cock! Face paint! Cock-cock-cock! Face paint!" It's just probably 250 times saying the word "cock."

I did that at *SNL* as the final thing in my audition and as I walked out, Lorne was right there and he said, "Thank you for coming." And I said, "I'm sorry about all the cocks." I didn't know what else to say! And that was it. And then I found out I got the job!

"I'm sorry about all the cocks."

LORNE MICHAELS

That cast of Kristen, Fred, Will, Jason, amazing. Then six people leave, because it's their time. Then you have to introduce a whole new group of people, and people say, "Well, they're not the ones we love." You say, "Trust me."

I used to say that all babies are ugly unless they're your baby, and then after a while, three, four months into it, people go, "What a cute baby." When they first come out they're not necessarily great-looking.

JENNY SLATE—COMEDIAN, WRITER, PRODUCER, ACTOR

They were like, "Lorne wants you to come back to meet with him, but it doesn't mean that you're hired; and don't expect anything, and you'll probably wait for, like, three hours to see him and just sit there." I was like, "Oh, okay, this is so psycho."

I got there and waited for, like, ten minutes and then I went in his office. He asked me, "Where are you from?"

I said, "Massachusetts."

He was like, "Have you worked with wigs a lot before?"

I thought he meant Kristen Wiig, and I was like, "I've never even met her, but I really admire her."

He was like, "No, wigs."

I was thinking, "Oh, this sucks." I just kept telling myself, "He's just a man, he's just a man. You have so much life in front of you, that's all that matters. Don't worry about it."

So I was like, "Oh, duhh," and I remember saying, "Oh no, sorry, I don't know, no, yeah, I've worked with wigs in my one-person show, but I don't do that a lot."

Then he says, "Well, I think you'd be a great addition to the show, and we're going to get you an office."

"So . . ." I wanted him to say it. "So I'm going to be on *Saturday Night Live*?"

He was like, "Yeah."

"That's so great. I know you've seen this happen a million times before where people are like, 'I can't believe it,' but this is my childhood dream and I'm so excited."

He said, "Okay, but don't tell anybody because we haven't announced it yet," and I asked, "Can I tell my nanas?" He laughed.

I said, "Can I give you a hug?"

"Sure." And then we hugged and I went outside and Seth Meyers was waiting there. He asked, "What did he say?"

"He said I'm going to be on the show."

Seth was like, "Whoa, that doesn't really happen."

"He said I could have an office and stuff."

I went outside and I went into the courtyard of Rockefeller Center. . . .

Whoops, I'm getting emotional.

I called my parents and I said, "I'm going to be on *Saturday Night Live*," and it was really exciting.

I never cry, I just. . . .

You know what? It is a beautiful story and sometimes I forget that.

Because it is cool to achieve something that you've always wanted, and to do it kind of on your terms.

To call my parents, they were just so stunned. We were all so stunned. I came from this fucking haunted house with these two artists and just had this one dream, and went to college and didn't become an asshole. To just call them and make that phone call, honestly I forget about that, and it was really, really meaningful.

LORNE MICHAELS

When you do live television, the one thing you can't expect is for it to be perfect, but the Fortieth Anniversary show, that night, for me, watching all of the people who created and built the show working together, and also being in the audience for each other was as close to perfect as it was ever going to get. The feeling in the room was so warm and supportive. You realize that it's, in the cliché sense, it's a family. You can't explain that experience of doing it, except to other people who have done it.

MORTALITY

"I Wouldn't Want It to Go Away"

I don't want to die. I don't want to live forever either. That sounds terrible.

I have no idea what happens after we die. I don't think about it much at all. I'm guessing probably nothing. It's the transition from life to nothing that terrifies me.

Being terrified of death is part of the human condition. Depending on how you look at it in terms of accepting that it's the one undeniable truth of life, it can be motivating or completely devastating. It can make you appreciate life and savor it or it can render almost everything pointless. I fluctuate between the two, depending on how much coffee I've had and what petty bullshit is consuming me. That death is part of life is annoying and sad. Denial is childish, but I can't think about it too much because it's just too fucking depressing. I choose to let myself be consumed with petty bullshit and not get too close to people. I think these will buffer the coming end of others and me.

I'm fortunate that I haven't had to deal with much death around me, yet. As of this writing, my parents are still alive, which on most days seems like a good thing. I haven't had to deal with someone too close to me having prolonged illness and dying. I'm old now, so I know it is coming. Just thinking about it right now is horrifying. I can barely handle when my cats are sick. I know they are going to die, but I've had them for twelve years, and as of today they are alive.

My best friend, Dave, from high school died suddenly. I went to his funeral. When I looked at him in the casket, it was shocking and awful, but I knew that it was real. He was dead. I appreciate that Jews don't view the body, but it was actually helpful in believing it was real and getting closure. I mean, I don't think my grandparents are still alive, but actually seeing them dead would have really driven the reality home. I guess the idea is to remember them alive without that image. Seeing Dave dead didn't rob me of my memories of him alive; it made them more special.

When I talk to people about death it's usually about the death of their parents or loved ones. Al Yankovic, Jack Antonoff, and Mike DeStefano shared some particularly heartrending examples. I try to empathize and absorb any sort of wisdom about dealing with that inevitability, but I don't think there is any real preparing for it. Especially if it happens when they are young, like Molly Shannon, who lost her mom when she was four. I can feel their grief and sense how they've had a lifetime to deal with it and how it defined them, changed them for the better or crippled them for life.

It seems that how we deal with the knowledge of death and the death of people we love really dictates how we live our lives on a core level. That, and having children, which I don't have. So I'm in the dark about a couple of life's massive emotional upheavals and responsibilities that bring pain and joy. If I really think about it, protecting myself from these things by not engaging has probably crippled my ability to feel the full joy and depth of being alive. I guess there's always time. Wait, there isn't. See, I'm sad now.

BOB ODENKIRK—ACTOR, WRITER, DIRECTOR, COMEDIAN

If you're not lucky enough to die young, and just get to be a flaming asshole, you will be humbled. Everybody gets humbled, everybody.

JANEANE GAROFALO—COMEDIAN, WRITER, ACTOR

Perhaps I should have taken better care of myself as a younger person, but I didn't, and this is the way it is. Honestly, I do not mind aging. I don't love some of the stuff that comes with it, but I've got no problem with telling people how old I am. I have no problem with birthdays. I don't have angst over "Oh my God. I'm turning forty-five." That stuff does not bother me, but I don't love waking up in the morning with my back cracking and my ankles hurting, and stuff like that. That is less appealing.

PRESIDENT BARACK OBAMA

I used to play basketball more, but these days I've gotten to the point where it's not as much fun because I'm not as good as I used to be and I get frustrated. I was never great, but I was a good player and I could play seriously. Now I'm like one of these old guys who's running around. The guys I play with, who are all a lot younger, they sort of pity me and sympathize with me. They tolerate me, but they know. We all know that I'm the weak link on the court, and I don't like being the weak link.

TOM SCHARPLING—COMEDIAN, WRITER, RADIO AND PODCAST HOST

I think it is a very bad thing to have a 4 on the front of your age at this point in history because you saw three lifetimes' worth of changes crammed into twenty years, and it's the wrong twenty years to grow up with.

Part of your current daily routine would take half a year not too long ago.

MARGARET CHO—COMEDIAN, WRITER, ACTOR

I want to age really dignified, like Amy Tan. I want to be really thin. I want to have kind of a very sharp, short bob haircut that's gray. I want to wear sort of Mandarin collar shirts all the time and be really, really Amy Tan about it. Teach. Do a lot of workshops. A lot of workshops and a lot of tai chi. I'll be at a university or teaching at a school, although I don't think I can do that because I don't even have a high school diploma.

NORM MACDONALD—COMEDIAN, WRITER, ACTOR

I love super old people because they help you with perspective. I love country songs and shit, but there's this myth about the old guy that never forgot about the girl and he's drinking and shit. That's not true. When you meet old people, you ask, "Hey, is your heart broken?"

"Huh? What?" They don't care. It's all like comedy to them. They have incredible perspective.

Then I was thinking if I could only get that perspective instantly. Just pretend you're a fucking old man and forget stuff instantly.

RUSSELL PETERS—COMEDIAN

You know how you find out what's inappropriate? Talk to an old person. They always just say what they see. There's no malice involved. They just say what the fuck they see.

My dad was born in 1925. He would say things when my friends would come over, and 95 percent of my friends were black. They would come over, and my dad was like, "Russell, there's some Negro here at the door," and I'm like, "Dad, what are you doing?" and you would think my black friend would be like, "What the fuck did you say?" But he'd be like, "Eh, what are you going to do? He's old." There's no malice. It's just, it's really about intent.

RAY ROMANO—COMEDIAN, WRITER, PRODUCER, ACTOR

I remember when I was living in New York and it was ten degrees out and I drove past an old woman at a bus stop at about ten at night, so the buses aren't coming frequently. This was in Queens. She was an old woman. Ten degrees, maybe fifteen degrees, and I'm driving somewhere and I can see her. I think to myself, "That woman could die tonight. At fifteen degrees, she's eightysomething years old." My conscience tells me, "I got to go back and make sure because whatever."

I go around the block and I open my window as I drive by and I just go, "Are you okay?" She's a little startled, like, "Who's this guy talking to me?" She says, "What? What?" And I ask, "Are you okay? It's very cold out. Are you okay?"

She doesn't know, creepy guy talking to her. I saw that I startled her so I drove away, she said she's okay. Then I started thinking, "I just startled her in fifteen-degree weather. What if her heart's skipping beats?" So I had to go around again just to make sure she's calming down.

I went around again and she saw me go around again. Now I'm fucking stuck going around the block all night.

BOB SAGET—COMEDIAN, ACTOR, WRITER

I went through a lot of metaphysical stuff in my twenties. I went to past life therapy. I sat there and went, "Oh, I was a pharaoh when I was fourteen." Then I started getting into drugs, so I was fine after that.

My outlook now is to not be afraid of death. This is a stupid thing to say for a mortal—if you can stop your fear of death or at least stop thinking about it for a while, you can give some thoughtful moments to the things that actually mean something to you.

TERRY GROSS—RADIO HOST

I think about death a fair amount. I'm not obsessed about it or anything. Part of the meaning of life is knowing that you're going to die, that's part of where you derive meaning, knowing that life is a measured amount of time, so you have to use that time wisely.

Marc

Yeah, something like that.

JULIA SWEENEY—COMEDIAN, WRITER, ACTOR

My daughter said to me recently, "You know, Dad's side of the family, they don't even believe in an afterlife. They don't talk about people dying that much. But your side of the family, they all believe in this afterlife"—even though she knows I don't—"you're totally comfortable talking about how this person's going to be dead and soon we'll all be dead and soon we'll all be in the ground." And I think that's healthy. I like it.

I am trying to think about death a lot. I think it gives me a more palpable sensation about being alive. My new thing is when I see babies anywhere, I think, "When that baby's my age, I won't be alive." And it gives you a little tingle. I don't know why that makes me feel calmer.

LENA DUNHAM—ACTOR, WRITER, DIRECTOR, PRODUCER

Sometimes if I'm in the middle of a conversation I think is stupid or unnecessary, the first place my brain goes, is like, "You know we're all going to die someday, you idiots. Why are you being so lame when you're just going to die? What do you think, you're going to live forever because of your stupid green juice, you bitch?"

WILL FORTE—COMEDIAN, ACTOR, WRITER

Every once in a while I will go very big picture on stuff. Ultimate big picture is realizing you're, at some point, going to die. What does it matter anyway? That's the biggest picture. Slightly pulled back from that big picture. I'll go there. "What does it matter?" All I care about are really my family and friends. That's what I really care about.

I remember when my grandma died, and the ultimate big picture thing, I thought, "This is going to happen to all of us. Why do I spend one moment of my life worrying about anything? I should just be not worrying about anything ever."

ROBIN WILLIAMS—COMEDIAN, ACTOR (1951–2014)

One time on TV, David Letterman leaned over to me during a commercial break and said, "Do you find yourself getting really emotional after this heart surgery?" I said, "Yeah," and I started to cry. And then he said, "We're back." I went, "Oh, fuck. I'm not going to break down. I'm not going to pull a Barbara Walters."

I think you get more emotional because literally they've cracked the armor. Guys are like, "Fuck you, man, I'm armored up." Then, the moment they peel you open and it's like literally you have this scar here. They opened you up and literally to the world, went inside, fixed the box, and then sealed you back up again, and said you're back. You're very conscious of it because there's wires and shit and you're literally so vulnerable in a weird way.

MEL BROOKS—COMEDIAN, WRITER, DIRECTOR, PRODUCER, ACTOR, MUSICIAN

The war was, on the surface, a patriotic and exciting phenomenon. Unconsciously, the idea of maybe dying, it was very complicated.

When you're a soldier, and there's any kind of shooting— We'd broadcast and I'd be on the radio. I give them coordinates. I'd start with Y, Tango, you know, Dodge, Easy, Over. Then I'd say, "Can you see the white church? Can you see the steeple, the white church? A little to the left of it. The Germans, go shoot them." I would end up talking like that.

We were in a command car or a jeep, highly mobile. Less than a minute after we broadcast, the road was straddled with gunfire—bang, bang, bang, bang—big shells. They'd get radio coordinates and take the shot at where we just were.

Marc

Dealing day-to-day with the idea that you could get blown up must have driven you nuts.

Mel

It did. We talked to each other. Soldiers would talk to each other. There was a guy from Jersey City. He said, "You know, Mel, it's like a newsreel. We're in a newsreel." I said, "You're right." I never forget it but you're right, we think we're in a newsreel. We don't pay attention to body bags inside.

STEPHEN TOBOLOWSKY—ACTOR

There was a period of time for a couple years, I was doing the TV show *Heroes*. I was slowly losing my voice. I didn't know how or why. It was scaring me because I'm an actor. I didn't know what it was. Eventually it got to the point where I couldn't talk. I went to the head of Cedars-Sinai, like head and neck and everything, and he said, "Well, you have a growth on your vocal cord," and that was enough to make me piss my pants and I was terrified.

I went to see my brother in Dallas, who's a doctor. He sent me to a friend of his who said, "You need surgery yesterday. Why have you not had surgery?" I had surgery. I couldn't speak for like two months. I couldn't speak, I couldn't sneeze, I couldn't whisper. I had to write. When I was pissed off I had to write in red ink. I had no options but just to write. When I was recovering from this, I remember I was getting these dull headaches at the same time, so with the fact that I couldn't speak, I couldn't work, I had dull headaches, I naturally thought I had a brain tumor.

Yeah, so the doctor sent me to a head and neck specialist. The head and neck specialist did X-rays of me, a whole CAT scan of me and told me, "Well, you have advanced arthritis of the neck so bad that the spine of your neck is 180 degrees curved the absolutely wrong way. You have ossification of the vertebrae." I'm going home thinking, "Not only can I not talk, but now I'm crippled! I've always been a healthy guy, why do I have this ossification of the neck?" Well, to recover from the throat surgery I was told to go somewhere where I could be quiet, so I thought I could go fishing. But that's a bad idea because when you catch a fish, you scream, "Oh, shit!" and I can't do that.

The other thing was to go horseback riding in Iceland, which I'd been to before.

Marc

Sure, that's a common thing that people do when they're stressed out. I've heard that horseback riding in Iceland is at the top of everyone's list.

Stephen

Oh, it's beautiful. You get on that horse and ride. My wife and I, we were riding to an active volcano, very close to the one that exploded.

Marc

Also, another nonstressful thing to do, to ride a horse directly into an active volcano. It's all making sense, Stephen.

Stephen

The last day of the trek, I get up on the ridge of the volcano and a wind comes and lifts me and the horse off the ground and threw us! The head of the riding group ran over and I was getting back on my horse and he said, "Are you okay after the fall?" Then I said, "What fall?" He said, "Get off the horse."

They drove me over to a little town and the woman said, "You know, I'm putting you in a neck brace. We're sending you to Reykjavík to be CAT scanned." They CAT scanned me there. I had a broken neck. The guy said, "Yeah, you've, you've fractured a vertebra." They put me in one of those soft collars like people get when they have whiplash.

Marc

Or when they want to make money off a doctor in court.

Stephen

Yeah. I'm getting on the plane going back from Iceland to New York and there's a guy there who happened to be a surgeon from Mount Sinai Hospital in New York. He loved me from *Deadwood* and said, "Man, have you found out a way to get onto the plane without waiting with the collar?"

I said, "Well, actually, I just broke my neck here."

This guy turned pale, and he said, "Are you kidding me?"

I said, "No, sir."

He said, "Well, you are in the wrong collar. You could die on this flight. You have to be in a hard collar. This is not gonna keep your neck stable. You have to hold your neck the entire time you're on the flight. Don't pick up a bag, don't move, don't do anything."

He said, "Do you have a head and neck specialist?" Voilà! I happened to have a head and neck specialist. Who in the world has a head and neck specialist? I had one who just did a whole series of X-rays on me, like, three weeks ago!

I said, "Yes, I have a head and neck specialist in Los Angeles."

He said, "You go to that head and neck specialist immediately."

I went back to New York holding my neck the entire way. I went from New York to LA holding my neck the entire way. I go to my head and neck specialist and he does another series of X-rays. He turns pale.

He said, "They misdiagnosed you in Iceland. You don't have a broken vertebra. You have five broken vertebrae from C2 to C7. You have a fatal injury. Your C4 vertebra is crushed." The same as Christopher Reeve.

He said, "I want to show you why you're alive." He took me over to his computer, where he had the picture of the X-rays. There, on the X-rays, he said, "Do you see your neck? Because of the arthritis in your neck, because the curve of your neck was 180 degrees different than it should have been, it made the force of the blow go into your shoulders instead of into your spinal cord. Because your vertebrae were ossified, it protected your spinal column. You are alive because of your malady."

Now, when you have a broken neck, and a lot of people out there don't know this, you have to remain vertical for three months. I mean vertical. You cannot lie down. When you go to bed, you have to sleep vertically. You have to lean up against the wall like you're in a bus stop. The neck brace can never come off. I made the mistake once of taking the brace off, thinking, "Well, I can lie down." The world went away. My vision went dark, I suddenly couldn't breathe, I couldn't move. Fortunately, I screamed. Ann put the brace back on and I sat up again, but I realized that was the last time I was ever going to be horizontal for the next three and a half months. It was a nightmare. It isn't just pain. It stops your central organs from functioning. Your heart stops, your breath stops, and if one of those vertebrae, as they're healing, slips, you're in blinding pain. You lose your vision, you lose your hearing, you lose your ability to breathe, you feel your heart stopping. It's a nightmare of darkness.

After this, I went to prayer services twice a day for a couple years because I lost my mother. Not because of my neck. It was during this period of time. There is one of the psalms you read in the morning service that God counts the number of stars in the sky. He heals the brokenhearted. He knows the secrets of the ocean.

I asked my doctor, I said, "How does this neck brace thing work? How do I heal? How does this happen?" He said, "Well, the brace holds the broken ends together, and after a month the ends get kind of sticky. Then after two months the stickiness becomes a soft bond. After three months it becomes a hard bond, then it's solid." I said, "No, that ain't my question. I get that. How does it happen?"

He said, "Oh, we don't know."

I realized, God heals the brokenhearted, and that's when I think, Oh, I get it. The astronomers say they don't know the number of stars in the sky. You can't talk about God because who knows what it is? Who knows what the concept is, but I felt it when I had my broken neck. I said, "I got it. I got it now." It's that life force that connects me and you and all of us together that you want the other guy to do better. You want the other guy to heal. It's that thing, the force of positiveness that moves us forward in the universe.

I mean, that's the only thing I could say it is and the broken neck made me see the wonders of it all. It made me see things I never saw before. I know people who have cancer and people who have heart disease and people with broken necks, they say it's a blessing. I'll join that long list of people with the same boring kind of thing and say, "Yeah, it was a blessing. The broken neck was a blessing."

JOSH HOMME—MUSICIAN

I got this MRSA infection, which is an antibiotic-resistant staph. I couldn't shake it because my immune system was so destroyed. People die of that all the time. In fact, down the hall someone died of it while I was in the hospital, and I was like, "Oh, no. What have I done?" Then when I was having surgery to try and fix it, they lost me trying to get the oxygen tube down my throat and reoxygenate my blood. I choked to death.

There was no tunnel.

When I woke up I knew something was wrong, someone had hurt me. Really something was stolen from me or I had lost something because it took a couple of years to recover. I've always heard music in my head since I was a little kid. When I woke up this time, I heard nothing for a couple of years and it affected me.

Marc

Oh my God. They told you you died?

Josh

Yeah. My doctor was like, "Whoa. I lost you. I thought you were going to stay lost."

I knew it. I could feel it in my body. When you get defibrillated, you're being electrocuted. You wake up and you feel like you've been beat up. Feels like you've been in a car crash. Then I was kind of contagious and in bed for four months and you can't hug your little kid. Your mind starts to play tricks on you. I'd never been knocked down that hard. You're in your tower without the Rapunzel hair.

I was stuck in a room for four months. I had to have these tubes in my leg and it was painful. Then all of a sudden after two months in bed you go, "I've got two months left. How do I do this?" It did the greatest thing it could ever do to me. It zeroed me. I was below zero. I had to crawl back up to zero, and I'm really thankful for it because I know what's important.

MEL BROOKS

I was on a show once, and the announcer who was interviewing me said, "So, when you were only two and a half or so, you lost your father." I took a pause.

I said, "No, no, no, no. He was dead. He wasn't lost. We knew just where he was. He was in the back. Finally, they took him away and they put him in some cemetery, but we never lost him. We were never that careless with our father. We cared about him."

JON HAMM—ACTOR, DIRECTOR

My dad had a lot of sadness in him. His first wife passed away suddenly. My mother, his second wife, passed away at a very young age. They were divorced at that point, but still, that's a bummer.

Marc

You remember your mom passing away.

Jon

Yeah. Vividly. No fun. She had cancer and it was no good. She was single. I was living with her. She got custody and I'd go every other weekend to my dad's. She had just massive, rapid abdominal cancer. This is 1980 in St. Louis. Obviously, it's not like we were living in the Mayo Clinic or anything, or Manhattan where there's up-to-date blah blah blah. There was just no treatment. It was kind of like, well, let's cut it out. We'll see what we can do.

They took out a bunch of her colon and they didn't get it all and it was in her liver, in her stomach, and that's a wrap.

It was not fun. It was not a good time. You're ten, so you have no mechanism to deal with it either. There's just nothing. You have family and you have friends, but your friends are ten. We're not going to get a beer and commiserate. It's going to be, "You want to play kickball?" All right. That's all we got.

It's the lamest expression in the world, but it is what it is and you can't do anything but get through it.

LESLIE JONES—COMEDIAN, WRITER, ACTOR

The conversation my dad and I had before he passed was, because, like, he used to always give my brother favor and I used to be like, "You never had to take care of me. My brother, you had to bail out of jail, you had to do all kinds of stuff. You never had to take care of me. I never came to you to borrow money. You never had to take care of me, ever. Even when I dropped out of school, I took care of myself, and I was just always wondering why you were always so fucking hard on me."

He said, "Because of just what you said, I never had to take care of you. Your brother, I've had to take care of him." He was like, "You're the one thing that I'm going to be proud that I had, and you're so funny. It was all worth it because you are really funny."

It was good to get there before he passed.

"WEIRD AL" YANKOVIC—MUSICIAN, ACTOR, DIRECTOR

It's always hard for me to relive my parents' deaths because it was the singular most traumatic thing that ever happened to me and I still feel the pain to this day. The shock has worn off, for the most part, but it's a pain that I still carry with me.

I was on the road and I got a phone call from my wife, in tears. I thought at the time that if she called up in tears, "Oh, her bird died. This is horrible." It turned out, my parents both had passed away because of the flue being closed in their house and they had the fireplace going. They both died from carbon monoxide poisoning.

It was, obviously, horrible. I could barely function, but I figured I had a responsibility. I had a show that night. I was in the middle of a tour. I had a small army of people depending on me, so I put my blinders on and I went into denial mode. I basically went on-stage every single night, did the full show, acted like everything was just fine, but afterward—no meet and greets, no nothing. I just went and collapsed and just was a sobbing mess. In a way, it kind of got me through it because I needed denial at that point. It was just too much for me to accept. I was able to, for a couple hours every night, to have a break from the horror of my situation. Every now and then I'd have a lyric talking about my mother or whatever, and then I'd be like, "Ohhh."

I've heard from so many people over the years that my music has gotten them through a very hard, trying time of their life. I thought, "Well, maybe it'll do the same for me." In a way, it did. Here's the thing, I always knew intellectually that someday my parents were going to pass away and I'd have to deal with it, but I never thought it would be out of the blue and at the same time.

Also, I thought I'd be able to deal with my grief very privately, but instead, it became a worldwide news story. I didn't want people walking on eggshells around me. I didn't want people treating me differently. I was doing a comedy show every night. I didn't want people going there and feeling sorry for me.

I think the first night, I don't even know if my crew knew. I think maybe the guys in my band knew. Then, it became a headline on CNN, so at that point everybody knew. We had a slide that we showed before the show started, saying: "Tonight's performance is in honor of my parents." It was sort of like dealing with the eight-hundred-pound gorilla and getting it out there. At that point, we did the show as normal. The outpouring of support from the fans was just unbelievable. I didn't ever think I'd want to share my grief with people, but it really was cathartic and was nice to know that people had my back.

MOLLY SHANNON—COMEDIAN, ACTOR

My dad raised two kids by himself. My mom died when I was four and a half, so it was hard on him. He was a single dad left with a four-year-old and a six-year-old. My little sister Katy was also killed in that car accident, and he was driving.

It was a station wagon, and it was late at night, and he was going to drop my cousin off, and my aunt let our cousin's friend go with us too. My dad and I talked about it later. I think he would have liked my mom to drive, but she was like, "No, you can drive."

I don't know if he nodded off. I don't know what happened, but at that time, they didn't have breakaway lampposts, so he just smashed into it. Nowadays they'll bend, or they'll break away. My mom was in the front and he was in the front. My sister and I were in the very back of the station wagon, so we were bruised up, but my baby sister, Katy, and my cousin Fran were in the middle, so they were killed. It was very sad.

We went to the hospital, and I remember having a fantasy that they were still alive. My sister and I were in beds next to one another in the hospital, and developmentally there's such a big difference between a six-year-old understanding what's going on, and a four-year-old. I was really out of it, in fantasy, like, "They must be somewhere else up there, on a different floor." My sister kind of knew what had happened, and kind of had to answer questions and talk to people. She was the one that was the most with it. Basically, I remember thinking, "I want to go see Katy." I really wanted to see my baby sister, because I thought she must be with the other babies.

There were a lot of kids on our floor and I was helping them. They didn't have parents coming to visit them, so I helped those kids. I remember playing with them, and helping them, and I think that's instantly where I went to. Then there were all these people bringing us toys and all that stuff. I was like, "Why are all these people bringing us toys?" Relatives bringing us toys, and then I said, "I really want to go see my mom and my sister now." I assumed they were alive. I finally put on my robe and wanted to go see them.

They were like, "I'm so sorry. . . ." I think an aunt told me or something. "We're so sorry, but they've gone to heaven." I was like, "What? Can we get there? Could we fly there, or take a hot air balloon, or could we take an airplane?" I just couldn't accept the fact that we couldn't get there. I kind of kept on that for a long time.

It's very complicated, but I think there's no way that you can take that in. It would just annihilate you when you're that little, so you just kind of go into some fantasy of waiting and waiting.

Then in the night, I remember screaming, "I want my mommy!" I just remember feeling so deflated.

Marc

Did you envy people who had moms? Did you have anger?

Molly

I was so close to my dad that I didn't really feel that way, but I remember if a teacher put her arm on me, I was like, "That feels so good." It made me feel really shy. I think for teachers like in third grade, I didn't want to get too close, so I would act really bad, just so I could be in control. I was like, "I could act bad so that way I'm in charge." Does that make sense?

I think when you're that little, you feel like you must have done something wrong to make them leave. You're too self-centered, so you think you must have done something wrong.

I have a different take on everything now. I feel so lucky. I feel like I don't take things for granted at all, because I feel like, "Oh my God, I pulled myself up out of the wreckage, and I created a life for myself, and now I'm a mom, and I have children, and I got help for myself so that I can start my own family." It's a miracle. My sister and I talk about it. We feel really lucky. It might not have gone that way, you know?

ARTIE LANGE—COMEDIAN, WRITER, ACTOR, RADIO HOST

My father was a very blue-collar guy. He climbed roofs for a living. He got to about ninth grade, my father. He grew up on the street in Newark. The toughest, most street-smart guy I ever knew in my life. I looked up to him. He was like my best friend but too much of a best friend. You find that out later in life.

He fell off a roof a week after my eighteenth birthday and became a quadriplegic.

I worked with him. My job was to hold the ladder and that day . . . I sound like I grew up in the 1940s sometimes, but I used to hustle pool. My buddies and I used to play nine ball and we used to go to the local county college and go into the game room. It was free fucking money. We would pretend we didn't know each other and we'd get into a nine ball game. If you hit the five in, it was twenty bucks. The nine was thirty. My buddy would set me up to shoot them in and the third guy would pay me. Then I'd split the money with my friends, until a guy found out and we almost got our ass kicked.

That day I was supposed to hold the ladder and I didn't go to work with him. I told him I was going to look for a job and I went to shoot pool. I shot pool all day. I got home and my mom said, "He fell off a roof." He put the ladder on top of a picnic table to get to the top of the roof and he went to swing a hammer and it fell. He fell thirty feet on his head and became a quadriplegic. Had no insurance. Nothing. We went broke. He lasted four and a half years before he died. I think he offed himself through the help of crazy friends that he had. There was no autopsy.

Marc
You felt guilty?

Artie
God yeah, that I wasn't there to hold the ladder. For a long time.

He would ask me to kill him every week. He's like, "Just fucking shoot me." He couldn't move from the neck down. We had to feed him. It's a living hell. He always said God was punishing him. He was an atheist, my father. My mother, big Catholic. My father would always say to me, "Don't tell your mother I told you, but there's nothing fucking up there." He'd always say to me, "Do all the shit, get the confirmation, but there's nothing up there." Then when you're a quadriplegic for four years, he started to think maybe there is.

If there is a heaven or hell, I hope God gave him his hell here.

JACK ANTONOFF—MUSICIAN, PRODUCER

I had two siblings, now one is dead. My youngest sister, about eleven years ago, died of brain cancer. It's terrible. It's just the worst thing ever.

We have this argument a lot in my family. When you get that question—How many siblings do you have?—what do you say? So I usually say, "I have a sister."

She was thirteen, I was eighteen. My entire life is based off that moment. Music, everything. It was the single most important thing that ever happened to me and probably will happen to me. Something froze there, and I think I'm constantly looking back on it. I'm thirty and I'm dealing with that at thirty. At forty, I'll be dealing with that at forty. I don't think that goes away. I wouldn't want it to go away.

MIKE DESTEFANO—COMEDIAN, DRUG COUNSELOR (1966–2011)

When I was twenty-one, I found out I'm HIV positive. I was diagnosed with HIV. This is twenty-three years ago, and that's what changed my fucking life. That's what just changed every priority. When you know that you've got four or five years to live, for real, you change shit.

I met my wife at the support group, the AIDS support group that we went to. I used to walk around and look at women that were in this particular building, the Gay Men's Health Crisis, and I'd go, "Oh, I hope she has AIDS!" That's the way it was back then, it was like, "Please, I hope she has AIDS."

I met this beautiful girl, Fran, and she had been a recovering addict as well, and she was also positive. One thing that the HIV thing gave me was, it gave me that sense of "I don't give a fuck, I'm not afraid of anything," and that's what I was always looking for as a kid. I wanted to be a gangster so I could be unafraid. I was on the fence. I lived on the fence most of my life. I was a kid riding my bicycle and I saw these two guys giving a cabdriver a beating, and when I say a beating, they were slamming his fucking head in the door of the car, they were fucking pulverizing this guy, and I remember looking at them, going, "I want to be like them," and then I looked down at the guy that was being hit, and I felt bad for him. I was like, "This poor guy." Then I spent the rest of my life trying to figure out, "Which one am I going to be? Those are the only two fucking paths." That was like, "This is what I have to choose from."

We move to Florida because of the health. We were dying. We came down here, I was twenty-two, she was a little older than me, she was about twenty-eight or twenty-nine, and we literally came to Florida like two old people would do. That's what my life was at that time. I didn't know how long I would live. Back then, people got the virus, they died in four to five years. I expected that to happen.

I noticed her getting sick during playing tennis, which is weird. We're playing tennis back and forth, and she wasn't moving as quick as she was. I said, "What's the matter?" She says, "My legs hurt, I have pains in my legs." We went to the doctor, and it was a thing called neuropathy, which meant that her immune system was really low and fucked-up. It was causing nerve damage in her body. That was the beginning of it. It was the beginning of such a long and fucking painful deterioration. It was a slow, fucked-up time for me back then.

It was about a five-year period of slow deterioration, and then these rapid, fucked-up things, where she had pneumonia like fifteen times, she was in the hospital, and she was given her last rites a few times and survived it and came back. It was just a brutal, brutal time.

I was her caregiver. I never thought of leaving her. I never even considered it. Today, it's the greatest decision I've made. It's the greatest thing I've ever done, was care for my wife. I'll never do anything that great again. Fucking HBO specials, whatever you want to give me. Nothing will be better than that, because it was such a deep reckoning within myself that I am not a piece of shit. That I don't deserve to stick needles in my arm. I am a good person. Look what I'm capable of. I'm capable of deep love and commitment. That was my whole life, was taking care of her.

I was not in the room when she died. I had been by her side every night. Her mother had been in town the night she died, and her mother wanted to stay with her alone, and I left her there, and I went home, and that's the night that she passed away. It's not a very big deal to me. I know what I did for her.

During her last days, she was in the hospice. I had just gotten a Harley, my first Harley. I rode up on one today. I love motorcycles. She came out and saw it, and she got upset. She was angry at me and she went back inside all pissed off. This gay dude that worked there— That's a group of people that, without them I wouldn't be alive. Gay men fucking saved my ass. The AIDS organizations, they're all run by gays. The hospices, the nurses were all gay guys. They've got some deep well of love within them that's just incredible.

So she goes inside, and she was pissed off that I had the motorcycle. This gay guy, let's call him "Bill." I say, "Why is she so mad at me?" Bill says, "Well, she just feels like you're moving on with your life and you don't love her anymore, you have this motorcycle. You don't need her anymore." That was a strange thing, and I realized how much I did need her. I loved her, she was my best friend. What I did was, I went home and I brought some of my work shirts back to the hospice, and I brought them into her room and said, "Franny, my shirts are a fucking mess, I need you to iron them for me." She got all, "Fuck you, I'm in hospice," you know. I left, I come back twenty minutes later, all the shirts are ironed, she got up, and then she's like, "Where's the motorcycle?" Now she's excited about it. I guess that guy was right. She just wanted to know that I still needed her, like I loved her, you know what I mean? People don't know they're dying. They feel like, "I'm alive right now." Dying is an event, they pass away at one moment. Up until that moment, they are alive, and they want to be loved, and they want to give and share in that case.

Now she wants to see the motorcycle. I take her out. She wants to sit on it. I put her on it. She wants to start it up. She's wearing a paper dress, essentially, she's got her morphine pole next to her and she's sitting on this Harley; I'm worried about her burning her frigging leg off. She says, "Can you just take me for a little ride around the parking lot?" I'm like, "No, I can't." Then it just hits me, I'm like, "No, you have to. You're in this moment, you have to do this motorcycle ride." Fuck, of course I will, yeah. I'm riding around the hospice parking lot, and then my friend comes barreling in in this van who's a cripple in a wheelchair, laughing, saying, "What are you doing?" I said, "I'm riding Franny around." Franny's like, "Can we just go out on the street a little bit?" She's holding the pole! It was a pole with four wheels on the bottom, and we're riding around this hospice! You can hear the goddamn wheels clanging and banging. It was insane.

I pass the front door and all these nurses are standing out front and they're all crying. They're watching us and they're fucking crying. I didn't know why they were crying. I was like, "Why are they crying?" I didn't get what they were seeing. I didn't know, because I was just in it. I was living it. I knew my wife, who had suffered, the suffering that she had been through in her life. She was a prostitute, she was a fucking heroin addict, she was beaten by fucking pimps, and this is her past, you know? Then she ends up with AIDS, and she's dying. All she wants is a fucking ride on my motorcycle. What a gift, you know?

Next thing you know, we're on I-95. Women, it's never enough for them. We're on I-95, she unhooks the fucking pole, and she's holding the morphine bag over her head, with her gown on that's flying up in the air. You could see her entire fucking naked, bony body, with the morphine bag whipping in the wind, and we're passing by these guys in their Lamborghinis and shit, and I'm looking at them like, "What kind of life are you living? Look at me! I'm on top of the world here!" That was the last thing I did with her. I feel so blessed and lucky. You can't ask for a better moment and memory than that.

It's beautiful stuff. The biggest things that we're afraid of really can be the most beautiful if you look them right in the fucking eye and you don't flinch, because there's something really beautiful behind it, you know?

AMAZING JOHNATHAN—COMEDIAN, MAGICIAN

About six years ago, I got diagnosed with a heart condition. Cardiomyopathy. It's degenerative. They said it's because I might have had a virus when I was a kid.

Now I've been given a time stamp. Two years. Maybe a year to two years. Right now, my heart is failing, and they can't get me a transplant because I'm diabetic and they won't give it to a diabetic.

I have a whole thing I got to wear that is a defibrillator that's over my heart. It's a real pain in the ass to wear it. I got electrodes all over the place. If I pass out, this thing will detect that, and I have thirty seconds to shut it off. If I don't shut it off, it shoots this blue jelly all over me, conductive jelly, and zaps me.

It warns people, stay away from me. People will start to touch you and shake you, "Are you all right?" It will stop their heart and start mine.

It's kind of like the ultimate practical joke.

If you ask me if I'm partying, fuck yeah, man. If I can get my hands on anything right now, I'd do it. The pain level in my hands and my feet right now, it's so bad. From my heart not pumping blood to my extremities. My hands are always tingling. I can't walk more than twenty feet.

You'll see me looking for heroin in about two months. Wouldn't you, if you were dying?

MIKE DESTEFANO

I've got to be honest, part of this having HIV, and my wife dying of AIDS and, there's this one part of it that I love, that I can look at anybody and say, "Really? Is that your fucking problem? Fuck you!" You know what I mean?

"What do you got, herpes? You fucking cunt. Get a real disease!"

"I got hepatitis."

"Give me your hepatitis, I'll give you what I got." There's something cool about that, having the worst fucking disease.

I'm in a hospital, I ended up with pneumonia, had nothing to do with HIV. I end up with this double pneumonia. My wife's still alive; she's home very sick. I'm fucking worried about her, lying in the hospital. She decides to get in the car and drive to come visit me, crashes the car on I-95. They tell me, "Your wife's in the emergency room." Downstairs of the hospital that I'm in with pneumonia. My wife's down there, my wife who's dying of AIDS is in the hospital from a car wreck that flipped over. Then the phone rings again, my mother tells me, "Dad got a brain tumor."

This is all in a ten-minute fucking period. This is a bad day. If someone says, "Oh, I'm having a rough day," yeah, tell me about it. Let me fucking hear about your bad day, you fuck. I love having that power. I don't know why, I just do.

PAUL THOMAS ANDERSON—WRITER, DIRECTOR, PRODUCER

I remember talking to an oncologist on the phone who was essentially telling me that there was no way my dad was going to make it, and one of the first things that popped into my mind was, "You're telling me that frogs are falling from the sky." I remember that kind of popping into my mind. I thought hearing that your dad is going to die is as bizarre as hearing that frogs are falling from the sky.

SAM SIMON—WRITER, DIRECTOR, PRODUCER, ACTIVIST, PHILANTHROPIST (1955–2015)

Cancer is a battle. I have good days and bad days. People tell me that I look great, and I don't have looks cancer. I will be a good-looking corpse. I've always been good-looking. My noble features will not be affected by this horrible disease.

I was given three to six months to live six months ago, and I just got my scans back. After six months of chemo, which is just so awful. I can't even tell you. Right now is the best I feel, because I'm a week on chemo drugs, and then I get a week off, and over the course of that week, the last couple days I'll start feeling pretty good, and then Wednesday morning I go in and I start the whole thing over again.

But the scans say that my tumors have shrunk, and what does that mean? I don't know, because my doctor refused to explain it to me. He said, "Look, we're meeting on Wednesday. Can't I just do this on Wednesday?"

Does it mean they're going to all shrink and go away? Does it mean the chemo . . . I don't know, but I will accept it. He told me it was good news and he told me he was very happy with it, so I'll just take his word for it for a week.

Marc

Do you think about it a lot?

Sam

I would say it enters my mind every three minutes. You think about it constantly. Most of the time I don't feel good and most of the time I can't really do anything. With dogs, I've had to euthanize all my dogs. People get upset about euthanizing animals, but I love my dogs, and I've killed every one of them. I've done it when the time was right, and what does that mean? It means you write down the three things your dog likes the most, and when they can't do that stuff anymore, it's time to put them out of their misery.

One of my three things would be lying in bed and watching TV.

By that criterion, I will never be euthanized, but I do wish I could do something. I can't drive. There's a lot of stuff I just don't feel up to.

I always had authority issues, and I always felt rules didn't apply to me. I always thought I was special, and I've always been kind of combative. My whole life, I've been labeled as someone that has a bad attitude, but now that I have cancer, all those qualities have helped. My doctors, they say, "You have a really good attitude about this," and it's all the stuff that made me a shitty person.

Now when this doctor said I have three to six months to live, for whatever reason, when the doctor said that, I just didn't believe him for a second. I plan on getting better. I'm not sure exactly what that means.

You just get thrown into this. I've been feeling sick for a long time. I went in and got some tests. I was misdiagnosed with a virus or something, but I didn't get better. I went in. They found something in my blood.

Then I meet the doctor. For the first time, I meet him, and he shows me my scans, and I don't know what I'm looking at. I say, "Whoa, that's really cool." He goes, "All the white parts are cancer."

"Oh. Fuck."

"It's in your liver. It's all through your connective tissue. It's in one kidney. It's in your colon, and it's in your lymph system."

As a writer, I should avoid clichés, but I was in the moment, and I said, "Is it curable?" That's what you ask, and he said, "We don't use that word." I went, "Oh, fuck. That's not good." Because they'd be happy to use it if they cured anybody.

I said, "How long do I have?" Another cliché.

"We don't answer that question."

I got upset. I said, "Look, I'm not going to hold you to the answer. I don't know what these rules are. This just seems ridiculous to me. Just, as a hypothetical question, if you saw this scan on somebody, worst-case scenario, how long do they have?"

He says, "Well, I suppose under those circumstances, I can answer the question. I would say you have between—"

Then his cell phone went off.

There was some confusion between him and his wife over who was going to pick his daughter up after judo class, and he straightened that out, and then he says, "Where were we? Okay."

That's when he said three to six months.

Then he said, "Are you all right?"

I say, "What?"

He says, "Your eyes look unfocused," and I said, "Well, yeah, that news you gave me, with your great bedside manner, that stuff you broke to me so gently. I'm about to faint."

TOM GREEN—COMEDIAN, WRITER, ACTOR, TALK SHOW HOST

Everywhere I go, when I'm on tour, there's always inevitably one kid every week, and he'll come up to me and go, "Hey, man. You know, I have testicular cancer." I had it, and we talk about it, and it's sort of an emotional thing.

On the other hand, every time I go anywhere, someone else will probably yell out of a cab, "Hey, how's your nut, Tom?" You know, "How's your ball doing, buddy?" Which happens so frequently that you wouldn't even believe it, and people think they're being funny. Because I made a joke about it myself.

I don't think people always realize that part of the reason, I think, we make jokes sometimes about things that are scary is because we're sort of using it as a self-defense mechanism. Cancer is scary, and crazy, and sort of surreal, and it changes you forever. You sort of realize that, you know, we could potentially be dead at any moment, so. . . . On one hand, you're like, "Okay, this is great," you know, "Let's live life for the moment. Let's be positive. Let's enjoy every moment, because life is short." On the other hand, you're also in a panic.

You feel that sort of very real possibility that something could go wrong with your body, which you don't normally think about when you're twenty-eight. We're going to die. It's definitely going to happen, but I always assumed it would be, "Okay, I'll live to be eighty, like my grandparents, and I got a long time to screw around until then." But no.

Now I'm completely cancer-free, and there's no issue or no chance of it returning.

They go in from above. They don't, like, hack apart your scrotum or anything like that. The sack is completely intact. They go in from above, they kind of reach in, and they—this is what I say—they shuck it out like an oyster, is what they do. I looked at the prosthetic balls, I looked at them. My doctor said, "You know, some people elect to do this, but I wouldn't necessarily say it's important." I'm glad I didn't do it. I can't imagine having a piece of plastic in there, because you'd be squeezing it all the time, but then you'd be probably squeezing, like, the scrotal skin, would probably be getting it all bruised up. I'm glad I didn't get it.

The thing that happened with the cancer, which I think is something that I'm really only kind of figuring out now and I'm still kind of coming to grips with it, is that it was just a physically very demanding thing. It took a major toll on my body, on my physical energy level, and so I went from being this sort of really hyper person to being more calm. I have a bit of a lack of energy.

I remember the first time I went snowboarding again after I got sick, and I used to be really into snowboarding and skateboarding, and we'd go snowboard all day, and I went snowboarding, I couldn't even get to the bottom of the hill without, "I'm going to sit down, take a breath."

It took quite a while for me to kind of realize that I was kind of going through some stuff that wasn't really anything about the beating the cancer, it was just, I have to kind of find a way to kind of get my body healthy again. In the last year or so, I've really kind of figured I have to get out there and exercise. Look after myself a bit more.

MEL BROOKS

You know, they say, "Well, shuffle off this mortal coil. The table is needed for somebody else. We need that table." As long as I feel okay, as long as I have energy, and as long as I still love singing and comedy and entertainment and people, and some food. As long as I still have an appetite, it's great.

I mean, I'm not complaining.

LIFE LESSONS

"Messy for Everybody"

Here's what I've learned:

Try to shut up and listen, and listen with your heart.

If you don't know something, admit it. Don't pretend like you do. Learn.

Don't exhaust yourself with anger at things you have no control over.

Most of the shit you are reacting to most of the time is stuff that your brain is making up, and you have some control over that.

If someone needs help, try to help, if you can.

Be honest.

Be nice.

Learn and know your limitations and work from there.

Talk to people. It helps everyone involved.

No yelling.

Get your yearly physical.

Try to accept who you are.

Don't hurt yourself because you don't like yourself.

Apologize.

MEL BROOKS—COMEDIAN, WRITER, DIRECTOR, PRODUCER, ACTOR, MUSICIAN

I've been having fun. You know, what do you live for? Occasionally, you live for a grilled cheese sandwich, and fun.

CONAN O'BRIEN—TALK SHOW HOST, COMEDIAN, WRITER

I used to believe that worry was a talisman against something bad happening to you. I'm a worrier, and I'm a guy that prepares, and I'm a guy that really tries to plan it out and make sure that I take care of everything. You can do that, and things can still go to shit, so you relax a little bit as you get older because you realize it's no guarantee against things, so why not try and enjoy it a little more?

BRUCE SPRINGSTEEN—MUSICIAN, SONGWRITER, AUTHOR

If you want to live a life, you've got to realize you are not going to be the writer of your own script. Life is something that happens. You don't happen to it. It happens to you. You've got to allow it, in all of its often-uncontrollable chaos, to come into your life. The way you reach adulthood is, you realize that you have the power to withstand the hurricane forces that uncontrolled events bring into your life.

What comes with those uncontrolled events? Love, happiness, fulfillment, satisfaction. You let all those things in too, which if you are a control nut, you squeeze out, because what's more dangerous than love? There's nothing more dangerous than that. You don't know what the hell's going to happen.

RUPAUL CHARLES—ACTOR, DRAG PERFORMER, SINGER, MODEL, WRITER, TELEVISION HOST

My acting teacher told me the best advice I'd ever gotten from anybody ever and since. He said, "Ru, don't take life too effing seriously." That is the key to navigating this life. Don't take it so seriously, and that's when the party begins.

If you take that red pill and you start your journey, you're going to discover, like Dorothy—all roads lead to Oz—that you get up close and you look behind that curtain, you go, "You're the wizard? Really?"

Then you get to know the wizard, and you go, "Okay, so everything was all in my head. I imagined this whole thing?" That's wherein lies the party. That's where you can really have some fun. The only thing you have to watch out for is other people who feel threatened by your party.

JASON SEGEL—COMEDIAN, ACTOR, WRITER

You have this idea of I need to get there, but then you find out "there" keeps moving. If your impulse is I need to get there, that's never going to go away. It's been the past few years when I've realized I'm good. Everything is going great, and let's focus on life stuff.

KEVIN HART—COMEDIAN, ACTOR

I find a positive in anything negative that happens, because I know it happened for a reason. For me, I refuse to treat people like shit because I see that things come full circle.

JIM NORTON—COMEDIAN, ACTOR, RADIO HOST

I take pictures with celebrities. I didn't do it for a long time and then I met Richard Pryor. He was my idol, so I got an autograph. I always regret not taking a photo, but I am happy that I got an autograph. With the photos, it became something I started to do.

Ozzy was one of the first photos I took. I probably was with Jim Florentine. We met Ozzy. Jim's like, "Get a picture." I was like, "Yeah, I should get one."

Then it became addictive. I noticed that sometimes I got good stories out of it, sometimes I didn't. It just became this fun thing. And if I'm ever saying, "I feel sorry for myself, my life is not this or that," it's like, "You fucking cunt. Shut up, you fuck. Look at what you're doing. You're meeting your idols. You're having fun. Shut your fucking mouth." It was like a visual slap to my fucking spoiled face. You're one of the lucky ones, man. I get so mad at myself for that fucking sense of entitlement or "I deserve more. I should have more." To me, the photos are a way of saying, "Look at what a fun life you had there. It's fucking fun what you do."

BRUCE SPRINGSTEEN

Your desperation has to be greater than your fear. Your desperation, your hunger, your desires, your ego, your ambitions have to be greater than your fear of complete humiliation. So as long as you have that equation correctly balanced, you're going out there, my friend, no matter what happens. Because you have to.

CONAN O'BRIEN

I swear to God this is true. Get yourselves into situations where you don't have a choice. I really believe that's the definition of accomplishing a lot of things in this life. I have some part of me, I'm not a brave person. I don't even think of myself as someone who has a lot of guts, but I will get myself into situations where the house is on fire, and there's only one way out, which is through the front door. Then, people later on give you credit for going through the front door, and you say, "Well, there was really nowhere else to go."

In '93 when I replaced David Letterman from complete obscurity, I got myself into a situation, and I was very aware that, "Man, this is a fucking serious situation I'm in." The only way out was to survive it. That's the only way out, because if I had been taken off the air after six months, I would just become a Trivial Pursuit question.

JUDD APATOW—COMEDIAN, DIRECTOR, WRITER, PRODUCER

I often think it's ridiculous that in this business, at some point you start to make a living at it, because it is the perfect example of something that you would do for free. I say to my kids, "I don't know what you want to do for a living. I just lucked out that the thing I do pays well, but I would do it anyway. It's just it happened to be a weird jackpot, but if it was like, eighteen grand a year, I probably would be doing it right now and we would be in a tiny apartment together."

BOB ODENKIRK—ACTOR, WRITER, DIRECTOR, COMEDIAN

I told my little daughter this the other night. We were talking about some comedy scene that I'd showed her or she'd seen, and I said, "So you see, honey, that's what comedy is. Comedy is about honesty." Because that is a very core truth to me. For me, comedy has always been a way to be honest about shit. Like, just fucking say what you're thinking.

GARRY SHANDLING—COMEDIAN, WRITER, ACTOR (1949–2016)

Needing to know the answer is an addiction. The truth actually is in the silence. People are afraid to have a silent moment. Silence is all the truth and all the wisdom in the world. You've got to stop fucking talking. Everybody is fucking talking and jumping up and giving their opinion too quickly.

JIM NORTON

I'm just trying to tell the truth. I'm not always right. I think most of us bat about .500. We're right half the time, wrong half the time. Whenever we're talking about the war or we're talking about health care or any real issues, half the time people will agree with you. Half the time, they won't. Half the time, I'll be point on. Half the time, I can be proven wrong. It doesn't matter as long as I'm truth-ful about the way I feel about it. Anyone who's so married to an ideology that their opinions about things won't change just because it doesn't go hand in hand with the ideology is fraudulent anyway.

BOB SAGET—COMEDIAN, ACTOR, WRITER

My mother said, "When you grow up, not everybody is going to like you," and I said, "I need names." Now I have the list. I know who they are. You can just Google.

MARIA BAMFORD—COMEDIAN, ACTOR

My favorite movie is *Ratatouille,* because the message is, "No matter how much people are disgusted by you, you've got to follow your dreams."

SARAH SILVERMAN—COMEDIAN, WRITER, ACTOR

I'm dreaming. I'm just sitting at home and dreaming and not feel-ing shitty about not knowing what's next, but realizing instead that we're just looking through a pinhole and we don't know what the fuck's coming up next. Instead of going, "Oh my God, what if I never have another show? What if, what if, what if?" You don't have to predict what's going to happen. What's going to happen will un-fold. The future's going to happen whether you predict it or not.

In the meantime, why don't you sit there and realize that every-thing that's happened to you so far, you have not been able to predict? Just know that whatever's coming is not anything you're going to know right now. If you go, "Oh, there's nothing out there. There's no opportunities for me." That's how it's always been. You know what I mean? We're looking through a pinhole, and we don't know what's out there.

GARRY SHANDLING

We are all making decisions based on fear. We have to be very, very, very careful. The other thing we're addicted to in America is the idea of security and trying to make everything permanent and solid and secure, when in fact, life itself is impermanent, not solid, but purely energy as proven by quantum mechanics.

The idea of trying to make it something secure and going as far as putting up walls around it is ignorance. It's just ignorance. That's all based on fear. We should do what we can to prevent terrorism, but this incredible panic about protecting what we have is what a human being on his own can't do. There is nowhere in any religion, any philosophy, where it says once you have the stuff, make sure no one else gets it. We should be embarrassed.

RUPAUL CHARLES

There are two types of people: the people who believe the Matrix, lock, stock, and barrel, and the people who understand that this is all just a construct. This is all illusion. Those are the two types of people, and I'm always looking for the other people who were going, "Yes. It is illusion." Against the mediocrity, the cultural expectations of Middle America and the American dream.

TOM SCHARPLING—COMEDIAN, WRITER, RADIO AND PODCAST HOST

I always have to think about just the next thing, and the thing after the thing, and the thing after that. I try to go for these walks, and I just leave my phone behind, and I'll listen to music, and I'll just try to reclaim it like a half hour at a time.

Does your leg ever feel like you feel the vibration and you don't even have your phone in your pocket? What's going on with that? That's a new thing for the human condition. "Oh, yeah, I felt my upper thigh vibrate. Oh, my phone's not in my pocket." What is that? That's like a sickness.

WHITNEY CUMMINGS—COMEDIAN, WRITER, PRODUCER, ACTOR

My favorite quote, and I'm really into quotes that I don't know who said them, this one quote kind of changed my life. "Comparison is the worst form of violence against yourself."

Marc
Wow.

Whitney
I know.

Marc
How about when I hit myself in the head with a hammer?

Whitney
I don't know. That's self-love in a lot of circles. That to me is a healthy relationship.

"Comparison is the worst form of violence against yourself." I used to run around and say, "She has more than me, I should have more than her," but that is just a way to self-abuse.

GARRY SHANDLING

I started to box about eleven years ago. The reason is twofold. One is it's out of my comfort zone completely. I never was a kid who got into fights. The idea of really being in a ring where someone is going to start throwing punches was crazy to me. The main reason is that you don't have time to think. It becomes completely intuitive. Someone is throwing a punch, you have to counter or you move or step back or you move but you can't think about it. When you land a punch, you can't think about it.

Marc

Are you good at it?

Garry

Well, I'm sure getting better than I was, which is better than getting worse.

Marc

Do you wear headgear?

Garry

I do. I wear headgear that goes from my head down to my knees. It's the biggest one they've ever seen.

TOM SCHARPLING

I go down to Princeton a lot, and I'll go down and walk around the town. It's an amazing town. It's absolutely beautiful. The campus is amazing. I'll just walk around. I'm looking at this school, and it's like, "Why didn't I go here?" It haunts me.

There are times I'll go down there and be like, "It's a really great place for me to get my head straight and take in the beautiful campus and everything." There are times where I walk around it and I'm just furious. It's in my backyard. Bill Bradley was my hero as a kid. He went here. If I'm writing my story out, this is like a lock in terms of what my arc should have been. I walk around and it just haunts me. This school that should have been. This should have been my life.

Then I just start to think, "Man, if I went here, I probably would not be where I'm at now." I wouldn't trade that. I'm happy I'm where I'm at now, and I'm happy that I've got the skill set to stick up for myself in whatever weird version of sticking up for myself I do. I still do it in terms of a career. You navigate through things and you take punches. You get back. I don't know if I would have that if I had gone to an Ivy League school and had the normal, ideal experience. I don't know if I would have the skill set I've got now that is helping me get to do exciting things.

ANDY RICHTER—COMEDIAN, WRITER, ACTOR

The only thing I really believe in is some form of yin and yang. Just in some sort of equalizer. Just the fact that if something's really good and something's really awesome, there's a price for it. It's going to suck. It's got to suck somehow. It's got to be awful in many, many ways.

RUPAUL CHARLES

Coming down here on the 101, there was an accident across the freeway. But everyone on my side was slowing down to look. It's like, "You know what? Govern your ass. Handle your shit, lady-kins, because you're the problem." Everybody wants to look. It's like, "It's an accident." Part of the rebel or the whatever in me is like, "I will not look. I will not be part of the problem. I won't look. I won't look."

PAULA POUNDSTONE—COMEDIAN, WRITER, ACTOR

I went backpacking with my daughter on Mount San Jacinto about two years ago now. In fact, it was February. We were in twelve feet of snow. We had the experience of getting dehydrated. I think because of the altitude and stuff. We weren't gone long. It wasn't long enough to risk life, but it did take us days to recover after we got home.

One thing that I noticed as we were hiking. We'd planned for this trip for a long time. It was a good thing to be doing. It was spectacular scenery, of course. We're hiking along, and I'm noticing myself sort of sinking like a rock emotionally. I couldn't figure out why. I'm like, "Wait. I'm where I want to be, doing what I want to be doing, with whom I want to be doing it. What's the matter?"

Later, when I realized that we didn't drink enough water, it actually was one of the most eye-opening things of my entire life. Do you know it's really important to drink water? As it turns out. I drink a lot of diet soda. That does not help. I still drink a lot of diet soda. I know it's not good for me, but I do enjoy it. I drink a lot of water now because it actually is connected to your emotional well-being, which is why, when you go to a therapist, they never say, "Would you like a glass of water?"

I realized that lives are complicated and all, but to some degree, some elements of happiness and balance are so much easier than I ever thought them to be. Drink some water and get a decent night's sleep, and it's the darnedest. All those years, all the therapy, all the angst, all the journaling, all the miserable phone calls. I look back on it now just with deep humiliation. It's like, "Okay. Drink some water and go to bed."

PENN JILLETTE—COMEDIAN, MAGICIAN, WRITER, ACTOR

My parents never had a drink of alcohol, never had any drugs. I've never had a sip of alcohol or any drug. They would never talk about it. They would never say, "So-and-so shouldn't be drinking." That never came up. Never a discussion of someone being a drunk. Every time someone says, "Why don't you do drugs or drink?" they always want to make my father and mother into alcoholics, and see this horror of when I was a child. No one wants to accept the opposite. They want to have some traumatic moment. They want to have me be AA or something. I think because it's just the story that's told most, especially in the U.S. It's not the international story, but kind of the American story, like that atheists are bitter.

One of the first questions you'll get, if you're an out-of-the-closet atheist, is, "I guess you were really fucked over by Christians, and they treated you badly." "You went to Catholic school," or they'll go the other way and say, "Something really bad must have happened in your life." In my experience with hardcore atheists, it tends to be if your family was so perfect that it made *Leave It to Beaver* look dysfunctional, that puts you on that road more. Because it's the absolute truth. If your love from your parents is unconditional and constant, and they just nurture you properly, then you become twelve feet tall and bulletproof.

When people talk to me about the eternal love of Jesus Christ, I just go, "Jesus Christ going one-on-one with my mom, my mom wins." My mom's love was so unconditional, so pure, and provable, provable with apple pie, provable with smiles, provable with being there for me every single time I needed her. There's proof.

LORNE MICHAELS—PRODUCER, WRITER, COMEDIAN, ACTOR

I have a family, which is really, as cliché as it sounds, the most important thing in my life. You sort of realize that you don't have your work in lieu of a family. You just have this and a family. It's a different feeling. One feeds the other. If you cannot care about the people you work with, you probably are going to have a hard time caring about the people you live with.

I think the reason I watch Yankee games is because there's something about when you follow baseball, you understand why you need a third baseman. If somebody hits it in that area, and you don't have anyone, you're going to be very embarrassed.

There's something about knowing you need others in order to be remarkable, that's a big deal.

BRUCE SPRINGSTEEN

You've got to prepare yourself for good things to come into your life, and also the bad things that come when you open yourself up to the world at large. That was the biggest change that happened in my thirties, that I had to make. It was like going back to learn my first chord on the guitar. I had to learn the first chord on myself and build it just the same way I built the craft of playing and singing. Slowly, step by step, angry, sometimes joyful, until finally I was able to put together a me that other people, once they got to know me, would be able to stand. Once I was able to do that, then kids come along and a wife and a relationship and you do your best to try and not fuck those things up as you go, which is not easy to do. But suddenly, you wake up one morning and there's a life there.

CARL REINER—COMEDIAN, WRITER, DIRECTOR, PRODUCER, ACTOR

You know what's interesting? Downtrodden people, you can't take music away from them. You can make yourself happy by singing or writing a song. You can't take that away from them. You can take physical things away from them, but a sense of humor is necessary to get through life. You'll kill yourself if you don't have a sense of humor. How did the people live through the Holocaust? They must've found something worth living. I'm sure humor might've been on the line. It saves people.

AIMEE MANN—MUSICIAN, ACTOR

My attitude is, life is messy for everybody. It's hard out there, man, and I get it. I certainly understand and have compassion for why you make decisions that don't seem smart and end up damaging other people, because sometimes the right answer is not obvious, and everybody's crazy. Everybody's operating at a deficit, and everybody's operating out of obsession and fear and desperation and longing. Life is messy. It's not easy for anyone.

PRESIDENT BARACK OBAMA

The more you do something, you lose fear. I was talking to somebody the other day about why I actually think I'm a better president and would be a better candidate if I were running again than I ever have been. It's sort of like an athlete, you might slow down a little bit, you might not jump as high as you used to, but I know what I'm doing and I'm fearless. You're not pretending to be fearless.

Also part of that fearlessness is because you've screwed up enough times that it's all happened. I've been through this. I've screwed up. I've been in the barrel tumbling down Niagara Falls, and I emerged and I lived. That's such a liberating feeling. It's one of the benefits of age.

It almost compensates for the fact that I can't play basketball anymore.

ACKNOWLEDGMENTS

Marc and Brendan wish to thank all WTF guests, past, present, and future, especially those whose contributions were used in this book. Thank you for your humor, generosity, and honesty. Thanks to John Oliver for writing the foreword. Thanks to Frank Cappello, Ashley Barnhill, Sam Varela, Sachi Ezura, Anastasia Kousak, Ashley Grashaw, and Jesse Thorn for your assistance on WTF throughout the years. Thanks to all the folks at Midroll, Libsyn, and iTunes who help get the podcast out into the world. Thanks to John Montagna, Nathan Smith, Dima Drjuchin, Jim Wirt, Travis Shinn, and Martin Celis for your personal artistic contributions to WTF. Thanks to Joanna Jordan, Abigail Parsons, Kelly Weber, Lindsey Johnson, Clare Bonsor, and Elizabeth Walid for getting many of these people to talk to us. Thanks to Colin Dickerman and James Melia for being great editors. Thanks to the rest of the Flatiron team, including Bob Miller, Marlena Bittner, Liz Keenan, Nancy Trypuc, Molly Fonseca, Erin Gordon, Steven Seighman, David Lott, Emily Walters, Shelly Perron, and Keith Hayes. Thanks to Henry Sene Yee for designing the cover. Thanks to Laury Frieber for making sure we didn't break the law. Thanks to Daniel Greenberg for representing us so well. Thanks to Olivia Wingate for being there at the very beginning. Thanks to David Martin and Kelly Van Valkenburg for making sure everything got signed. Thanks to Harvey Altman and Rob Urio for making sure everything got deposited.

Marc: Thanks to all the people who listened to me, talked to me, and put up with me. Without them I literally wouldn't know who I am or if I exist. I also want to thank Sarah Cain. She's a trouper. I love her.

Brendan: Thank you, Mike and Dorothy McDonald. My gratitude is the least I can give you in return for raising me so well. Thank you, Ian McDonald. You were the first person to teach me what was funny and why—a quality older-brother move. Thank you, Marc Maron. I have the career of my dreams because of your talent, your trust, and your friendship. Thank you, Owen McDonald. You are the greatest thing I ever produced. Thank you, Dawn McDonald. You are the reason I strive to be my best every day. I love you. Sorry I had to go away for days at a time to work on this book. I'll be around more now.

INDEX